E-Innovation

E-Innovation

Trends and Applications

Edited by
Moonmoon Bhattacharya

2010

Icfai Books
The Icfai University Press

E-INNOVATION – TRENDS AND APPLICATIONS

Editor: Moonmoon Bhattacharya

First Edition: 2010
Printed in India

Published by

The Icfai University Press
52, Nagarjuna Hills, Punjagutta
Hyderabad, India – 500 082
Phone: (+91) (040) 23430–368, 369, 370, 372, 373, 374
Fax: (+91) (040) 23352521, 23435386
E-mail: info@icfaibooks.com, icfaibooks@icfai.org, ssd@icfai.org

ISBN: 9788131405970

Editorial Team: Arindam Basu and R Madhavi

Contents

Overview

"Innovation has nothing to do with how many R&D dollars you have. When Apple came up with the Mac, IBM was spending at least 100 times more on R&D. It's not about money. It's about the people you have, how you're led, and how much you get it".

– Steve Jobs, Fortune, November 9, 1998,
US computer engineer & industrialist (1955 -)

The greatest test of innovation lies in its successful adoption by enterprises across the globe. In the wake of the new millennium, innovation, adoption and diffusion of innovative technologies and practices have become vital to the growth and development of the global economy. Today, the enterprises worldwide are focusing on innovation to sustain competitive advantage. Innovation introduces new products, promotes the development of new production processes and encourages organizational changes. Through the adoption of advanced tools, technologies and practices, the industries are enjoying improved production capabilities, thereby increasing their productivity and expanding the lines of innovative goods and services.

We are aware that the present decade is governed by enormous growth in personal computing, evolving web environments, the Internet, improved communication networks, newer digital applications and consumer-friendly data-access devices. All these have created a radically new electronic environment worldwide. These technological inventions are enhancing the way enterprises collaborate and manage information, thereby leading to a global electronic market-place. Driving the speed of technological change are the innovations in Information and Communication Technologies (ICTs). Research reveals that ICT-based innovations are favorable to both large and small enterprises to sustain competitive edge. Driving the design and creation of all ICT artifacts is the field of software engineering, which is expediting developments in all technology sectors worldwide. This collective change to innovation driven by ICTs is called 'E-Innovation'.

In this present competitive scenario, it is essential for the Managers, IT professionals, Academicians and Practitioners to track and leverage the innovative activities of the e-world. This book presents a holistic view of the emerging phenomenon of electronic innovation and draws upon latest trends, practices and experiences, with focus on e-business innovations, through a mix of articles and cases.

Section I: E-Innovation: An Overview

Discourses on innovation are ubiquitous and the most frequently cited innovative activities include research and development, tactical planning and new product development. This section provides an overview of the widespread phenomenon of innovation and ascertains its role in the e-world.

Although research and development plays an important role in the innovation process, mere investments in R&D do not make an enterprise innovative, until these expenditures fetch profitable returns.

The curtain raising article "**Making Innovation Pay**" by *James P Andrew* and *Harold L Sirkine* from Boston Consulting Group, nails down the significance of innovation in firms for gaining competitive advantage, superior shareholder returns and, above all, cash. This article affirms that the companies, which had mostly increased their R&D spending, failed to see any major return on their investments. The authors identify the problem – "that Innovation is an act, not an idea" and successful or profitable innovation relies on a series of actions that transform an idea into cash returns: the Innovation to Cash (ITC) process. The article further suggests that this entire process, which runs across organizational boundaries, play a pivotal role and demands managerial attention. If not carefully managed, the enterprises suffer from lost profit, wasted resources and little or no growth. The article recognizes that the managerial challenge is to have the rigor and discipline to consistently evaluate and manage the inherent trade-offs, across an entire portfolio of diverse innovation efforts. For the purpose, the article asserts the significance of managing and revitalizing the portfolio of "cash-curves", besides linking innovation with strategy. Finally, the essence of the article is to ensure the accountability and also making innovation pay.

Evidently, the large, small, medium and micro enterprises are vastly adopting ICT infrastructure and opening the doors for technology innovation. The second article "**E-Innovation: An Emerging Paradigm**" by *Moonmoon Bhattacharya*, reiterates the significance of innovative activities and explains how businesses worldwide and across most sectors of the economy depend on sustained innovations to attain competitive advantage. This article defines e-innovation as an evolving strategy for proactively responding to the present climate of continuous, radical change. It explores e-innovation as an emerging discipline that combines competitive intelligence, strategic planning, design and new product development. The article also recognizes software as a key driver of e-innovation and elucidates the dominant models of open and global sourcing. It further affirms the role of the Internet in the entire e-innovation process. Instances of e-innovation of large enterprises like INTEL, IBM and Procter and Gamble have been explicated. Lastly, the article explores e-business as a key driver of e-innovation, describes the role of ICTs in the entire innovation process, defines the models of innovation in e-business and explores the emerging trends.

The third article **"The Knowledge Based View and Open Innovation: Strategies from Open Source Software"** by *Scott Gallagher* and *Joel West*, affirms the knowledge-based view as an alternative way of conceptualizing a firm. The focus of the firms in 'Open innovation' is to identify, exploit and integrate external knowledge with the internal R&D activities, which has been suggested as a new paradigm for corporate innovation. Depending on the knowledge-based view, the article develops four innovation strategies—pooled R&D, spinouts, selling complements and attracting donated complements. It illustrates how the large enterprises depend on these strategies to support their innovation strategies in the software browser, operating system and server and also in the game markets. Examples of innovative enterprises include IBM and Dell.

The fourth article **"Recent Productivity Growth: The Role of Information Technology and Other Innovations"** from the Federal Reserve Bank of India, authored by *Martin N Baily* critically speculates on the role of Information Technology investments as a major driver of productivity and growth in the US Economy, since the mid-1990s. Although the article links productivity with innovation and asserts that technology and especially IT are critical drivers of productivity, it was initially skeptical whether the contribution of IT to growth had been overstated. This article further suggests that, in addition to IT, a high level of competitive intensity encourages the enterprises to innovate. The article derives lessons from McKinsey case studies on the enterprises like Wal-Mart and Costco, which relied on IT to improve their supply chains. The article further highlights the innovative applications like Enterprise Resource Planning (ERP) which has experienced mixed results of both success and failure.

The fifth article **"Does Electronic Business Create Value for Firms? – An Organizational Innovation Perspective"** by

Youlong Zhuang, applies the theory of organizational innovation to one specific type of electronic innovation-electronic business. This research-based article explains innovation along seven dimensions: organizational focus, radicalness, centrality, adaptability, uncertainty, pervasiveness, and communicability. Here, the innovative use of e-business has been linked with the firm's performance. The study, which has taken data from the InformationWeek and The Compustat database, reveals significant differences between the performances of innovative firms and the performance averages of their respective industries. The article identifies the attributes of e-business innovation, affirms the linkage between e-business innovation and the firm's performance and assists the researchers in building e-business theories. Besides, it also helps the practitioners to better understand the e-business innovations. Lastly, the findings of the study will help the managers to choose their appropriate level of involvement in e-business and plan their e-business strategies.

Section II: Emerging Trends

"The Internet, World Wide Web, and Web browsers have brought us to the brink of a new way of doing business, and electronic economy, an e-economy, if you will."

Alan H Karp, Hewlett-Packard Laboratories, Palo Alto, California.

Presently, the interactive qualities of the internet and the advanced IT applications have transformed the business-consumer relationships across enterprises worldwide.

The sixth article **"E-Business Driving Innovation"** authored by *Niels Bjørn-Andersen*, reinforces the importance of ICT investments in improving a firm's competitiveness and fostering innovation. The article also states that all ICT investments do not lead to e-business developments. The author writes "for example, an internal system for managing personnel may represent a considerable investment in ICT for a large firm, but would not have an impact on the firm's key business processes". While e-business entails trading over the internet, the utility of ICT tools in e-business is to manage a firm's relationship with its customers and suppliers. The article reaffirms that more than one quarter of world trade is conducted using ICT tools and that, in the next five years, the same will rise to one-third of the global trade. While B2C (Business-To-Consumer) trade represents only one-tenth of the total volume of e-business, B2B (Business-To-Business) trade is, by far, the more significant area of e-business. Lastly, the article reveals results of a recent survey conducted by CRITO across ten nations regarding ICT uptake.

E-Service was initially predominant in the B2B sector because B2B deals with relationships and it involves and impacts areas like information technology, marketing, human resources, information systems, finance, etc. The seventh article "**Business Case Modelling for E-Services**"authored by *Wil Janssen, René van Buuren* and *Jaap Gordijn*, affirms that innovative ICT-based services help the companies to develop their operational efficiencies and differentiate themselves from their competitors. Since most industry players lack adequate resources for designing innovative-ICT based services, they increasingly rely on the networks of cooperative organizations for developing these services. Various studies discuss the disappointing success rates of inter-firm cooperation and the costs and risks that are involved in it. It is, then, that the practitioners and academics pay attention to the concept of business models and business networks. This article intends to bridge the gap between business models and business strategy on the one hand and business architecture on the other.

The eighth article "**ATM: Innovative Vehicle of Tomorrow's E-Banking**" by *C Rama Gopal*, talks about the virtual shift of the banking industry from the traditional brick-and-mortar model to innovative e-banking solutions like ATMs, in recent times. Initially, the article talks about this popular e-banking tool as a means of teaching e-banking to the customers at minimal cost. As the banks need to market new products and increase their delivery channels to attract new customers and retain the existing ones, these ATMs fulfill consumer needs through the established concept of 'anywhere, anyhow and anytime' banking. The article, describes how technology plays a vital role in reducing the time to market new products. Lastly, the article sheds light on the future scope of E-banking and describes how ATMs will deliver the real solution through innovations in infrastructure and technology.

The ninth article titled **"RFID and the Innovation Cycle"** by *Yossi Sheffi*, explores several disruptive technologies and mapsout the path from the early phase of innovation to total implementation. While explaining several disruptive technologies, the article applies the evolutionary steps through early innovation to wide adoption to a recent disruptive technology, viz: Radio Frequency Identification (RFID). The article speculates on the probable future adoption and impact of this technology and infers that the widespread implementation of RFID for managing supply chains is likely to continue until the end of the decade. The article envisages how RFID is posed to change the future retail operations and describes how the trend towards suburban large malls might be reversed in days to come. Finally, it predicts that RFID in combination with other emerging technologies will lead to a sixth "digital sense" enabling humans to sense their locations and conditions digitally.

The tenth article is based on the **"The European E-Business Report 2005"**, the 4th Annual Synthesis Report by the E-Business Watch of the European Commission, summarized by *Hannes Selhofer,* Enterprise and Industry Directorate General. This executive summary portrays the relevance of ICTs and E-Business in ten sectors of the European Union (EU) in 2005 and explores the emerging trends. The report reveals that the extent of diffusion of ICTs and E-Business in the EU differs considerably between industries and within sectors, the opportunities and challenges are different for small, medium-sized and large firms. Besides, geographical disparities in the adoption of ICT within enterprises and their readiness for innovation exist within the EU, especially among the smaller companies. The various policy implications of E-Business have been dealt with in conclusion.

The eleventh article titled "**International E-Business Developments**" by *Hannes Selhofer*, summarizes the main results of the special report "Overview of International E-Business Developments", published by e-Business W@tch in July 2005. The article compares the status quo of e-business monitoring activities in the major economies of the world. It further identifies the major national monitoring initiatives along with their institutional set-up and features the main results. The major economies outside Europe, namely, Australia, Canada, Japan, Korea and the USA, have been selected for this purpose. The findings for these countries are then compared to the equivalent activities in the EU. The study concludes with some policy recommendations for the future international e-business monitoring.

Section III: Applications and Cases

The third section is a mix of articles and cases. While the articles delve into the applications of e-business and present a global scenario on the readiness for innovation, the cases revolve around large global innovative enterprises like Google and Apple.

The twelfth article "**E-Tourism: An Innovative Approach for the Small and Medium-Sized Tourism Enterprises (SMTEs) in Korea**" by *Chulwon Kim*, talks about e-tourism, innovation and growth. It highlights the internet revolution of recent times and how internet is facilitating the distribution of tourism information and sales. It also discusses the Small and Medium Tourism Enterprises (SMTEs) in Korea and how these enterprises, with well-developed and innovative websites, can now enjoy 'equal internet access' to the international tourism markets. The article further probes into the problems and solutions pertaining to the electronic commerce in the tourism industry. Finally, it suggests recommendations for the decision-makers, entrepreneurs and practitioners in the tourism industry, particularly the SMTEs in the Korean e-tourism market. These recommendations are in the form of e-commerce strategies that can be applied to other countries as well.

The thirteenth article **"Walk, Don't Run: E-Business Readiness in Canadian SMEs"** by *Michelle Saulnier* and *Philip Rosson*, reports the results of exploratory research on the readiness of Canadian Small and Medium-Sized Enterprises (SMEs) to engage in e-business. The study is based on field interviews in 15 SMEs in Nova Scotia and the analyses of their websites. It reports the status quo of e-business implementations, supply and demand chain actions, website features and compares the results with those of other jurisdictions. The article suggests that e-business readiness is an emerging area of business activity and, like most other business innovations, it is closely linked to internet implementation. Therefore, the degree to which managers consider e-business as a vital factor to their business is most strongly correlated with Internet implementation.

One of the keystones of the Irish economy is the agribusiness industry. The fourteenth article **"E-Business Developments in the Irish Agribusiness Industry"** by *Paul Brandon, John O' Connell, Dermot Ruane* and *Padraig Wims,* reports the levels of e-business development and website adoption amongst Irish agribusinesses through an exploratory research that aims to assess the likely future developments of e-business in the Irish agribusiness industry. At the same time, the research compares the status quo of e-business developments in the Irish agribusiness industry with those of other countries. The study also focuses on B2B transactions over the Internet and explores the wider uses of e-business, like internet, intranet, extranet and e-mail. The article lays down future e-business strategies and suggests that those having websites are strategically well positioned in the e-business world. Finally, it predicts that e-procurement is likely to be the next significant phase of e-business implementation.

The widespread application of ICTs and e-business are being increasingly appreciated by the government to enhance the delivery of its services to the citizens through e-government solutions. The fifteenth article **"Improving Citizen-Government Interface Through Innovative E-Governance: A Study of India"** by *Y Pardhasaradhi*, examines and analyzes the improving citizen interface of the Government of India through electronic means and cites the example of Andhra Pradesh (AP), where IT is leveraged as a significant tool for governance. It further analyzes the innovative E-Seva (Electronic Citizen Services) initiative of the AP government. In conclusion, it talks about three significant dimensions of e-seva, i.e., new mangerialism, Public Private Partnerships (PPP) and practicing innovative technology to benefit the citizens.

The following two cases delve into true product innovators like Google and Apple, who have topped the 2006 list of innovative enterprises.

The sixteenth case "**Google in 2005: Innovating to Stay Ahead**" by *A V Vedpuriswar*, explores the product innovation strategy of Google as a means to sustain the lead. Google is well-known for its search engine and has been ranked as one of the most innovative enterprises in the e-world. Having completed its IPO successfully in 2004, the company has been widening its product range in order to minimize its dependence on its search service. In doing so, it faced stiff competition from bigger rivals like Microsoft. Therefore, it has been relying heavily on innovation inorder to sustain competitive edge. The case revolves around the prime question "will google be able to sustain the lead?"

The seventeenth case "**Apple's New Operating System, "Tiger": Riding on the Success of iPod?**" by *Shalini*, highlights the product innovation strategy of Apple and discusses Apple's plans to promote 'Tiger' by leveraging the brand value of iPod. In April 2005, Apple released its new version of operating system, 'Tiger', for its Mac computers. With 200 innovative features, 'Tiger' has set in as the most advanced powerful and user-friendly operating system for the Apple's Mac users. While analysts have opined that Apple had launched 'Tiger' about the same time, when the company was enjoying the success of iPod, others are skeptical whether the company can make 'Tiger' as successful as iPod, especially when Microsoft's new operating system 'Longhorn' is about to be launched.

Today, the spread of electronic innovation is driving the success of global economy. As these innovations are likely to take on many shapes to enhance the effectiveness of business operations in the enterprises worldwide, it is apparent that business innovations these days are closely linked to e-business innovations and the factors like e-business readiness are the indicators of e-inclusion at the grass roots level.

Besides providing an immense learning value to the academicians, researchers and students of management and information technology, the book, it is hoped, will enlighten the managers, IT professionals and executives about the incident of e-innovation. It will also help the readers to understand the latest trends in e-innovation, applications of e-innovation and related technologies in the e-world.

Section I

E-Innovation: An Overview

1

Making Innovation Pay

James P Andrew and Harold L Sirkine

The article states that companies, which had primarily focused on cost reductions in the past several years, are now turning their focus to innovation to sustain competitive advantage. These companies are seeking "organic" resources of revenues. Often, companies who merely increase R&D expenses fail to see any major change in the return on their investment. The article refers to the problem is that innovation is an act, not an idea. That successful innovation results from a series of actions that transform the ideas into cash returns—the Innovation To Cash (ITC) process has been explored in the article. Managing the entire portfolio of cash curves, linking innovation with strategy and ensuring accountability is discussed at length. Lastly, the article differentiates between the innovation efforts of a company i.e., whether to be innovative or be an innovative enterprise.

After years of focusing intensely on cost, quality, and productivity, companies seem to have rediscovered growth. In every industry, senior executives are turning to their organizations and asking for new "organic" sources of revenues. They want more innovation and they want results—now. But at the same time they also worry that their efforts will not deliver, in terms of either growth or profitability. Through often, companies, increase R&D spending, but fail to see any major change in the return on their investments.

The problem is that innovation is an act, not an idea. Too many people believe that an insight will carry the day. Rarely are they right.

Successful innovation—which is to say, profitable innovation depends on the entire set of actions that are required to turn an idea into cash returns: the Innovation-To-Cash (ITC) process. This process cuts across organizational boundaries and presents many difficult choices. It must be explicitly, and thoughtfully, managed. When it isn't, the damage shows up in companies' results—lost profits, wasted resources, and little or no growth.

Let's be clear, though the managerial challenge is not to "integrate" all the separate steps and functional decisions of the ITC process. Rather, it is to have the rigor and discipline to evaluate and manage the inherent tradeoffs—consistently and across a whole portfolio of different innovation efforts. This takes real collaboration and problem solving, not just better handoffs between functions.

Managing the "Cash Curve"

Despite the many uncertainties of innovation, it is possible to assess, at the outset, the likely impact of different approaches to managing the full ITC process. This is accomplished by examining the "cash curve" of an innovation. A cash curve depicts the cumulative cash investments and returns for an innovation over time. It runs from the very beginning of development, until the point at which the product or service is removed from the market. (See the exhibit "The cash curve")

Clearly, management's decisions affect the shape of the cash curve and also determine its dynamics. As a result, managers need to understand and openly discuss how, say, "pushing" the curve in one place horizontally or vertically is likely to move it someplace else—and how other actions can enhance or dampen that movement.

Consider the example of a manufacturer which is trying to develop a product that is new to its market. Because it knows its customers well, has manufacturing

The Cash Curve

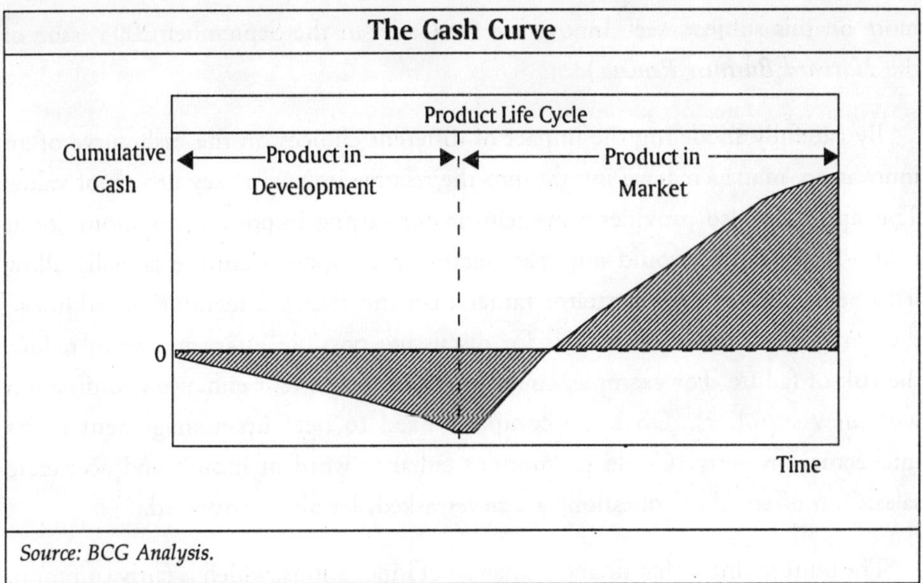

Source: BCG Analysis.

plants around the world, and has solid design expertise, the company's first inclination is to go it alone. After all, why share the margins? However, because the product is a breakthrough, plants would need to be re-tooled and some new critical R&D skills acquired. Moreover, marketing and launch expenditures would be higher than normal. In addition, new technology in the product and customers' lack of familiarity with its application would add time to development and slow market penetration. When all this is considered, the cash curve our company creates for that its breakthrough may not look so good after all.

There are, however, other ways to bring the innovation to market, with different effects on the curve. For instance, could risks be shared and market penetration accelerated by "orchestrating" the process? This could mean acquiring, rather than developing in-house, some of the required technologies, and focusing instead on design and marketing. Or it could mean turning to other organizations to handle the manufacturing or supply chain activities. Indeed, there are three basic ITC approaches to consider—the Integrator, the Orchestrator, and the Licensor. Each approach has different strengths, weaknesses, and requirements, so each is better or worse suited for different innovations, situations, and companies. (For more on this subject, see "Innovating for Cash" in the September 2003 issue of the *Harvard Business Review.*)

By carefully modeling the impact of different choices on the cash curve of an innovation, managers have insight into the relative impact of key drivers of value. This approach also provides a mechanism for raising important questions about risks—for instance, would our manufacturing company's culture actually allow it to be a successful Orchestrator rather than the classic Integrator? In addition, the curve offers managers a basis for discussing possible interventions to reduce the risk of failure. For example, could project management enhance coordination with new suppliers? Does the company need to beef up management of its intellectual property? Could promotions enhance word of mouth and accelerate sales? Too often, these questions are never asked, let alone answered.

The bottom line is that financial analysis of innovations, which is fairly common, combined with a dynamic view of the cash curve, which is rare, blends strategy and execution. It can make the difference between developing another inconsequential product or service and winning big—because it gives the top management team a language for and an appreciation of interrelated financial, market, and technology risks. In the end, executives have a common ground to make better trade offs and break compromises.

Not Just One Curve, But Many

Of course, it's not a matter of managing just one cash curve. To grow consistently, companies need a much more consistent series of hits, both big and small. This means coming to grips with a full portfolio of innovations, aligning investments explicitly with the overall strategy, and ensuring that someone is actually accountable for the performance of the entire process.

Revitalizing the Portfolio

To get more out of innovation spending throughout a company, management must successfully handle an entire portfolio of cash curves. It must decide on the right balance of spending across a range of initiatives: maintenance projects (in essence, keeping market share), incremental projects (gaining share), and breakthrough projects (entering completely new markets). Which mix is right, given the competitive environment? Where do you want to be? Where do you need to be? What will you get there? Then, how do you align your resources and, more important, your people with these different priorities? No one can do it all.

Trade offs need to be made regularly and rigorously to maintain the desired balance in the portfolio. Too often, companies let the "walking dead" (projects that should be killed) live far too long. As a result, winning projects are often starved for resources, frequently in the name of "balance," "fairness," and "hedging our bets." Bad projects and virtually every company has some—can be extremely controversial. Typically, a manager has invested so much in a project that he or she cannot bear to see it fail. Using the cash curve as a lens to evaluate such projects can make it clear that they will never pay off. Fewer projects, with bigger potential pay offs and faster development tracks, should be the goal for just about any company in any industry.

Linking Innovation with Strategy

Decisions about innovation shape a company's future. The outcomes determine cash flow and competitive position. But too often, innovation is managed in a largely random fashion, rather than explicitly linked to strategy. Investments of capital and great people (always scarcer and more valuable than money) are typically based on budgets, not on strategic goals.

Like any major investment, innovation needs to be focused on clearly defined objectives. This requires a view on where innovation is possible and to what degree. It means understanding whether the ideas can be developed within a company or whether the company must look outside. It means selecting an appropriate strategic approach, such as fast follower or first to market—because each may be right in different situations, depending on the objective. It means understanding how different investments in different types of innovation—breakthrough versus incremental versus maintenance match up with the overall strategy. Most of all, it means accepting the risk of being wrong, but doing everything possible to be right.

Again, companies also need to decide precisely when and where to use different innovation approaches. Each of the three ITC approaches represents a different way to allocate risk and cash flows. Thus, the choice is highly strategic yet often poorly considered, if it is considered at all. Already, though, some leading companies are using all three. More companies will need to learn how to do so.

Ensuring Accountability

In many companies, no one "owns" innovation; instead, it is the responsibility of many. Too often, this means that no one is actually accountable for the "cash" part of innovation. ITC must be subjected to the same culture of accountability and measurement that governs other processes. Accountability for results, authority to make things happen, and a clear view of current performance are critical, if a company is serious about generating more cash.

It is impossible, however, to manage something that can't be measured. Innovation is often seen as something that just "happens," and trying to track its progress seems either futile or a restraint on creativity, or both. Often, management defaults to a single number or two that are easily measured for example, corporate revenue growth. Yet the ITC process must be measured, and measured rigorously. A carefully constructed suite of measures is required. Inputs such as time, people, and cash need to be carefully tracked by project and product. In addition, measuring the performance of the process itself (for instance, the time to market relative to certain benchmarks) is important. Is the process performing as designed? Finally, critical output metrics such as new cash generation, market share in new segments, and true new markets entered provide essential information.

In the end, it is undeniably difficult to measure innovation, and no suite of metrics will ever be perfect. But companies should measure the performance of their ITC process, if they want anyone to manage it and be accountable for it.

None of this is to say that ideas and creativity don't matter. They do. But ideas are not innovations. We hear far too many executives talk about their great ideas and bemoan their inability to profit from them. Companies must make a basic choice about their innovation efforts—whether to be innovative or whether to be an innovative enterprise. After all, there is a world of difference between the two. The former produces lots of great ideas, but often has little to show for them.

By contrast, innovative enterprises use their ideas to produce competitive advantage, superior shareholder returns, and, above all, cash. There are precious few of these companies, and they stand apart from the pack. They manage the innovation-to-cash process aggressively and well. They grow. And, most of all, they make innovation pay.

(James P Andrew is a senior vice president and director in the Chicago office of The Boston Consulting Group and head of the innovation and commercialization area for the firm's Operations practice.

Harold L Sirkine is a senior vice president and director in BCG's Chicago office and head of the firm's global Operations practice.)

The Ten Types of Innovation

Innovation Category	Innovation Type	Description of Type	Business Example
Finance	1. Business model	How you make money?	Dell revolutionized the personal computer business model by collecting money before the consumer's PC was even assembled and shipped (resulting in net positive working capital of seven to eight days).
	2. Networks and alliances	How you join forces with other companies for mutual benefit?	Consumer goods company Sara Lee realized that its core competencies were in consumer insight, brand management, marketing and distribution. Thus it divested itself of a majority of its manufacturing operations and formed alliances with manufacturing and supply chain partners.
Process	3. Enabling processes	How you support the company's core processes and workers?	Starbucks can deliver its profitable store/ coffee experience to customers because it offers better-than-market compensation and employment benefits to its store workers – usually part time, educated, professional, and responsive people.
	4. Core processes	How you create and add value to your offerings?	Wal-Mart continues to grow profitably through core process innovations such as real-time inventory management systems, aggressive volume/pricing/delivery contracts with merchandise providers and systems that give store managers the ability to identify changing buyer's behaviors in and respond quickly with new pricing and merchandising configurations.
Offerings	5. Product perfor- mance	How you design your core offerings?	The VW Beetle (in both its original and its newest form) took the market by storm, combining multiple dimensions of product performance.
	6. Product system	How you link and/or provide a platform for multiple products?	Microsoft Office bundles a variety of specific products (Word, Excel, PowerPoint, etc.,) into a system designed to deliver productivity in the workplace.

Contd...

Contd...			
	7. Service	How you provide value to customers and consumers beyond and around your products?	An international flight on any airlines will get you to your intended designation. A flight on Singapore Airlines, however, nearly makes you forget that you are flying at all, with the most attentive, respectful, and pampering pre-flight, in-flight and post-services you can imagine.
Delivery	8. Channel	How you get your offerings to market?	Legal problems aside, Martha Stewart has developed such a deep understanding of her customers that she knows just where to be (stores, TV shows, magazines, online, etc.) to drive huge sales volumes from a relatively small set of "home living" educational and product offerings.
	9. Brand	How you communicate your offerings?	Absolut conquered the vodka category on the strength of a brilliant "theme and variations" advertising concept, strong bottle and packaging design, and a whiff of Nordic authenticity.
	10. Customer experience	How your customers feel when they interact with your company and its offerings?	Harley Davidson has created a worldwide community of millions of customers, many of whom would describe "being a Harley Davidson owner" as a part of how they fundamentally see, think, and feel about themselves.

Source: Doblin Inc. Chicago

2

E-Innovation: An Emerging Paradigm

Moonmoon Bhattacharya

The article explores e-innovation in a rapidly evolving marketplace and asserts its significance as a strategy for continuous innovation. Besides recognizing software as a key driver of e-innovation, it affirms the role of the Internet as a giant-bottom-up innovation machine. Lastly, the article ascribes e-business as a key driver of e-innovation, highlights the role of ICTs in the entire innovation process, defines the models of innovations in e-business and explores the recent trends.

1. Introduction

The present era is an age of continuous innovation. This is evident from the global scenario of rapid technological advancements. Nowadays, in order to sustain competitive advantage, even the conservative companies are shifting their focus from cost reductions to innovations. In a survey[1] conducted by the Boston

[1] The BCG 2004-2005 Senior Management Survey on innovation was electronically distributed to executives worldwide in late 2004 and the survey was closed in February 2005.

Consulting Group[2] in 2005, it was found that 90%[3] of the senior executives favor generating 'organic growth'[4] through innovation and 74% of them have plans to spend more on innovation. Companies like Apple, 3M, GE, Microsoft, Sony, Google and IBM, were ranked as the most innovative ones by the executives.

In the 21st century, the growth of personal computing, worldwide web, networks of cellular and satellite telecommunications, consumer-friendly data access devices, etc., have created a radically new global environment. Besides, the intellectual developments, offered by the innovative tools of the computer and the Internet, are transforming the world into a global electronic market place. This market place is expected to promote collaborative thinking and offer corporate and individuals, innovative ways to manage information. It is perceptible that the revolutions in Information and Communication Technologies (ICT), which are driving the speed of technological change, will determine the future of business, health, education, society, telecommunications, media and entertainment. Thus, to compete in this rapidly evolving environment, the enterprises should be ready with tactics and strategies. (Cotton, Bob, 2002).

It is quite apparent that software engineering is driving ICT advancements in the present decade. According to Bob Cotton (2002), "Underpinning ICT development is software engineering and the design and creation of code to control, coordinate, and run applications upon all the new computers, micro processor devices, consumer electronics products, telephone and computer networks, digital cameras, MP3 players, e-books, mobile phones, and other ICT artifacts." And despite the existence of a strong proprietary software industry, software engineering practices are historically rooted to community[5] and sharing. The Internet itself is the result of an open and collaborative effort of the Advanced Research Projects

---

2 Founded in 1963, the Boston consulting group is a general management consulting firm that is a global leader in business strategy. See *www.bcg.com*

3 940 executives and managers from 68 countries and major industries had participated in the 2004-2005 Sr. Management BCG Survey.

4 "Organic growth is the rate of business expansion through increasing output and sales as opposed to mergers, acquisitions and take-overs." See *www.investordictionary.com*

5 Community of software developers refer to the web-connected programmers (software developers.)

Agency (ARPA) in the early 1990s. Since then, the Internet has evolved as a giant bottom-up innovation machine[6].

A major manifestation of how the Internet will help the future innovation on a global scale is the open source movement in software development. This movement, which implies an open access to software code, is facilitating radical revolution[7], thereby increasing the potential of distributed innovation[8] across the globe (Kogut, Bruce and Turcanu, Anca, 1999). It plays a major role in the e-innovation process.

"E-Innovation represents a powerful model for the organization of research and development, for the arts, for the creation of a global community of innovators. And it raises significant implications for expansion of creativity in every domain." (Kogut, Bruce and Turcanu, Anca, 1999).

The first section of the article describes software as a key driver of innovation and explains the dominant models of open sourcing and global sourcing with relevant examples. The second section of the article defines e-innovation in a rapid and fast evolving marketplace and explores e-innovation as a strategy for proactively responding to an evolving environment whose main attribute is change. The third section explores e-business as a key driver of innovation; defines the models of innovations in e-business and explores recent trends.

2. Software Drives Innovation

Software represents the wave of challenges driven by the rapid pace of technological development. Today, it is difficult to imagine any industry that is not depending on software for value-creation. The software industry which is a proliferation of the 'digital revolution' is accelerating developments across all the sectors, ranging

---

6 The Internet is behind the philosophy of bottom-up innovation because it allows an increasing number of innovators to collaborate across time-zones, thereby promoting openness and cooperation that characterize the open source movement.

7 "Our claim is that there is ultimately a more radical revolution in the open source movement than the murky and contentious issues surrounding property rights and proprietary ownership of code."(Kogut,Meitu,2000)

8 "This is the use of networks and collaborative conceptual and concept development tools or groupware, the use of open-source development techniques and the building of responsive mechanisms for encouraging innovation in distributed (modularized) outsourced software development. Distributed innovation can be employed for hardware product development too." (Cotton, Bob, 2002)

from electrical engineering to genetic research and biotechnology. An increasing reliance on software to match and integrate customer needs tends to make the enterprises software intensive. Recently, music, movies, games, information, financial services, automobiles and telecommunications, are all becoming software-centric industries. The increasing awareness amongst all the sectors to become software driven entities has generated a worldwide demand for software engineers.

For decades, the scarcity of software engineers in the US and in many industrial countries has led to a global search for software production to match the high productivity requirements in this area. In the earlier days of computing, software engineering organizations thought that by simply hiring more staff (engineers), it was possible to expedite software engineering tasks. However, in the early 1960s and 1970s, IBM and other software firms realized that the strategy of simply recruiting more staff was expensive because of the increased costs of training new programmers, matching them to the pace of developments, as well as managing and coordinating their work.

Thus, during the early 1970s and 1980s, software production methodologies and processes were improved and considerable educational resources were dedicated to develop a pool of skilled software programmers. In the 1980s, as new set of programming languages emerged, modularized[9] software development became popular, making outsourcing modules an easy task. This rationale of the software development process put greater emphasis on the architectural design[10] of the project and the innovative task of defining and evaluating customer needs. Modules of tasks were sorted at the architecture-design stage, and the complex modules were outsourced to specialists, or teams in the same organization.

The search for a cost-efficient process, coupled with the decreasing communications costs (and Internet use) and increasing network bandwidth[11] led to the outsourcing of modules to dispersed locations through a global

---

9 The entire program is made up of modules of logical and functional building blocks of programs.

10 The software architecture of a system comprises its software components, their external properties, and their relationships with one another. The term also refers to documentation of a system's software architecture.

11 "The amount of information or data that can be sent over a network connection in a given period of time. Bandwidth is usually stated in bits per second (bps), kilobits per second (kbps), or megabits per second (mps)." (*www.tecrime.com*)

24-hour software production cycle. For instance, the programmers developed software modules in Japan and then passed them over to their teams in Europe and the US through the 24-hour global software cycle. However, the total costs of coordinating such diurnal projects were sensitive to the least efficient operations in the production-line and as a result, the 24-hour development cycle could not be fully exploited.

Kogut and Meitus of Pennsylvania University's Wharton school, in an important paper[12] have suggested two main models (global sourcing and open sourcing) for coping with the increased demand of software engineers. The Internet, which is primary to both the models, is the virtual platform that enables the software engineers across the globe to participate and develop new software.

2.1 Model 1: Global Sourcing

The first model is that of global sourcing. It deals with the sourcing of software from software engineering firms across the world. Offshore sites are created, either by launching in-house subsidiaries overseas or outsourcing (contracting out) to offshore suppliers. For instance, the financial services division of an American firm sub-contracts widely to Indian software houses like Wipro, Infosys and Tata Consultancy Services.

Global sourcing reduces the cost by employing people across time zones[13], often by outsourcing routine modules to sites where wages are lower and the sophisticated ones to the sites having the requisite expertise. As a result, a 24-hour (diurnal) global software development cycle becomes possible and the offshore sites tend to benefit from an improved production-cycle time. Thus, the dominant strategy for offshore sourcing is to lower the costs by assigning routine tasks to offshore sites as well as expand the pool of software engineers. This effort enables this model to express a cost-speed trade off by lowering the costs and speeding up the development time.

12 Kogut & Meitu (2000). "The Emergence of e-Innovation: Insights from Open Source Software Development". A working paper of the Reginald H Jones Center. The Wharton School. University of Pennsylvania.

13 Time differences around the world. "A time zone is a region of the Earth that has adopted the same standard time, usually referred to as the local time." See *en.wikepedia.org*

However, Kogut and Meitu have pointed out that this type of diurnal development relies heavily on centralized planning and co-ordination of global teams. It further underpins the fact that the initial innovative task of design and new product planning is also centralized in the leading and post-industrial nations of the west. In this situation, the software engineers in the developing countries tend to remain underutilized and the innovation engines of the west continue to be expensive.

Global sourcing had made the people skeptical about whether innovation is location dependent. "The implicit model of innovation is that good ideas come from innovators usually located near customer needs. These innovators create the architecture and the design. This is no longer a model of coordinating productivity. It is a model of getting the best ideas. But maximizing creativity is often like stirring the witch's brew: the recipe is unknown." (Kogut & Meitu, 2000)

Kogut and Meitu have noted the role of Indian software houses like Wipro and Infosys, who are taking part in the global innovation process by developing their own products, besides providing software developments services to the US firms. Over the years, Indian firms that have been operational in the US have been more innovative by being directly located in the 'customer demand zone' or the end-user's market. So by moving onshore, these offshore firms can better understand and hence better define the customer's needs. The idea is to share the locus of innovation between the offshore and onshore sites.

Exploring the possibility of virtual development is the next thought. For instance, Trinitech, Inc. is an Irish software firm, which realizes that in order to develop innovative software, it must start its operations in the customer's market. So, the company expands its operations across Princeton, San Jose, Frankfurt and Dublin for developing software on a global scale. Work done by engineers at Dublin is virtually passed over to their teams in Princeton and San Jose at the end of the working day. The Internet which facilitates the coordination between global teams, allows the innovation process to be fast and inexpensive.

Thus, the emerging process which encourages innovation and creates opportunities for web connected programmers like the community of software developers from across the world to meet and develop new (and innovative) software products on a global scale is termed as e-Innovation.

2.2. Model 2: Outsourcing and Open Sourcing

The second model proposed by Kogut and Meitu, shifts the focus from the centralized model of innovation to accommodate the bottom-up innovation potential promised by the Internet, which allows an increasing number of innovators to virtually meet and innovate on a global scale. Thus, model 2 of e-Innovation harnesses distributed innovation by allowing natural intelligence to be distributed widely and controls the monopoly of the wealthiest firms or countries.

This is accomplished in two ways. Firstly, by outsourcing innovation, say for example, to the software providers in Russia, India or Eastern Europe, so that innovation is not centralized to the expensive software companies of the west. The central theme of outsourcing innovation is that the software industry is global in nature and innovation is not centralized to the countries with main markets. Irrespective of whether the software engineer is physically present in the customers market, or he designs the software, writes the technical briefings and finally delivers the solution to the customer through the Internet. The customer might never meet up the software engineer. Thus, the proximity between the software engineer and the customer is no longer a primary condition of innovation.

For example, an Indian firm like Wipro which works as a supplier to firms from the main market aspires to be innovative in spite of being located far off from the final market. However, the basic problem has been the conventional perception that the innovations are designed by customers located in the final market. Kogut and Meitu have cited the instance of a customer from the final market of San Diego who requests the Wipro center at Bangalore to develop a software product. The Indian software engineer defines the customer requirement, designs the architecture and finally delivers the product to the customer through the net. This happens without the engineer meeting the customer.

Alternatively, software companies may choose to have offshore operations at sites where labor wages are lower, while controlling the software design and innovations in-house, or even encouraging bottom-up innovation by developing software modules. For instance, software firms like Netscape and Adobe inspired the developers to build software modules, by supplying the software development tools and tutorials through the Internet. Similarly, PalmPilot, which is the Personal Digital Assistance (PDA) of 3 Com, have formed a global network of around 3500 innovators (programmers) for developing PalmPilot. 3 Com provides the freeware[14] and shareware[15] through the net.

Secondly, this model relies heavily on open source development to promote the bottom-up innovation effect of the Internet. According to Kogut and Meitu, the open source software development allows software innovations to be practiced in a distributed community. It is a radical move from the traditional style of proprietary coding. The advantage is the creation of a global pool of programmers – hackers or other software engineers, who are connected through the web.

The open source approach encourages the company or individual to release the initial source code of the program (like the browser or operating system) through the Internet. For instance, in 1998, Netscape had published the source code for Communicator 5.0 to compete Microsoft in the web-browsing category of products. A prominent example of open source software is the development of the operating system LINUX. In the early 90s, Linus Torvald, a Finish hacker had posted a question on an Internet newsgroup, intended for the minix (compact version of UNIX) developers. This initiative was a part of his hobby and was intended at developing a free operating system for PCs which later became the LINUX (UNIX like) operating System. Thereby, Torvald became the key player of the open source movement. The open source approach, which promotes the 'open innovation paradigm' (see box), guides the firms with flexible innovation strategies to meet market demand and customer requirements, while taking into account the company's objectives.

The process of global sourcing and open sourcing can be coupled with other traditional methods of new product development to yield a workable e-innovation strategy.

---

14 "Software that is available free of charge for personal use." See *www.educationworld.com/help/glossary.shtml*

15 "Computer software developed for the public domain, which can be used or copied without infringing copyright. Programmers typically get paid a small one time fee from users who find the software useful." See *www.tamu.edu/ode/glossary.html*

The Open Innovation Paradigm

Throughout the 20th century, enterprises depended upon closed innovation or centralized innovation wherein successful innovation was the monopoly of central R&D organizations, such as AT&T's Bell Labs and innovation was more in-house in nature. However, in the present era, this centralized approach to R&D is becoming outdated in most of the industries and the firms are depending on external resources for new product ideas, technologies and means to innovate and compete. The logic behind the 'Open innovation' paradigm is that valuable information and ideas will be lost if not widely disseminated. Thus, in the case of open 'innovation', the role of R&D extends much beyond the firm's boundaries. According to Henry W. Cherbourg, "Specifically, companies must now harness outside ideas to advance their own businesses while leveraging their internal ideas outside their current operations. That fundamental change offers novel ways to create value — along with new opportunities to claim portions of that value."

The collaborative development of software by a worldwide community of web connected software developers has led to the open source approach. This approach results in the exploitation of ideas and Intellectual Property (IP) and often leads to the development of improved software. A renowned example is the development of the operating system LINUX.

By opening up a firm's boundaries, 'open innovation' allows the flow of external knowledge into the firm, thereby enriching the firm's knowledge base. This results in the creation of flexible innovation strategies which are capable of addressing market demands and matching company requirements. For example, innovative companies like Procter and Gamble, has a Global Technology Council and an internal network entitled the Innovation Net. Here, the entrepreneurs explore the Internet, global patent databases and other potential sources, which help the company to innovate. IBM is another example of an innovative player in the IT market, whose continual success depends upon the steady development of its research strategy. Driven by the forces of globalization and emerging technologies like e-business, IBM has sustained stiff competition over the years, by investing in research and development and focusing on market and customer demands. Thus, open Innovation helps firms to boost their revenues by harnessing relationships with external firms.

3. E-Innovation

Nowadays, due to shorter innovation life cycles, increasing expenses on research and the lack of adequate resources, the companies are increasingly adopting innovative strategies to sustain competitive edge and e-innovation is a tool that allows businesses around the globe and across most sectors of the economy to gain competitive advantage.

According to Bob Cotton (2002), "e-Innovation is the emerging art of harnessing the bottom up power of globally networked individuals and teams to conceive better products, and to create them and bring them to market more efficiently, through a combination of internal design, planning and new product development methodologies and global innovation-sourcing and open sourcing (open-source software development)." He has further pointed out that in the present environment of continuous radical change, the methods of product design, strategic planning and new product development must continuously evolve in order to adapt to the change. This proactive response to change results from the convergence of several disciplines and processes like product design, planning, technology scanning, forecasting, creativity, new product development and market intelligence, to name a few. So, the strategy for proactively responding to an environment whose main attribute is change is called 'e-Innovation'.

The converging business processes that lead to e-innovation broadly combine competitive intelligence, strategic corporate planning and new product development and these disciplines have emerged, over the past five decades. Competitive intelligence is a subject that deals with technology scoping[16], research analysis, forecasting and market intelligence. While strategic corporate planning focuses on the processes of new business development and new product development, new product development stems from idea generation, design, production planning, software production and marketing plan.

The explosive growth in global software development reinforces the ability of e-innovation to contribute to the phenomenon of global innovation. Although the software sector is pivotal to the global economy, it is important to acknowledge that the implication of e-innovation extends far beyond the software sector like in the manufacturing or service sectors. According to Kogut and Meitu "e-innovation is not just possible only for software, but for all fields in which cooperation can be arranged by modules and there exists a wide understanding of a common language and culture."

Nowadays, every business benefits from a real-time business environment. The internet is allowing this real-time business environment to flourish and it is changing the way in which businesses communicate, produce and trade. With an increasing number of businesses accessing the internet, and adopting e-business

---

16 Technology scoping deals with scanning or scoping the technology environment to identify the technology developments those are important with respect to the company, marketplace, products and plans.

solutions, the conventional linear supply chain is getting integrated into a network of suppliers, business partners and customers. The repositioning of business to addresses and benefit from the opportunities created by massive networking and ubiquitous processing is called e-business. It is being vastly adopted through out the economy primarily because such tools and applications help the firms to gain competitive advantage. These 'innovative' e-business solutions are designed and created by the 'software engineers' in the software laboratories who carefully identify and define customer's needs, re-enforces the role played by the software industry in driving the design and creation of all ICT artifacts. ICT connectivity is gaining prevalence in businesses of all sizes. This clearly indicates that ICTs are vital technologies that must be in place to harness innovation. In the subsequent section, the article will define e-business and explore e-business as a tool that drives electronic innovation.

4. E-Business and Innovation

E-Business is defined as Internet-mediated integration of business processes, applications, and information systems. (Tiwana & McLean, 2001). Thus, e-business involves the use of an array of tools like the intranet, extranet, portals, mobile, content management, etc. The OECD[17] defines e-business as "automated business processes (both intra-and inter-firm) over computer mediated networks."

According to Waddell and Singh (2004) "e-business is a revolution that brings with it new ways of dealing with customers and business partners, new revenue streams, new ways of processing information, new organization structures, new skill sets, electronic supply chains, new standards and policies, new collaborations and the need for adaptable business strategies." From this viewpoint, e-business is an innovative tool that opens new markets and creates new product opportunities for organizations. By transforming the traditional way of doing business, e-business redefines the existing business processes and transforms the internal processes of an organization. In doing so, continued impacts on innovation, competition and economic growth can be realized.

[17] Organization for Economic Cooperation and Management. (OECD) is an international organization which handles economic, social and governance challenges in a globalised economy.

E-Business innovations deal with change and the rapidity of change plays a key role in the entire innovation process. Although, e-business has the capacity to redefine the business processes of an organization and harness innovation, the positive outcome of implementing e-business will be fully realized with effective management of related changes. E-business implementations deal largely with changes in company culture often expressed as a system of shared meaning within an organization determining the way employees act. (Singh, Waddell. 2003). Hence change management[18] plays a crucial role in determining the success of e-business. E-business in some organizations have revealed dissatisfactory results in the past not because of drawbacks in any technology or tactic but because the organizational staff were resistant to change. To cope with organizational change, organizations implementing e-business must train their staff to acquire the skills needed to use e-business tools. Proper training and learning mechanisms play a crucial role in effective change management. This signifies that human resource and skills play a major role in determining the successful adoption of e-business tools.

That various policy instruments support e-business innovations has been reiterated by a recent conference background paper[19]. The paper has outlined the kind of policies that enable e-business innovation in large as well as small and medium enterprises. Recent trends in public governance of e-business and innovation in Europe has revealed a close relation between e-business and innovation policies. The paper has defined innovation policy as "a set of policy actions to raise the quantity and efficiency of innovation activities – thus, the creation, adaptation and adoption of new or improved products, processes or services." In today's climate of continuous change, a modern innovation policy, besides technological innovation, must also focus on organizational innovation. Therefore, since e-business facilitates business competitiveness, it has to be closely linked to innovation.

---

18 "Activities involved in (1) defining and instilling new values, attitudes, norms, and behaviors within an organization that support new ways of doing work and overcome resistance to change; (2) building consensus among customers and stakeholders on specific changes designed to better meet their needs; and (3) planning, testing, and implementing all aspects of the transition from one organizational structure or business process to another.", *www.gao.gov/special.pubs/bprag/bprgloss.htm*

19 European Conference on Innovation and e-Business. 26 –27 May 2005. Charlemagne Conference Centre Rue de la Loi 170, Brussels. Output Paper. Technolpolis Group.

4.1 Innovation Models in E-Business

Existing literature on technological innovation confirm to the fundamental idea that innovation can be classified as incremental, radical, architectural or modular, each having different competitive effects. The various classifications of innovation depend upon the impact each one will have on the established potential of the firm. This idea leads to the classification of innovation on the basis of its impact – on components and the linkages between the components.

Henderson and Clark have pointed out the difference between a product as a whole (the system) and the product as a set of components. For instance, a fan's major components (parts) are the blades, the motor, the blade guard, the control system, and it is the total architecture of the fan that determines how the various components will work collectively. The example guides us to the definition of a component. According to Henderson and Clark, "a component is defined as a physically distinct portion of the product that embodies a core design concept and performs a well defined function."

Knowledge of both components and architectures are essential for successful product development. Component knowledge describes the core design concept of a component and the physical implementation of the design concept in a particular component. Architectural knowledge on the other hand, is the way that various components of a product are integrated and linked together to form a coherent whole (the product in its entirety).

'Architectural' innovation alters the architectural knowledge of a product and leaves the component knowledge of the product unchanged. This type of innovation reconfigures the existing system by linking components in a new way.

For example, in the mid-1970s, Xerox had faced stiff competition from small copiers, which were more reliable than the traditional products i.e., the copiers of Xerox. Although Xerox was the inventor of the core technology, the company took around eight years to launch a competitive product in the market. During that period it lost significant market share. It was during this time that architectural innovation faced Xerox.

According to Henderson and Clark, "Incremental innovation introduces relatively minor changes to the existing product, exploits the potential of the established design, and often reinforces the dominance of established firms" and radical innovation "is based on a different set of engineering and scientific principles and opens up whole new markets and potential applications."

Thus, while incremental innovation improves an existing product design, radical innovation creates a new set of core design concepts, which are implemented in components and then linked together in a new architecture. Radical innovation can create new markets and can often jeopardize established firms by allowing new firms to enter markets successfully. An exemplar would be *Kroger.com* which sells grocery coupons through an Internet integration of coupon systems.

Yet another type of innovation refers to the changes in the core design concepts of a technology, while leaving the architecture of the product unaltered. This type of innovation is called 'modular' innovation'. An instance of modular innovation can be seen at *Amazon.com*, where a business model is based on modular e-commerce.

The differences between the components and the architectures suggest that the objects are basically modular to some degree.

Both the business models and e-business information systems are a collection of components. So, e-business innovations can be categorized in any of the four quadrants of Figure 1. It is helpful to differentiate between innovations at the business model level with that at the systems level. Tiwana and McLean (2001) have suggested that the knowledge of components and organizational architectures can be destroyed by innovations at the business model level. This leads to the classification of the e-business model innovations as modular, radical, architectural or incremental. Systems level innovations, on the other hand, are mostly architectural and these innovations deal with the facilitating systems that participate in the innovation process. For instance, the facilitating system at *WebGrocer.com* refers to the web-connected logistics system. This system which facilitates the re-combination of existing technologies in new ways, leads to architectural innovation at *WebGrocer.com*.

Figure 1: Business Model and Systems Level Innovation Models

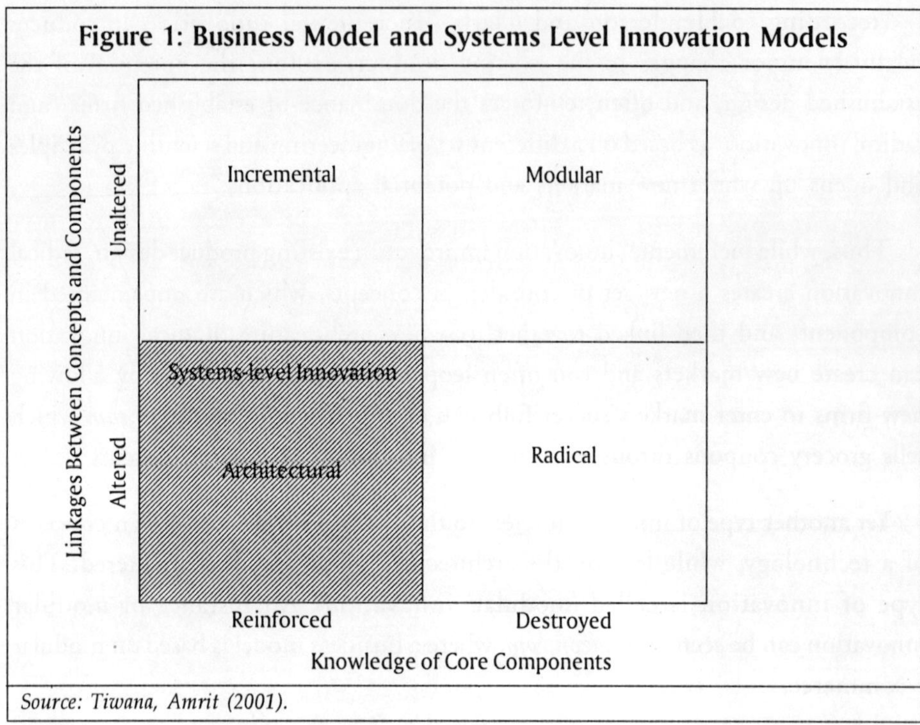

Source: Tiwana, Amrit (2001).

4.2 Emerging Trends in E-Business

A result of a recent survey conducted by e-Business Watch in 2005, has confirmed that although the performance of a firm depends upon the innovative activities of the firm, the relation between the two is independent of the company's size. Therefore, ICT-based innovations are useful for both large and small firms. Moreover, innovative activities help in bridging the digital divide between the large enterprises and the SMEs. Consequently, in today's era of innovation, SMEs are gaining competitive edge through sustained innovations.

Recently, the e-Business W@tch Report (2005) reveals an increasing trend towards the adoption of ICT infrastructure by both the large and small enterprises of the 7 European Union (EU)[20] member states. Deployment of ICT network infrastructure reveals further advancements in Internet connectivity and that 96%

[20] The European Union (EU) is a family of democratic European countries, committed to working together for peace and prosperity Czech Republic, France, Germany, Italy, Poland, Spain and the UK

of employees interviewed from the 10 sectors[21], worked in enterprises which had an Internet connection. The adoption of the broadband infrastructure reveals an increase in the share of firms that uses Digital Subscriber Lines (DSL) across all sectors of the EU member states. Furthermore, the adoption of ICT networks like – Local Area Networks (LAN), Wireless Local Area Networks (WLAN), Virtual Private Networks (VPN) and Wide Area Networks (WAN) that facilitate intra-enterprise as well as inter-enterprise communication reveals significant signs of growth. The survey result also shows an increasing rate of adoption of Remote

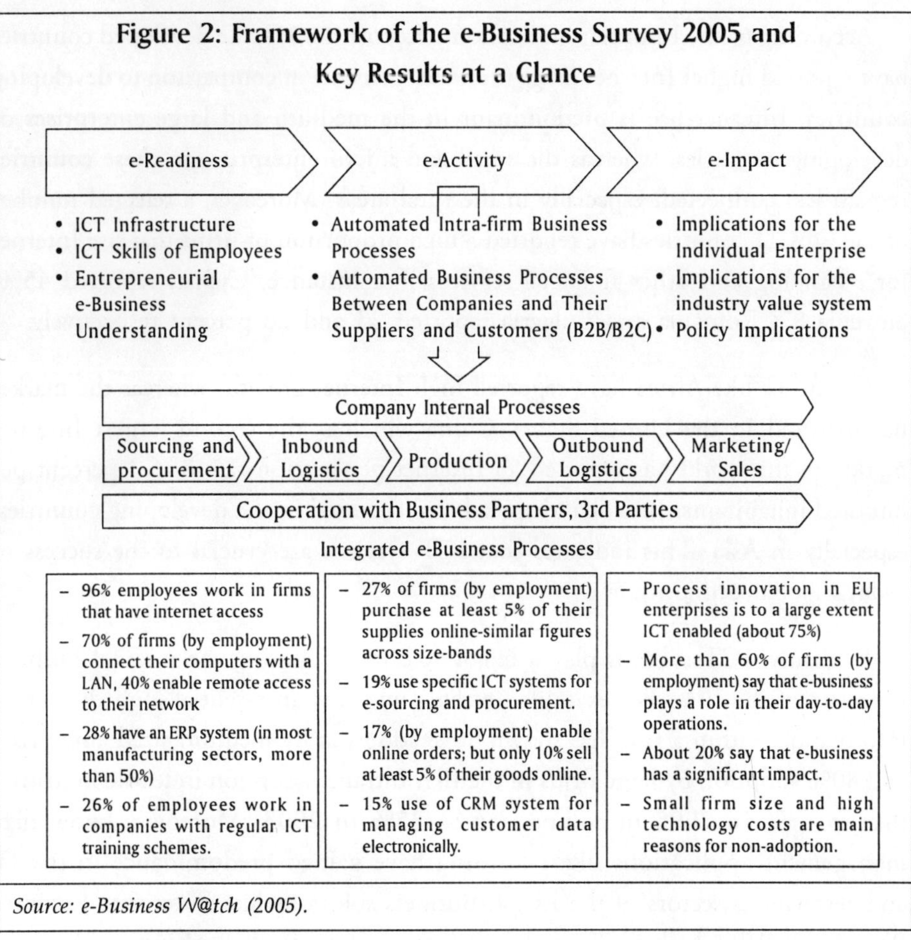

Figure 2: Framework of the e-Business Survey 2005 and Key Results at a Glance

Source: e-Business W@tch (2005).

21 The research was conducted in about 5200 enterprises across ten sectors of the 7 EU member states. The 10 sectors comprised of food and beverages, textile industry, publishing and printing, pharmaceutical, publishing and printing, automotive industry, aerospace, construction, tourism and IT services.

Access Solutions for tele work and mobile work. These solutions allow the field workers of a firm like the sales force and the managers (who travel frequently), to access the firms' computer networks from remote locations. Other mobile solutions like the mobile e-mail; mobile PIM (Personal Information Management) Mobile CRM (Customer Relationship Management) and Mobile Stock Recording (for recording the stocks of products at the site of the retailer using mobile devices.) systems are expected to gain prominence in most sectors of the EU member states.

According to the Information Economy Report (2005), the developed countries have reported higher Internet usage (up to 90 percent) in comparison to developing countries. Internet use is predominant in the medium and large enterprises of developing countries, whereas the small and micro enterprises in these countries remain less connected, especially in the rural areas. Moreover, a selected number of the OECD countries have reported a high proportion of firms that use Internet for e-banking and other financial services. For instance, Cyprus reported 45%; Slovenia 87, Romania and Bulgaria reported 23 and 26 percent respectively.

Countries like Africa have reported high Internet growth, whereas the market has matured in the United States. China which is the second largest Internet market in the world has reported an Internet penetration rate of 6.3 percent per hundred inhabitants. Broadband spread has increased in the developing countries, especially in Asia. This indicates that ICT systems are crucial to the success of today's global economy.

Evidently, ICT systems play a major role in integrating the internal business processes of the firm. For example, intranet which is an essential tool for sharing information within a firm has shown 50% adoption by medium sized enterprises and 80% adoption by large firms in the EU. Intranet adoption in textile industries rose to 45% in 2005 in comparison to 35% in 2003. Moreover, knowledge management applications like e-learning have gained predominance in the IT and aeronautics sectors of the EU. E-Business solutions like Enterprise Resource Planning (ERP) which facilitate the planning and controlling of internal business processes, is a key function of the internal ICT systems. These ERP solutions are pivotal to the "production and product related ICT systems, including systems for product planning, purchasing, inventory management, order tracking and finance."[22] Therefore, large scale deployments of ERP systems signify the extent of e-business maturity. Recently, the e-business report (2005) reveals an increase in ERP adoption across large, medium and small enterprises in the EU in comparison to the findings in 2003/04. The large enterprises where ERP adoption is predominant include the manufacturing, and retail companies. Other ICT systems for optimizing the firm's internal business processes include Electronic Data Management (EDM)[23] that can be linked to ERP systems. However, the adoption rate of EDM systems is quite low and only 9% of firms from all the sectors in the EU reveal adoption of these solutions.

E-procurement is gaining momentum in the manufacturing sectors across the globe. The key driver behind procuring supplies electronically is the intention to decrease the direct cost of supplies and increase the efficiency of the core processes inside the firm and allow communication with the suppliers. "E-procurement is the business-to-business purchase and sale of supplies and services over the Internet."[24] Furthermore, e-procurement systems rely largely on standardization and inter-operability of the (Business-to-Business) B2B procurement processes. For instance, documents like product catalogues, orders, payments and invoices need to be exchanged through a standardized format, so that the companies can benefit through considerable cost reductions. According to the survey conducted by e-Business W@tch (2005), 44% of companies from the 10 sectors practiced e-procurement in early 2005. B2B online trading confirmed an increasing shift towards online purchase, with 40-60% of the firms accounting for the same.

INTEL, a large innovative enterprise well known for designing and manufacturing microprocessors and integrated circuits, exemplifies a successful deployer of e-procurement solutions. A recent journal[25] describes the technological developments of INTEL to strengthen the Indirect Materials (IDM)[26] supply

22 European e-Business Report 2005, *www.ebusiness-watch.org*

23 "EDM (Electronic Document Management) is the management of different kinds and formats of documents in an enterprise, usually enabling a single view of (otherwise) multiple databases." (European E-Business report 2005)

24 European E-Business Report – 2005 Edition, *www.ebusiness-watch.org/resources/documents/eBusiness-Report-2005.pdf*

25 *Intel technology Journal* – 2005– volume 09 issue 03

26 Indirect Materials (IDM) can be defined as goods and services that are not directly used in the production of the Intel products.

chain. Intel's indirect material organization had launched the e-procurement program in 2002 in order to strengthen the IDM supply chain, because IDM expenses reported 60% of Intel's expenses with a major impact on INTEL's supply chain and bottom line profits. These e-procurement systems at INTEL constitute various innovative solutions which depend upon a global enterprise resource planning system and comprise e-catalogs and Internet negotiations. Internet negotiations or on-line negotiations allow multiple suppliers to bid in real-time. Since, this process utilizes the Internet, it reduces cycle time and provides cost advantage. E-catalogs on the other hand favor suppliers by linking the requisitioners to the supply base and that the deployment of these online catalogs at INTEL will continue till 2008.

Recently, Customer Relationship Management Systems (CRM), has gained worldwide predominance, especially in the large enterprises (See Figure3). These systems are integrated software applications that help the companies to gather and process information about customers. ICT systems also support online sales and marketing processes by applying specialized innovative software solutions

Figure 3: Companies Using a CRM System (2005)

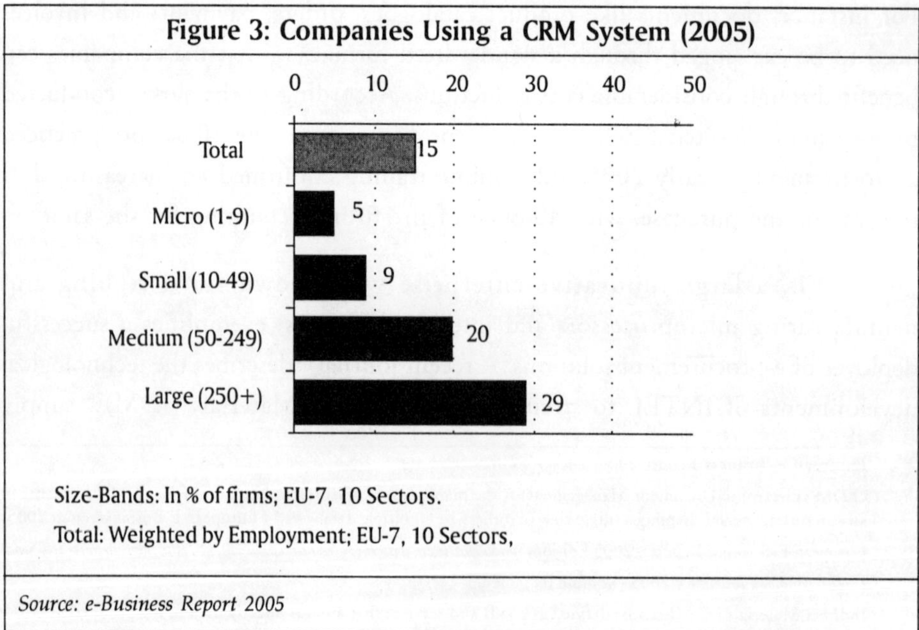

Size-Bands: In % of firms; EU-7, 10 Sectors.

Total: Weighted by Employment; EU-7, 10 Sectors,

Source: e-Business Report 2005

and services based on the Internet. E-marketing and sales have gained prevalence across the globe. (See Figure 4)

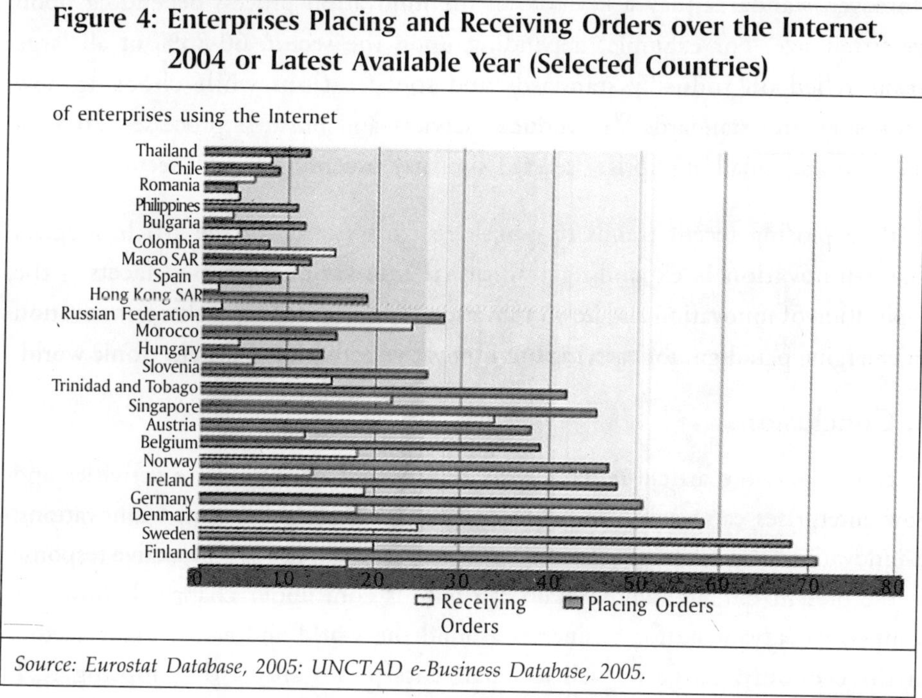

Figure 4: Enterprises Placing and Receiving Orders over the Internet, 2004 or Latest Available Year (Selected Countries)

Source: Eurostat Database, 2005: UNCTAD e-Business Database, 2005.

Looking into various ICT systems that facilitate e-business functions, it is evident that standards play a significant role in e-business inter-operability. Inter-operability is "the ability of e-business systems and applications to work seamlessly together, and for diverse information resources to be systematically and consistently accessible to applications, when required." While technical inter-operability allows different companies to interact using software solutions, Business Inter-operability (BI) on the other hand deals with collaboration amongst companies and how their respective business processes can be aligned to carry out business electronically. BI provides the trading communities with the semantics and agreements of inter-enterprise collaboration. The recent growth in the interoperable public networks and ICT systems implies that these systems are essential for carrying out worldwide business activities and public services. However, this increasing reliance of enterprises on these ICT systems demands appropriate security measures in the networks to ensure correct functioning of the value chains. The e-business reports (2005) reflects the adoption of ICT security controls like firewall and secure servers across all sectors of the EU. Moreover, standards play a key role in the innovation process depending upon the firm's size. For example, depending upon the sector, 60-85% of all large firms' relied on industry standards and specifications while choosing new technology and standards for products, services and business processes. 20-45% of micro and small enterprises reacted similarly excepting the IT sector.

By exploring recent trends in e-business, this section of the article suggests that e-innovation is expanding traditional innovation into two facets – the application of innovation and how innovation is delivered. This makes e-innovation an emerging paradigm for carrying out innovative activities in the electronic world.

5. Conclusion

In conclusion, the article reiterates the significance of innovative activities and how enterprises can attain competitive advantage through sustained innovations. E-innovation is an evolving strategy that enterprises can use as a proactive response to the present climate, whose main attribute is continuous change. It promises competitive advantage for businesses around the world and across many sectors of the economy. Large as well as small enterprises are vastly adopting ICT infrastructure and opening doors for technology innovation. The rapidity of technological advancements is characterized by advancements in ICTs, which are driving the pace of electronic innovations across the globe. Underpinning ICT developments is the field of software engineering which is driving the changes in the electronic market place. The article discusses the role of software in the innovation process and explores new processes of software development like global sourcing and open sourcing. Fundamental to both models is the Internet which is an enormous bottom-up innovation machine. Finally, the article explicates the role of e-business in innovation and draws upon recent trends, practices and experiences pertaining to e-innovation with focus on e-business.

(Moonmoon Bhattacharya is the consulting editor at Icfai Research Centre, Kolkata).

References

1. Brad Wheeler. "Open Source 2007. How did this happen?".
2. Cotton, Bob (2002). "E-Innovation." Capstone Publishing (a Wiley Company), Oxford, United Kingdom.
3. Gassmann, Oliver and Enkel, Ellen (2004). "Towards a Theory of Open Innovation: Three Core Process Archetypes." Institute of Technology Management, University of St. Gallen, Switzerland.
4. Ghiya, Kinnar and Powers, Marci (2005). "E-Procurement-Strengthening the Indirect Supply Chain through Technology Globalization." *Intel technology Journal,* Volume 9, Issue 3, 2005.
5. Henderson, Rebecca and Clark, Kim (1990). "Architectural Innovation: The Reconfiguration of Existing Product Technologies and The Failure of Established Firms." Administrative Science Quarterly. Cornell University Graduate School of Management.
6. Henry W. Chesbrough. "The Era of Open Innovation." *MIT Sloan Management Review,* 2003
7. "Innovation 2005", Executive Summary, Boston Consulting Group.
8. "Information Economy Report 2005". *www.unctad.org*
9. Kogut & Meitu (2000). "The Emergence of e-Innovation: Insights from Open Source Software Development." A working paper of the Reginald H Jones Center. The Wharton School. University of Pennsylvania.
10. M Singh, D Waddell – 2003. "E-Business Innovation and Change Management." Idea Group Inc (IGI).
11. "Open source: Open for Business", *www.csc.com*
12. Peyman Oreizy, Gail Kaiser, "The Web as Enabling Technology for Software Development and Distribution," *IEEE Internet Computing,* vol. 01, no. 6, pp. 84-87, 1997.
13. Rebecca Allinson, Alexandrea Rammer, Patries Boekholt and Jan-Frens van Giessel. "European Conference on Innovation and e-Business. 26 –27 May 2005." Charlemagne Conference Centre Rue de la Loi 170, Brussels. Output Paper. Technopolis Group
14. "The European e-Business Report 2005" edition.4th Synthesis Report of The e-Business W@tch. *European Commission Enterprise & Industry Directorate Journal. www.ebusiness-watch.org.*
15. Tiwana, McLean (2001). "Recombinant Knowledge Structures and models of E-Business Innovation." The 9th European Conference on Information Systems Bled, Slovenia, June 27-29, 2001.

16. *www.tecrime.com*
17. *medicines.mhra.gov.uk/ourwork/licensingmeds/types/thmpd/glossary.htm*
18. *www.sei.cmu.edu/architecture/definitions.html*
19. *www.trendchart.org*
20. *en.wikepedia.org*
21. *www.gao.gov*
22. *www.educationworld.com*
23. *www.tamu.edu*
24. *www.investordictionary.com*

3

The Knowledge Based View and Open Innovation: Strategies from Open Source Software

Scott Gallagher and Joel West

The knowledge-based view has been advanced as an alternative way to conceptualize the firm. "Open innovation" where firms focus on identifying, exploiting and integrating external knowledge into their internal R&D activities has been suggested as a new paradigm for corporate innovation. As such, the knowledge-based view may greatly inform scholarship and practice regarding the critical insights of open innovation.

We use the knowledge-based view to develop a typology of open innovation strategies centered on appropriability and knowledge/product alignment. From this, we identify four strategies – pooled R&D, spinouts, selling complements and attracting donated complements. We show how firms used these strategies to support their innovation strategies in the software browser, operating system, server, and game markets. We conclude with suggestions as to how these principles can be applied to other industries, as well as new questions raised by this study.

Introduction

Open innovation models stress the importance of using a broad range of sources for a firm's innovation and invention activities, including customers, rivals, academics, and firms in unrelated industries, while simultaneously using creative methods to exploit a firm's resulting IP (Chesbrough, 2003). Frequently contrasted to the traditional vertical integration model where internal R&D activities lead to internally developed products that are then distributed by the firm, open innovation offers the promise that firms can achieve a greater return on their innovative activities and their resulting Intellectual Property (IP). Here we define open innovation as systematically encouraging and exploring a wide range of internal and external sources for innovation opportunities, consciously integrating that exploration with firm capabilities and resources, and broadly exploiting those opportunities through multiple channels.

Of course, the use of external sources of innovation is nothing new and scholars have begun to develop an alternative view of the firm that places at its center the possession of knowledge. The advent of a Knowledge-based View (KBV) is especially appropriate given the rise of outsourcing and exceptionally useful for considering open innovation because of the KBV's focus on accessing knowledge rather than the acquisition of knowledge (Grant and Baden-Fuller, 2004). While it is admittedly not yet a full theory of the firm, the KBV models the firm as an institution for integrating knowledge, both internal and external (Grant, 1996). While Simon (1991) has noted that initially learning takes place within the heads of individuals, firms can become repositories of that knowledge in the form of machines, patents, policies, procedures, or even culture (March, 1991). Given the breakdown in the virtuous circle of innovation cited by open innovation proponents, where firms, e.g., Bell Labs, invested in basic research for its own sake, the KBV may be an especially useful lens to identity firm strategies for this environment (Chesbrough, 2003).

Over the past 20 years, an increasingly popular example of open innovation has been open source software, which involves collaboration between firms, suppliers, customers and makers of related products to pool software R&D to produce a shared technology such as the Linux operating system. The rise of this method of software production is especially interesting for the KBV with its focus on accessing rather than acquiring knowledge. Here we consider patterns of open source innovation as an exemplar for more general forms of open innovation, and how open source strategies used by firms can enhance firm performance.

Innovation and the Knowledge Based View

The pace of technological advance has often been sub-divided into two phases – invention (a scientific breakthrough) and innovation (commercialization of the invention). Nelson & Winter (1982: 263) attribute the distinction to Schumpeter (1934). This split parallels a similar bifurcation between research and development, where inventions come from basic research and innovations from the development group. Like Nelson and Winter, we use "innovation" in its broadest sense to refer to the entire process by which technological change is deployed in commercial products.[1]

From the perspective of the firm, two critical issues arise concerning innovation, its source and its exploitation. What is the best way to generate innovation? How can profits be maximized from the resulting innovations? One of the key insights driving the benefits of internalizing knowledge is that while useful knowledge is notoriously difficult to generate it can be shared at very low cost providing a firm with economies of scale as well as potential economies of scope (Grant, 1996). Of course, it can also "leak out" of the firm providing a means for rivals and imitators to benefit from the innovation as well (Teece, 1986). This section discusses the sources and uses of innovation.

Proprietary R&D as a Source of Innovation

One of the most successful innovation models to emerge was a "proprietary" model where large enterprises internalized their R&D activities. Historical accounts suggest that early R&D activities grew out of the need in many industries to maintain and improve production activities (Chandler, 1990). Because activities were frequently unique for each firm, investments in R&D were firm-specific and thus (as predicted by transaction cost economics) firms internalized their

---

[1] We do not attempt to define knowledge beyond the tautological "what is known." We are unusually pragmatic here because there is little philosophical agreement on exactly what is knowable.

R&D expenditures (Williamson, 1991). From such R&D firms naturally moved to exploit their accumulated knowledge to develop new products, thereby enhancing their economies of scope and in many industries large scale dedicated R&D functions emerged, providing a barrier to entry through economies of scale (Chandler, 1990). This logic suggests that firms should pursue internal innovation activities when they embody relatively specific assets.

Absorbing External Knowledge as a Source of Innovation

Of course, considerable knowledge is generated beyond the confines of the firm. Even the proponents of the proprietary model never claimed to explain all innovation activity. In addition to internally generated knowledge, von Hippel (1988) identified four external sources:

1) Suppliers and customers;
2) University, government and private laboratories;
3) Competitors; and
4) Other nations.

Firms that fail to exploit such external R&D may be at a severe competitive disadvantage (Rosenberg and Steinmueller, 1998).

Many models have been developed to explain how firms can exploit external knowledge. Perhaps the simplest method is to imitate a competitor: such free riding on the product and market investments of rivals is a common way for firms to overcome a first mover strategy (Lieberman and Montgomery, 1998). Consulting with customers can provide firms ideas about discovering, developing, and refining innovations (von Hippel, 1988). Public sources are also an important source of knowledge, for example government R&D spending was identified almost 50 years ago as an important stimulus for private R&D (David, Hall, and Toole, 2000). Similarly, university research is often explicitly funded to generate external spillovers (Colyvas *et al*, 2002). However, despite the potential for spillovers, developing absorptive capacity, via internal R&D investments appears to be an important prerequisite for converting external knowledge into internal innovation (Cohen and Levinthal, 1990).

The Knowledge Based View

The central question for "open" versus proprietary innovation approaches is essentially a question of where should the boundaries of the firm lie? As an emerging theory of the firm, the KBV has some potential to inform this issue. Since it can frequently be non-rival and non-exclusive many institutions exist in developed countries to attempt to facilitate a market for knowledge, e.g., patent protection (Spender, 1992). The KBV attempts to model the boundaries of the firm based on its ability to facilitate the creation and use of knowledge.

How do firms facilitate the creation of knowledge? Since knowledge creation requires greater specialization than is needed for its utilization, (e.g., a college professor contrasted with a college student) the firm coordinates the efforts of individual specialists and prevents opportunism (Grant, 1996). Therefore, the firm permits individuals to specialize in developing expertise, while establishing mechanisms to facilitate the coordination of the resulting knowledge in transforming inputs into outputs (Grant, 1997, p. 451). While it can be argued that this is a special case of Coase/Williamson transaction cost theory of the firm, KBV proponents note that the key is the emphasis upon the firm as an organization for managing team production, not simply minimizing transaction costs between team members (Grant, 1996). The historical record is consistent with this framework – despite the availability of external research organizations, firms developed internal R&D functions because of the specialist knowledge that built up around their production capacities (Chandler, 1990). Steve Jobs might have toured Xerox's PARC to see the idea of the mouse, but specialized Apple engineers created the knowledge to develop it, integrate it with the Lisa and then the Macintosh computers, and finally produce it efficiently.

What about the application of knowledge? The key insight of the KBV is that knowledge transfer is not always the most efficient approach to knowledge integration (Grant, 1996). For example, Steve Wozniak did not teach Steve Jobs how to build an Apple II, but they effectively combined their talents in the firm called Apple Computer (Grant, 1997). For thinking about vertical integration and diversification, the key insight is how well knowledge can be encoded, frequently in the form of a product, as it moves from one production state to another (Grant, 1996; 1997). While knowledge is created by specialists it frequently isn't specialized and can therefore provide economies of scope (Grant, 1996). So one item of knowledge, e.g., an effective management technique, may provide benefits in multiple markets or for multiple processes. Grant and Baden-Fuller (2004) utilize the idea of product – knowledge congruence with product and knowledge domains mapped onto a matrix.

The Open Innovation Paradigm & The Knowledge Based View

In contrast to earlier models and "fully integrated innovators" like AT&T (now Lucent) Bell Labs and IBM which do basic research through commercial products, open innovation celebrates success stories like Cisco, Intel and Microsoft, which initially succeed by leveraging the basic research of others (Chesbrough, 2003). Under this paradigm, firms exploit both internal and external sources of innovation, while maximizing the returns that accrue from both sources. This two-sided nature of open innovation, both generating and utilizing a firm's IP, goes beyond simple external innovation models.

Maximizing Returns to Internal Innovation

A concern unique to open innovation is the breadth of ways to best use the internal R&D capabilities of the firm to maximum advantage. Those capabilities can be used for

- generating innovations to be internally commercialized (the traditional model);
- building absorptive capacity and using that capacity to identify external innovations;
- generating innovations that generate returns through external commercialization (e.g., licensable patent portfolios); and
- generating IP that does not produce direct economic benefit, but indirectly generates a return through spillovers or sale of related goods and products.

Successful approaches will often combine a variety of these approaches. For example, to identify promising technologies Intel establishes research labs near promising university research groups, with open flows of information in both directions. If an innovation proves promising, Intel recruits the top academic researchers to help commercialize the technology and see it through to production (Tennenhouse, 2003).

This approach can be used cooperatively as well. For example, the GSM patent pool assembled by European telephone makers in the early 1990s. While the patents were often the result of (at times unrelated) basic research, contribution of a patent to the patent pool allowed firms to have favorable access to all of the IPR of the GSM standard, which created a cost advantage for European pool participants over potential Asian rivals (Bekkers *et al*, 2002).

Incorporating External Innovations

To benefit from external innovations two things are required. First, organizations need to identify worthwhile innovations, maintain the absorptive capacity to understand them, and be able to combine such spillovers with firm-specific internal knowledge to produce a product tailored to the firm's specific needs. However, even if external innovations are identified, that does not mean they will be incorporated into the firm's product strategies. A firm that was once highly successful at the integrated innovation model will tend to believe its innovations superior to any competing ideas from outsiders. For example, flush from its successful user-interface innovations of the 1980s, engineers at Apple Computer rejected external ideas in areas such as hand-held computers, adopting the phrase "not invented here" to describe such rejection (Kaplan 1996: 156).

Application of Knowledge Based View – Strategic Considerations for "Giving Away" a Firm's IP

Open innovation appears to have advantages for the creation and incorporation of IP that are not controversial, e.g., free ride if you can, or have been identified before, e.g., innovation comes from many sources (von Hipple, 1988). However, what also distinguishes open innovation is its focus on firms' maximizing the value of their IP, frequently by giving it away. This raises an interesting question, how can firms benefit by giving away their IP? Why should firms assign professionals, e.g., engineers, to work on products that are freely available to all? We suggest firms can benefit from giving their IP away in two primary ways, by economizing and by benefiting from the sale of complements.

Generating IP, supporting products that rely upon it, as well as monitoring and defending it entail costs for the firm. Economizing is simply attempting to minimize the costs of this entire portfolio by using a firm's IP strategically. If a firm's knowledge is incongruent with its product mix it should "export" it (Grant and Baden-Fuller, 2004). Licensing is the most traditional "export" method but licensing requires a willing licensee and all the problems of transferring information (Arrow, 1962), while at the same time costs are being incurred. Similarly, firms should seek to generate and access knowledge at the lowest possible cost. Collaboration, e.g., a strategic alliance, is a common way to share risks and reduce costs. However, this requires some knowledge and frequently IP contribution by the firm. So IP is just another asset to be used strategically by a firm. So just as an office building that a firm no longer needs can be efficiently sold at a loss or donated, so can IP.

Providing complements, e.g., selling razor blades to go with razors, can often be an effective strategy for firms. Many goods in computers and electronics fall into what Katz & Shapiro (1985) term the "hardware-software paradigm". As Teece (1986) notes, the base innovation ("hardware") requires an investment into producing complementary goods ("software") specialized for that innovation, in order to make the entire system useful. In many cases, these complements are more valuable than the core innovation. For example, makers of videogame consoles deliberately lose money or break even on the hardware so that they can make money from software royalties (Gallagher & Park, 2002). Therefore, in some cases giving away IP, e.g., subsidized video game players, can stimulate demand for a firm's even more profitable complements.

So giving away IP can clearly be beneficial. This leads to another question, what IP should firms seek to manage creatively, or "give away"? Here we rely on a key KBV insight – product-knowledge alignment. Obviously, where there is full alignment between products and a firm's knowledge they should focus on producing those products. However, even if a firm's knowledge is congruent with its current products it may find that it may want to seek outside knowledge. For example, the firm may want to expand into a foreign market about which it knows little, therefore it may form an alliance with a firm that has more knowledge about that market.

Therefore, we use the KBV to model the advantages of open innovation along how a firm may reap benefits (economizing versus selling complements) and how it should allocate its commitments to open innovation initiatives (degree of product-knowledge alignment). The next section takes the ideas of open innovation and applies them to several open source software projects.

Open Source as Open Innovation

Open source and other collaborative development techniques in the software industry offer examples of how the three key challenges of open innovation can and have been addressed by commercial firms. Open source also offers an approach to address what West (2003) refers to as an "essential tension" in information technology innovation – appropriating the returns from an innovation versus winning adoption of that innovation.

The term "open source" was coined in 1997 to refer a category of software where the source code is freely distributed. The term is defined to require free redistribution of the software, its source code, or any derived works thereof, while at the same time acknowledging the original author's ownership and contribution (Perens 1999; Raymond 2004). In popular usage, the term "open source" overlaps (and largely subsumes) the "free software" category as launched by Richard Stallman in 1984.[2]

While "open source" is explicitly an IP policy, it typically includes a development methodology where geographically dispersed programmers collaborate in the joint production of software through a set of virtual collaboration tools. Such programmers were originally hobbyist users, but increasingly have been professionals paid by employers that either intend to use the software internally or sell related products and services. To be effective, such paid collaborators must internalize the ethos of both their project and the employer (O'Mahony, 2003).

Meanwhile, the widespread dissemination of the necessary tools have both fueled the rise of specific open source projects, but also enabled other forms of

2 However, the "free" software contains IP restrictions intended to force sharing of any derivative works, while "open" software (e.g., Apache) allow private commercialization of related innovations (West 2003).

open innovation in the software industry, such as user scenario development for PC games.

Thus, open source as an open innovation strategy has two key components – shared rights to use the technology, and collaborative development of that technology. Here we consider four approaches from open source projects (and the non-open source PC games) where firms have both invested in and benefited from open innovation (Table 1).

Table 1: Open Source Projects as Examples of Open Innovation

Project	Product Category	Approach
Apache	Web Server	Shared R&D
Darwin	Operating System	Selling Complements
Eclipse	Programming Environment	Spinout
Jikes	Java Compiler	Spinout
Linux	Operating System	Shared R&D
Mozilla	Web Browser	Shared R&D, Spinout
Mysql	Database	Selling Complements
Openoffice	Business Productivity	Selling Complements
Sendmail	Mail Router	Selling Complements

Pooled R&D: Linux, Mozilla

A familiar model of open innovation is that of pooled R&D. Two highly visible open source examples are support for the Linux operating system through the Open Source Development Lab, and the Mozilla web browser. For both, firms donate R&D to the open source project while exploiting the pooled R&D of all contributors to facilitate the sale of related products. This is an example of firms' economizing in generating knowledge that is congruent with their future product knowledge matrix. We would also include simple free riding here except that the value of the IP offered by the firm is zero.

A simple example is the Mozilla open source project, a descendant of the Netscape Navigator browser offered for a wide range of systems – Windows, Macintosh, Linux and at least 7 Unix variants. This browser was the first commercial browser product, and held dominant market share from 1994 to 1996 ("Netscape Navigator", 2004). However, Navigator was rapidly eclipsed by Microsoft's Internet

Explorer, which gained more than 90% market share due to bundling with Microsoft Windows (Bresnahan & Yin, 2004).

Netscape created the Mozilla open source project in 1998, and in July 2003 terminated all internal development, deferring further work to the open source community. Unix system vendors such as IBM, HP and Sun were left without a browser, which they needed to sell Internet-connected workstations. Thus, each of the major Unix systems vendors assigned software engineers to work with the Mozilla project, both to help to keep the project moving forward and to assure that new releases are compatible with their respective systems (Dotzler, 2004).

The R&D cooperation in the Open Source Development Labs (OSDL) for Linux is more complex. Founded in 2000, the OSDL takes as its mission "To be the recognized center-of-gravity for the Linux industry, a central body dedicated to accelerating the use of Linux for enterprise computing" ("Corporate Overview," 2004). In its first five years, the consortium began work on three projects – data center Linux, carrier grade Linux and desktop Linux.

How did firms benefit? For firms participating in Mozilla, the quid pro-quo is straightforward – systems vendors maximize the returns of their innovation by concentrating on their own needs (such as platform-specific customization), and then incorporated the shared browser technology into their integrated systems. For the OSDL, firms contributed their specialized knowledge (e.g., in telecommunications operations or microprocessor architecture) to build a common platform. OSDL resembles other self-supporting industrial research consortia, where firms pool interests towards a common goal, and assume they can both cooperate in supporting that goal and compete in selling their respective products.

However, both Mozilla and OSDL differ from typical consortia in two ways:

- **Spillovers are not Controllable:** Many consortia incent membership by limiting access to the consortium's research output to member-participants. Open source licenses make this difficult if not impossible, allowing non-members to accrue many of the same benefits as members.
- **Contributions from Non-Participants:** The engineering contributions to these open source projects extend beyond the sponsoring companies to

include user organizations, academics, individual hobbyists and other interested parties. Unless the corporate contributions eventually dwarf the individual ones, the projects must continue to motivate such contributions to survive.

Given these factors, an open source innovation model is inherently more "open" than a typical R&D consortium, both in terms of exploiting information from outside the consortium, and sharing that information back out to non-member organizations and individuals.

Spinouts: Jikes, Eclipse, Beehive

Open innovation can release the potential of technologies within the firm that are not creating value. In some cases, the technologies are no longer strategic, as with AOL Time Warner's decision to spinoff Mozilla into a stand-alone open source project after firing its Netscape development team (Hansen, 2003).

But in addition to spinoff (and, frequently, abandonment), firms also have opportunities to release more value from their technologies by situating them outside the firm, but at the same time maintaining an ongoing corporate involvement. Here we use the term "spinout" to refer to all cases where firms transform internal development projects to externally visible open source projects. Spinouts are essentially firms economizing by giving away IP that is now incongruent with their current or expected product knowledge matrix.

If a firm gives away its IP, how can such spinouts create value? One way is that the donated IP generates demand for other products and services that the donor continues to sell. Two examples of this come from IBM and its efforts to promote the Java programming language developed by Sun Microsystems, that was widely embraced by firms competing with Microsoft in web-based technologies. In such a Java-centric world, IBM would still generate revenue from sales of hardware and supporting services.

IBM's first open source spinout came from a pre-production R&D project. In response to IBM's growing interest in Java, in early 1996 two IBM researchers began work on an experimental Java compiler, which they named "Jikes". They quickly developed a prototype that was more efficient than Sun's industry standard compiler. After customer requests for a better Java compiler, in December 1998 IBM announced the release of Jikes in open source form to allow external programmers to extend and improve the compiler. IBM continues to host the project website, but since 2000 development has been led by non-IBM engineers (Gonsalves & Coffee, 1998; Shields, 2004). Jikes has been widely adopted, and is now bundled with several distributions of open source operating systems.

A second IBM spinout came with Java development tools. In 1996, IBM purchased a Canadian software company that created such tools for its WebSphere application server product, IBM released much of this technology in open source form when it founded the Eclipse project in 2001 (Brody, 2001). IBM was joined by other software companies involved in web application development, including Borland, Red Hat, SAP and SuSE, and well as hardware makers HP, Fujitsu and Intel; in 2004, the project became an independent non-profit corporation ("Eclipse Forms Independent Organization," 2004), although IBM engineers retained technical leadership of key projects. As an IBM executive later explained, "It is not that we are looking to make more money off the platform. It is just that we are looking to accelerate the adoption of Java and the building up of it for all of us" (Southwick, 2004).

But despite this openness, Java rivals BEA and Sun chose not to join IBM's coalition, instead promoting the rival Java Tools Community (Taft, 2003). Meanwhile, in May 2004 BEA announced plans to create a "Beehive" open source project, in which key application libraries from its Web-Logic product family could be used with Sun's NetBeans, Eclipse, or other development systems.

The spinout thus makes sense for technologies that either are not yet commercialized (as with Jikes), or that will eventually become commoditized and thus of limited commercial value (as many predicted for Java development tools).

Both IBM and BEA donated internal innovations to create open source projects, which were intended to fuel adoption of the innovations. As with other organizations that sponsor open source projects, the benefits included:

- helping to establish their technology as de facto standards, which, at a minimum, reduces the likelihood of having to re-implement their technology to conform to competing standards;

- attracting improvements and complements that make the technology more attractive;
- together, the innovation and complements enable the sale of related products (such as other components of WebSphere and WebLogic); and
- generating mindshare and goodwill with the same audience that includes the potential customers for these related products.

Selling Complements: Apache, KHTML, Darwin

Earlier we noted the "hardware-software paradigm" and that in many cases complements are more valuable than the core innovation. Because of its tremendous economies of scope, firms may find that knowledge that has been developed for one product that is no longer profitable, provides value for some others that are quite profitable. IBM's business service and consulting business that started with its mainframes remains and important part of their firm. This is an example of firms giving away IP in order to sell complements that are congruent with their extant knowledge. Two open source examples are the Apache web server and the KHTML web browser engine.

Customers access IBM's WebSphere e-commerce software using standard web browsers, so IBM originally developed a proprietary http (web page) server. IBM later abandoned its server for the Apache httpd server, recognizing that it would be wasting resources trying to catch up to the better quality and larger market share enjoyed by Apache (West, 2003). Today, IBM engineers are involved in the ongoing Apache innovation, both for the httpd server and also related projects hosted by the Apache Software Foundation (Apache.org website).

Similarly, in 2002 Apple Computer decided to build a new web browser called Safari to guarantee one would be available for buyers of its computer systems. Instead of Mozilla, it incorporated the KHTML open source libraries, which in turn were developed to support the KDE desktop interface for Linux users (Searls, 2003). The move paralleled Apple's earlier use of BSD Unix as a foundation for its OSX operating system, in which it created a new open source project (Darwin) to share all modifications of the BSD code (West, 2003). For both Safari and OSX, Apple used open source and contributed back its changes, but the company did not release the remainder of the proprietary code for its browser and OS, respectively (Brockmeier, 2003).

In the case of the Apache, KHTML and Darwin open source projects, the firms adopting open source components had four common characteristics:

- there was pre-existing open source code being developed without the intervention of the focal firms;
- the "buy vs. build" decision to use external innovation was made easier because the code was "free";
- the firms were willing to contribute back to the existing projects on an ongoing basis, both to assure that the technology continued to meet their respective needs and to maintain absorptive capacity; and
- the firms could continue to yield returns for internal innovation by combining the internal and external technologies to make a product offering that was not directly available through open source.

Donated Complements: PC Game "Mods"

In other cases, firms make their money off of the core innovation, but seek donated labor for valuable complements. Although not a pure example of open source software, the solicitation of "mods" for PC video games demonstrates this principle. Firms give away the IP surrounding manipulating the content of their games in exchange for an expanded market for their games (in a sense the games are complements for the mods) and receiving product innovations that are incongruent with their extant knowledge. For example, it is not uncommon for "modders" to totally revise the games setting and characters to have it appeal to a new market that the original firm didn't anticipate.

The PC gaming industry competes with lower priced dedicated gaming platforms such as Sony's PlayStation2 or Microsoft's new Xbox360. The commercial publishers of PC games thus have decided to exploit the one key advantage they have versus the consoles – the ability for PC users to update and modify their games. To do this, publishers release editing tools for their games to encourage user mods that create different environments, scenarios, or even total rebuilds of the game; the users then freely distribute these mods on the Internet.

While mods do not directly generate publisher revenues, the novelty of the mods extends the relatively short demand period (measured in weeks or months) for most computer games. Meanwhile, the mods keep the name of the game in front of consumers for additional months. This is especially important because the publishers often need a year or so to prepare follow-on products and frequently multiple years to prepare a full sequel to the earlier successful game. This external innovation keeps the product current without tying up publisher innovation resources.

As with open source, a key issue for mods is motivating the contributors. The motivations parallel those for open source – direct utility, intrinsic reward or external signaling. Individuals (or virtual teams) contribute mods because of their creative nature, love of either the computer game they modified or the milieu they recreated via their mod (Todd, 2004). Students are also frequent contributors, increasing their enjoyment of a favorite game (direct utility) as well as signaling their value to potential employers.

The computer game industry highlights two key ideas for attracting external innovation that similar to those for open source:

- *creating an infrastructure* that encourages participation and collaboration. For open source, this is a project website and e-mail list, but for mods this would be a distribution site that highlights the mods. Modern technologies make the cost of such infrastructure quite low.
- *recognition for contributors*, including added visibility for the most popular creators. For example, since 2002 Apple has given annual awards for the best use of open source related to its OSX operating system.

However, the mods also help address one problem that's very different from those of business-oriented source projects. As with other entertainment products, novelty-seeking consumers eventually grow bored with a PC game; by combining the core game engine with new externally generated game scenarios, the external innovation extends the life of the core (internally developed) innovation.

Implications for Open Innovation

The goals and broad principles of open innovation are attractive, but to have practical value, managers need specific guidelines about how such innovation can be implemented. We suggest that what is distinct about open innovation is the systematic exploitation of external and internal innovation. Three key management challenges that emerge include maximizing returns to internal innovation, incorporating external innovation into internal development, and enhancing firm value by "giving away" IP.

We identified four patterns of open innovation in software that suggest approaches that address these challenges based on maximizing its returns and the product alignment of a firm's knowledge (Table 2).

Table 2: Open Source Strategies and Knowledge Based View

		Appropriating Value	
		Economizing	**Complements**
Product – Knowledge	Congruent	Pooled R&D	Selling Complements
Alignment	Incongruent	Spinouts	Donated Complements

- *Pooled R&D.* When the firm retains alignment between its knowledge base and seeks to economize pooled R&D is an optimal approach. This is nothing new and has been used in many industries, e.g., semi-conductors, but the open source examples offer new insights for coordination and governance of collaboration to support competing interests.
- *Spinouts.* When the firm has a useful innovation that does not appear congruent with its extant knowledge base, e.g., Xerox's Alto computer, spinouts are a way to exploit that knowledge at low cost. Since spinouts are valuable for technologies locked in. the laboratory, they are most relevant to the largest firms, which tend to both have the largest innovation budgets and also the largest bureaucracies that can monitor their commercialization, frequently via licensing, and prevent opportunism by licensees. While Xerox PARC is the poster child for "lost" innovations, Chesbrough and Rosenbloom (2002) note that in some cases Xerox was able to spinout the technology and participate (very successfully) in its commercialization and the view of PARC being an unmitigated financial failure for Xerox might be too harsh.
- *Selling complements.* Frequently the firm fully understands its product or service, but it is not particularly profitable. Firms have long sold support services around

public goods as well as exploited demand side economies of scale to sell lots of complements for a single core product, e.g., razor blades for razors. Ironically, while necessary for absorptive capacity, utilizing open innovation requires overcoming the "not invented here" bias of inhouse R&D in order to incorporate external innovations into internally developed products.

- *Donated complements.* Finally, firms may frequently find it useful to generate complements that they themselves do not envision or expect. Under these circumstances what von Hippel and Katz (2002) refer to as "user toolkits," where general purpose technologies are sold to users capable of generating their own modifications and improvements, become especially valuable. Such strategies are most feasible when selling to technically proficient buyers, whether corporate engineers or hobbyist-programmers.

Open source software as part of corporate open innovation strategies is still a comparatively recent phenomenon and there are some unresolved issues. Open source built on a confluence of ideology, professional norms and enthusiasm; some question the long-term sustainability of such motivations. Also, many projects have been created as challenges to an entrenched incumbent (e.g., Microsoft), and if such challenges are largely unsuccessful, vendor interest in sponsoring future open source efforts could wane.

Also, open source has yet to fully resolve the IP issues of accepting donations from a wide community of unknown contributors. Contributors to Linux have been accused by SCO of stealing copyrighted or trade secret-protected source code from SCO's proprietary Unix implementation. While such potential infringement has been attributed to ignorance, others have suggested that infringing "stealth" IP could be deliberately donated to projects to sabotage their success (Cargill & Bolin, 2004).

Further Research

In considering what "open innovation" means, there is a huge gap between the freeriding on basic research (e.g., Chesbrough, 2003b) and this study of the partitioning of software development between firms and open source projects. From our own study, we suggest that future research should consider whether these characteristics of open source are prerequisites for other forms of open innovation –

- feasibility of virtual teams as a way to organize innovation, enabling pooled R&D and other collaboration between organizations;
- a culture of open innovation throughout such teams that spans organizations;
- modularization of technologies and products, to allow the external production of components or complements; and
- formal IP mechanisms that encourage collaboration.

Our attempts to define open innovation uncovered questions beyond those specific to software. Two relate to the availability of external spillovers:

- *commercialization of public research.* Universities have increasingly sought to profit from their research spillovers, a trend encouraged in the U.S. by the Bayh-Dole Act (Colyvas *et al*, 2002). Will this restrict the flow of external innovations or provide an ongoing incentive for greater supply?
- *increasing conflict over patents.* The increasing scope and commercial value of patents has spawned various concerns that patents will inhibit traditional closed innovation (e.g., Jaffe & Lerner, 2004); the threat to external spillovers is likely greater.

Other questions relate to potential patterns for leveraging external knowledge:

- *role of process innovations.* Companies like Dell combine external product innovations with internal process innovations. Is the process of open innovation fundamentally different when it incorporates process innovations?
- *low R&D intensity firms.* Many firms have low R&D intensity, either due to size (e.g., small businesses) or industry characteristics (low tech). Are they pursuing "external innovation," "open innovation," or (as commonly assumed) "no innovation" strategies?

These are but some of the questions about how open innovation can be applied to a wide range of industries and contexts.

(Scott Gallagher, Assistant Professor, College of Business, James Madison University, Harrisonburg, VA 22807 USA. He can be reached at gallagsr@jmu.edu

Joel West, Associate Professor, College of Business, San José State University, One Washington Square, San José, CA 95192-0070 USA. He can be reached at Joel.West@sjsu.edu).

References

Arrow, K J (1962) Economic Welfare and the allocation of resources for invention, in The Rate and Direction of Inventive Activity: Economic and Social Factors, Nelson, R R (ed.), Princeton, N J: Princeton University Press.

Bekkers, R, Duysters, G and Verspagen, B (2002) "Intellectual Property Rights, Strategic Technology Agreements and Market Structure: the Case of GSM". Research Policy, 31, 7, 1141-1161.

Bresnahan, T and Yin, P-L (2004) "Standard Setting in Browsers: Technology and (real world) Incomplete Information". Standards and Public Policy conference, Federal Reserve Bank of Chicago, May 13-14.

Brockmeier, J (2003) "Is Open Source Apple's Salvation?," NewsFactor Network, April 21, 2003, URL: *http://www.newsfactor.com/perl/story/21318.html*

Brody, Steve, "Interview: The Eclipse code donation," IBM developerWorks, 1 November 2001, *URL: http://www.ibm.com/developerworks/linux/library/l-erick.html*

Cargill, C & Bolin, S (2004) "Standardization: a Failing Paradigm". Standards and Public Policy Conference, Chicago Federal Reserve, Chicago, USA. May 12 - 14.

Chandler, A D (1990) "Scale and Scope". Cambridge, MA: Belknap.

Chesbrough, H and Rosenbloom, R S. (2002) The Role of the Business Model in Capturing Value form Innovation: Evidence from Xerox Corporation's Technology Spin-Off Companies". Industrial and Corporate Change, 11, 3 (June), 529-555.

Chesbrough, H.W (2003a) Open Innovation, Boston, MA: Harvard University Press.

Chesbrough, H.W (2003b) "The Era of Open Innovation". *Sloan Management Review*, 44, 3, 35-41.

Cohen, W M & Levinthal, D A (1990) Absorptive Capacity: "A New Perspective on Learning and Innovation". *Administrative Science Quarterly*, 35, 128-152.

Colyvas, J, Crow, M, Gelijns, A, Mazzoleni, R, Nelson, R R, Rosenberg, N and Sampat, B N (2002) "How Do university Inventions Get into Practice?" *Management Science*, 48, 1, 61–72.

"Corporate Overview," Open Source Development Labs, April 1, 2004,
URL: *http://www.osdl.org/about_osdl/OSDL_overview_website.pdf*

David, P A, Hall, B H, and Toole, A A (2000) Is public R&D a complement or substitute for private R&D? A review of the econometric evidence. Research Policy, 29, 497-529.

Dotzler, A (2004), interview, Mozilla.org, March 8.

"Eclipse Forms Independent Organization," press release, February 2, 2004, URL: *http://www.eclipse.org/org/index.html*

Gallagher, S and Park, S H (2002) "Innovation and Competition in Standard-Based Industries: A Historical Analysis of the US Home Video Game Market". IEEE Transactions on Engineering Management, 49, 1, 67-82.

Gonsalves, A and Coffee, P (1998) Jikes! "More Open Source Code", *PC Week*, 15, 49, December 7, 6.

Grant, R M (1996) "Toward a Knowledge Based Theory of the Firm". *Strategic Management Journal*, 17, Winter, 109-122.

Grant, R M (1997) "The Knowledge-based View of the Firm: Implications for Management Practice", Long Range Planning, 30, 3, 450-454.

Grant, R M and Baden-Fuller, C (2004) "A Knowledge Accessing Theory of Strategic Alliances". *Journal of Management Studies*, 41, 1, 61-84.

Hansen, Evan, "AOL lays off Netscape developers," CNET News.com, July 15, 2003,
URL: *http://news.com.com/2100-1032_3-1026078.html*

Jaffe, A B and Lerner, J (2004) "Innovation and Its Discontents: How Our Broken Patent System is Endangering Innovation and Progress, and What to Do About It". Princeton, NJ: Princeton University Press.

Kaplan, J (1996) "Startup: A Silicon Valley Adventure", Paperback ed, New York: Penguin.

Katz, M L and Shapiro, C (1985) "Network Externalities, Competition, and Compatibility". *American Economic Review*, 75, 3, 424-440.

Lieberman, M B and Montgomery, D B (1998) "First Mover (Dis)advantages: Retrospective and Link with the Resource-Based View". *Strategic Management Journal*, 19, 1111-1125.

March, J G (1991) "Exploration and Exploitation in Organizational Learning". Organization Science, 2, 71-87.

Nelson, R R and Winter, S G (1982) "An Evolutionary Model of Economic Change". Cambridge, Mass.: Harvard University Press.

"Netscape Navigator", Wikipedia, April 16, 2004, URL: *http://en.wikipedia.org/wiki/* Netscape_Navigator, accessed May 22, 2004.

O'Mahony, S (2003) "Guarding the Commons: How Community Managed Software Projects Protect Their Work". Research Policy, 32, 7, 1179-1198.

"OSDL Members," Open Source Development Labs, copyright 2003, URL: *http:// www.osdl.org/about_osdl/members/*

Perens, B (1999) "The Open Source Definition" in Chris DiBona, Sam Ockman and Mark Stone, eds., Open Sources: Voices from the Open Source Revolution, Sebastopol, Calif.: O'Reilly, pp. 171-188.

Raymond, E "The Open Source Definition," Version 1.9, 2004, URL: *http:// www.opensource.org/docs/definition.php*

Rosenberg, N and Steinmueller, W E (1988) "Why are Americans such Poor Imitators?" *American Economic Review*, 78, 2, p229 - 235.

Schumpeter, J A (1934), TheTheory of Economic Development, Cambridge, Mass., Harvard University Press.

Searls, Doc "Surprise: Apple's New Browser Is a Sister to Konqueror," *LinuxJournal.com*, January 11, 2003, URL: *http://www.linuxjournal.com/article.php?sid=6565*

Shields, D (2004) "Personal Interview", IBM Corporation, May 24.

Simon, H A (1991) "Bounded Rationality and Organizational Learning". Organization Science, 2, 125-134.

Southwick, K "Big Blue's Mr. Web services," March 17, 2004, *CNET News.com*, URL: *http://news.com.com/2008-7345_3-5173667.html*

Spender, J C (1992) Limits to Learning from the West: How Western Management Advice May Prove Limited in Eastern Europe. International Executive, 34, 5, 389-410.

Taft, Darryl K, "Sun Mulls Joining Java Eclipse Effort," eWeek, September 1, 2003, URL: *http://www.eweek.com/article2/0,1759,1236123,00.asp*

Teece, D (1986) "Profiting from Technological Innovation: Implications for Integration, Collaboration, Licensing and Public Policy". Research Policy, 15, 6, 285-305.

Tennenhouse, D (2003) "Innovation Breeds Success at Intel". IEE Engineering Management, 13, 6, 44-47.

Todd, B (2004) "The Whys of Modding". Computer Games, No. 163, June, 38-40.

von Hippel, Eric (1988) "The Sources of Innovation". New York: Oxford University Press.

von Hippel, E and Katz, R (2002) "Shifting Innovation to Users via Toolkits". Management Science, 48, 7, 821- 834.

West, J (2003) "How Open is Open Enough? Melding Proprietary and Open Source Platform Strategies". Research Policy, 32, 7, 1259-1285.

Williamson, O E (1991) "Comparative Economic Organization: The Analysis of Discrete Structural Alternatives". *Administrative Science Quarterly*, 36, 2, 269-296.

4

Recent Productivity Growth: The Role of Information Technology and Other Innovations

Martin N Baily

The article critically speculates on the role of Information Technology investments as a major driver of productivity and growth in the US Economy, since the mid-1990s. Although the article links productivity with innovation and asserts that technology and especially IT are critical drivers of productivity, it is initially skeptical whether the contribution of IT to growth has been overstated. One of the reasons that the contribution of IT to growth may have been overstated is that the main tool by which we judge such contributions is growth accounting. This article further suggests that besides IT, a high level of competitive intensity encourages the enterprises to innovate. The article derives lessons from McKinsey case studies on the enterprises like Wal-Mart and Costco, who relied on IT to improve their supply chains. The article further highlights the innovative applications like Enterprise Resource Planning (ERP) which has experienced mixed results of both success and failure.

Source: Federal Reserve Bank of San Francisco Economic Review, 2004, pp 35-41. (www.iie.com)

The acceleration in productivity growth since the mid-1990s has been an exceptionally important development for the US economy. My remarks are going to run somewhat contrary to the view that information technology has been the overwhelming impetus to the acceleration in productivity growth in recent years. While technology and in particular Information Technology (IT) are obviously very important drivers of productivity.

A considerably less controversial point now is that productivity growth has accelerated. Obviously, there was a period when we wondered if the increase in productivity growth starting in the mid-1990s was just a cyclical effect. Now that concern seems to have gone away, in part because measured productivity growth now is even faster than it was from 1995 to 2000. Whether that will survive data revisions and changes in measurement methodologies remains to be seen. However, unless there are drastic revisions, it certainly looks as if the higher rate of productivity growth is staying around for a while.[1]

Has the Contribution of IT Been Overstated?

One of the reasons that the contribution of IT to grow may have been overstated is that the main tool by which we judge such contributions is growth accounting. This is obviously a valuable tool, but it has some pitfalls; in addition, it requires careful interpretation as to what it actually says about the recent growth period.

In concept, growth accounting is straightforward—it is a framework for allocating the growth in output to the growth in capital (plants, equipment, and software), the growth in labor, and the growth in Total Factor Productivity (TFP). In principle, growth in TFP stems from improvements in the ways capital and labor are combined in production processes. This might be thought of generally as changes in how workplaces are organized and managed.

In practice, however, we know that measured growth in TFP is affected by the errors in measuring capital and labor inputs. The potential mis-measurement of IT investment is one of the pitfalls of relying on growth accounting that I will come to in a bit. First, I'd like to discuss other reasons to be careful about the

---

[1] Fuller discussion of the issues discussed in this article can be found on the website *www.iie.com.*

empirical results relating to the 1990s experience that use growth accounting measures, especially ones using aggregate data for a single country.

One reason for caution is that the growth accounting results from the 1990s reflect the fact that there was essentially a "one-observation" correlation in the aggregate data: IT investment and labor productivity accelerated at about the same time. This convinced many people that the two events were related as cause and effect—the productivity acceleration must have been driven by IT investment.

However, before the 1990s productivity speedup, there was the 1970s productivity slowdown. Measured labor productivity growth went from an average of 2.8 percent during the period spanning the 1950s through the earlier 1970s, to an average of about 1.4 percent from 1973 to 1995. During the sessions at this conference, there were discussions about the host of reasons given for the slowdown. The one that was certainly the most popular when it was proffered in the 1970s was that the productivity growth slowdown was caused by the rise in oil prices. At that time there was a different one-observation correlation – productivity slowed down and energy prices went up at about the same time. Many people, me included for a while, believed that higher energy costs had caused slower productivity growth. It was not a crazy idea, indeed, there were good arguments, such as that rising energy prices would cause labor productivity growth to slow down, because labor would be substituted for energy-using capital. There were also objections to that story, of course, but what really caused the collapse of the energy-productivity story is that oil prices came back down in the 1980s and there was little or no improvement in trend productivity growth. That experience should sound a warning that one-observation correlations can easily collapse when a second observation comes along.

Another reason for caution in linking IT investment to the post-1995 productivity acceleration is that the growth accounting framework did not do very well in tracking productivity movements prior to 1995. There was a fair amount of IT investment going on well before 1995. Indeed, that investment inspired the famous Solow paradox—Robert Solow quipped in 1987 that he could see computers everywhere except in the productivity data.

Moreover, we now seem to be dealing with the reverse of the paradox – there was a severe slump in technology spending that began in 2000 and lasted into 2003, yet productivity growth has remained strong and may even have accelerated, from the first quarter of 2001, which is roughly the official cyclical peak, through the third quarter of 2003, productivity growth averaged over 4 percent a year. Later on I will talk about how investment in intangible capital may help, at least in part, to resolve this paradox. However, as with the oil price story, on the surface there appears to have been a breakdown in the one observation correlation between the productivity growth trend and its apparent driver.

A second concern about taking the growth accounting results at face value is the possibility of reverse causality in the 1990s. To a degree, it may have been the economic boom that created the big wave of IT investment rather than the wave of IT investment that created the boom. Investing in IT became the thing for companies to do. Profits were strong and IT managers had considerable influence over investment decisions. Hardware and software vendors hyped the benefits of their products, and no CEO wanted his or her company to be left behind in the hightech boom. Some of that investment did pay off in higher productivity, but there may have been a systematic tendency to overinvest. Expected returns were higher than actual returns over this period—hence, in part, setting the stage for the technology bust after 2000.

This latter concern, of course, is not directly related to any shortcomings of growth accounting, per se. Indeed, growth accounting is part of the basic tool kit of economics and is firmly established as a valid approach. The first question is whether or not to believe what the computer price deflators are telling us. Is it really true that quality-adjusted computer prices are falling rapidly, or are there problems in the methodology used for their estimation? There have been questions raised about the hedonic approach, but this does not seem to be a key issue quantitatively. The computer price deflators are built not only from hedonic regressions, but also from matched models. The matched model approach follows the price over time of the same computer or compares prices in different periods for computers that are functionally very similar. In addition, the price indexes based on the matched model approach have fallen about as fast as the prices based on hedonic regressions. It really does seem to be the case that quality-adjusted computer prices have fallen extraordinarily fast.

Nevertheless, it still is fair to ask whether the price deflators accurately reflect the effective use-value of IT capital in the production process. Many of us have voiced skepticism based on anecdotal evidence. Robert Gordon (2000) has argued that the latest version of Word run on the latest model computer does not do that much more than the previous version and does not increase the computer user's productivity by very much. Going beyond anecdotal evidence, one of the McKinsey Global Institute (2002a) case studies examined what happened when banks invested in new generations of faster, more powerful computers. The McKinsey team found that most of the lower-skill and middle-level employees (tellers, for example) were doing pretty much the same things in the same way with the new computers as with the old computers. The banks reported little productivity gain in their retail operations from upgrading their computer hardware.

If this case study evidence is correct, however, it poses an important puzzle. If the new computers and software yielded little in the way of productivity benefits, why did the banks invest so much in them? Both the hedonic approach to computer price measurement and the matched model approach reflect what customers (businesses or individuals) are willing to pay to get the latest technology. If people are willing to spend their own money to buy new hardware, they must expect a gain from the purchase. Is there some systematic bias or failure of expectations that could explain this puzzle? Or are we missing a dimension of the decision-making?

Part of the answer may be that it is difficult to infer the use-value of investments when there are network effects, and computer technology is one area where these effects are important. The value to a business (or to a consumer) of a computer depends a great deal on the compatibility of that computer with other people's computers. One reason that banks put very high-powered computers on the desks of all of their employees is that they follow replacement cycles. After a period of time some computers wear out and, more importantly, some computers become obsolete in that they are not able to meet the high-end technology needs of some employees. To maintain internal compatibility, a company undertakes a comprehensive upgrade so that the speed of the convoy, if you like, is pulled along by the fastest ship rather than going at the speed of the slowest ship. The reason a low speed computer, enters with a very low price when the Bureau of Labor Statistics collects its data is that many firms cannot choose to buy the less powerful computer since it would not be compatible with their other computers or with the software in use throughout the company. And the issue of compatibility may also extend outside a specific company to its suppliers or customers.

Though this argument is suggestive, but not proven. Still, in the presence of strong network effects, it is very difficult to assess the benefit of IT investment to one part of a business enterprise without considering the enterprise-wide effects. In the case of IT investment by banks, for example, we need to know the impact on productivity if lower-skilled and middle-level employees were to continue to use less powerful computers, while the rest of an organization upgraded its IT hardware and software.

Insights from the Use of Disaggregated Data

The severity of the pitfalls for empirical analysis I have mentioned are mitigated to some extent in studies that use disaggregated data. There are a number of excellent studies that use industry level data, but rather than going through a full literature review, let me mention work by Kevin Stiroh and by Dale Jorgensen, along with a paper that I wrote with Robert Lawrence.[2] These papers suggest that industries that had invested in IT hardware had indeed achieved faster productivity growth than other industries in the 1990s and had achieved greater productivity acceleration after 1995. Not all the industry evidence point the same way, however. In particular, an article by Jack Triplett and Barry Bosworth finds that the industries that had surges in labor productivity growth were not necessarily the industries that had surges in IT investments. Rather, more of the post-1995 increase in labor productivity growth on an industry level seemed to come from TFP than from investment in IT. They were using the growth accounting framework at the industry level and, not surprisingly given the

---

2 See, for example, Stiroh (2002), Jorgensen, Ho, and Stiroh (2004), and Baily and Lawrence (2001).

aggregate results, they did find that IT contributed to productivity in the 1990s as a whole. What they did not find at the industry level was that IT contributed especially to the post-1995 acceleration.

Going below the industry level, a study by Lucia Foster, John Haltiwanger, and Cornell Krizan (2002) finds that the exit of low-productivity establishments and the entry of high-productivity establishments generated most of the gains in retailing. That is a strong result, and it raises questions about the impact of IT. It suggests that investment in IT within existing retail establishments was not the main source of productivity increases in that industry. This is a notable result since retailing is a sector that has made one of the biggest contributions to overall productivity growth in recent years.

Key Drivers of Innovation: IT and Competitive Intensity

Detailed industry case studies also can shed light on the role of IT, especially how it is used in the business setting. For example case study evidence from the work carried out by the McKinsey Global Institute (2002a).

The analysis from the McKinsey case studies suggests that there is not one simple paradigm that can describe how IT affects business production processes and productivity. They looked at examples where IT investment did have a positive impact on productivity and found that the IT applications were used in very different ways across industries and even within sub-categories of an industry. For example, in retailing, the mass-market super center, big box discounters, such as Wal-Mart and Costco, used IT to improve their supply chains and to allow the stores to manage their inventories, purchasing, etc., more effectively. Among specialty retailers, such as J Crew and The Limited, IT allowed these stores to track changing customer tastes and match their own inventory mix to stock the right products for their customers (making sure the "hot" products are on the shelves). In both of these examples, IT is used to improve the supply chain, but it is serving a different role in each. For the discounters, its purpose was primarily to cut costs, allowing the stores to sell at lower prices. For the specialty stores, it allowed them to sell higher margin items with greater value-added.

Earlier I talked about banks and the apparent low returns they obtained from one part of their IT investment. Some of their investments clearly succeeded, however. Over the course of the 1990s, banking organizations saw a massive increase in the number of phone requests and inquiries from their customers (the number of phone inquiries rose from just over 1 million in 1994 to 2.3 million in 1998, a 24 percent annual rate of growth). The banks made major investments in computerized voice response units to handle the growth of calls. Customers would rather talk to a person than a machine, but without the greater use of IT, banks would not have been able to provide the same level of service profitably. There was, in fact, a large increase in the number of people employed to handle calls, as well (employment in this activity grew at 13 percent a year between 1994 and 1998). But it would have taken an even larger increase in personnel to handle all of the calls personally. With the IT investment, banks were able to expand their services and, at the same time, sustain overall labor productivity.

The design of chips is another example where the use of IT had a positive impact on productivity, but the way that was achieved is very different from the two previous examples. In developing a new chip, the constraint on performance improvement in the late 1990s was not merely the number of transistors that could be packed onto a chip. Over the long-term, the ability to manufacture chips with greater technological capability (to keep Moore's law going) is obviously important. But at that time, the binding constraint was the ability of companies to design chips that took advantage of the capability that was available. The complexity of chip design had increased very rapidly, almost too rapidly for companies to deal with effectively. Consequently, there was a development in electronic design and testing tools that helped companies such as Intel to its improved productivity.

These are all examples of how IT investment paid-off in higher productivity. There were a number of cases where the investment did not pay off. One example was already discussed, as banks upgraded the computers on the desks of tellers. Another example is investment in customer relations management software. As companies installed this software, they planned to collect reams of data on their customers that would allow them to customize their services. For example, customers would walk into a hotel, where employees would greet them personally, equipped with detailed information about what kind of rooms they liked and what services they might want. In some cases, the hardware and software were purchased, but were never really put into operation because of data problems or other difficulties. In other cases the hotels were not able to generate higher revenues through using the systems or at least they were not able to earn a positive return on their investment.

Another innovation, Enterprise Resource Planning (ERP) software, has had mixed results. It has had some successes, as evidenced by the growth of SAP, one of the leading providers of this software. But many of the efforts involving ERP did not improve productivity. A key shortcoming is that ERP tends to lock in a certain way of doing things making innovation more difficult. Another problem with ERP is that the technology has had difficulty dealing with the degree of data incompatibility within many firms, so the promise of total information integration frequently was not realized.

The case studies, then, suggest that IT has paid off in some cases, but not in others. That is to be expected, after all, in any area, some projects will pay off and others will not. However, three important lessons emerge from the case studies. First, the examples where businesses were successful in their IT investment were ones where the companies had already identified a specific problem to be solved or opportunity to be exploited. They then looked at their business system to figure out how it could be changed to solve the problem or exploit the opportunity. Then, as part of that process, they figured out how IT investment could contribute to the success of the improved business system. Successful IT applications also typically occurred where outcomes could be quantified and monitored. The second lesson, as I stated earlier, is that when IT works, it can work very differently from industry to industry and even from firm to firm within an industry.

The third lesson is that, for many productivity-increasing innovations, IT investment was not the most important component. For example take the case of the retail sector. Generally, companies can obtain labor productivity increases by building larger stores, such as the big box stores. They can also lower their costs by efficient national and global sourcing where, again, scale is an important benefit. Large purchasers are able to obtain lower prices from suppliers, thereby adding to their margins and value-added per employee. In retailing and many other industries, figuring out what consumers want and what they will pay for allows companies to develop new designs that add value to their products and increase productivity. The auto industry is such an example, where (for better or worse) companies alized that customers would pay premium prices for SUVs and minivans. By shifting the mix of their output, auto makers were able to increase their value-added per employee.

Let me clarify here. Clearly, IT has become part of the backbone of business operations, so it does have a role in all of the preceding examples; e.g., in the case of product design, computer-aided designs are important, so IT was certainly a facilitating technology for the innovations. But the key point is that the source of the productivity increase was not primarily major new IT investments, nor, I suspect, were these innovations driven to any great extent by the decline in computer prices.

In general, improvements in workplace organization that affect the way offices are run, the way work flows are organized, and the way workplaces are configured can often have very large payoffs in productivity, and they do seem to have done so, based on the industry case studies. Is there any unifying catalyst for such innovations? The one thing that comes through consistently is that competitive intensity puts a lot of pressure on companies to innovate and improve their productivity. McKinsey Global Institute's (2001) study suggested that this explains the acceleration in productivity that took place in the 1990s. That is a tough case to make, because there is no smoking gun that says competitive intensity suddenly strengthened in the mid-1990s. A better case to be made is that there was a lot of deregulation in the US, starting in the 1970s and continuing into the 1980s and 1990s that steadily increased competitive intensity. In addition, there has been a substantial increase in the volume of trade and the extent of globalization in the last twenty years, with a large volume of foreign direct investment coming to the US in the 1990s. In a large country like the US, the benefits that are thought to come from globalization often occur as best practice companies expand their operations throughout the country. It is the progression from regional competition to national competition that increases competitive intensity. In short, there is a pretty good case that competitive intensity in the US economy was greater in the 1990s than in earlier periods, and competitive intensity remains high today.

It may simply be that the forces driving faster productivity growth after the mid-1990s—both IT improvements and increased competitive intensity were building over a number of years and that business cycle effects or quirks in the data resulted in an apparent pickup in productivity growth starting in the second part of the 1990s. In reality, faster trend labor productivity growth may have been coming down the pipeline before 1995, masked perhaps in the early years of the decade by recession and then by very rapid job growth.

Intangible Capital

There is an emerging body of economics literature looking at investment in intangible capital, which is relevant for understanding productivity trends and for interpreting growth accounting results. Robert Hall, Eric Brynjolfsson, and Robert Gordon have all been leaders in this area. The existence and importance of intangible capital can be used to explain the Solow paradox of why productivity remained slow in the 1980s and early 1990s, even though computer investment was growing rapidly. And it can explain why productivity growth remained rapid after 2000, even though IT spending slumped.

The argument is that it takes time to learn how to apply new technologies effectively and that learning takes resources (people). The buildup in such knowledge is investment in intangible capital, and the resulting knowledge stock is part of an economy's intangible capital. Based on this view, the explanation for the Solow paradox is that, even though companies were investing in IT, measured productivity growth was not increasing, because companies also were employing many people to figure out how to use the new technology and how to reorganize their companies to take advantage of the new technology. It was not until after 1995, that the pay off in increased productivity in business operations was large enough to offset the drag-on measured productivity from the employees whose output was intangible capital investment. One way of looking at this is that there was (and still is) a measurement error. Spending on tangible capital is counted as investment in GDP, while spending on intangible capital is not.

After 2000, the effects went in the other direction. Under pressure to sustain profits, companies cut back drastically on their investment in IT and cut back similarly on their investment in intangible capital. Measured productivity soared as companies reduced employment, but this came at the price of reduced intangible investment. If this story is correct, then the prospects for future productivity growth may have been compromised. Companies are taking advantage of their past investments and are not building the basis for future growth.

This is an interesting and valuable story, and it can help to explain some of the surprising shifts in productivity trends. In some ways it is quite consistent with the industry case study results which was described earlier. Productivity growth is not coming just from how many computers a company bought this year, or even the stock of computer capital. It also comes from how well companies use information technology. Further, intangible capital does not have to be associated only with IT. Investment in designing new business systems or reorganizing the workplace or developing new products or new markets, all can be considered investments in intangible capital. For individual companies, investments in advertising and brand development are important sources of intangible capital. How these contribute to aggregate productivity is less clear.

There is no question that intangible capital is important. That part of the new thinking is solid.[3] The only question about this view is whether the new theory is being presented in quite the right way. One of the lessons from the case studies is that the companies that went out and bought IT and then sat down to figure out how to use it often did not succeed. The innovation should be the starting point, that is, when someone figures out how to improve operations or add value to a company's products. The IT investment that pays off is the investment that follows that innovation. Maybe this nuance would lead to the same place empirically, but it is important to get the story straight. In addition, there is skepticism among the business consultants that I talk to about whether the cutbacks after 2000, really involved the elimination of valuable intangible

3 Of course the importance of intangible capital in the form of R&D investment has been appreciated for a long time.

capital accumulation. The alternative view is that, in the downturn, companies eliminated low-return activities that probably should have been cut earlier (at least from the viewpoint of shareholders). Either way, there has been a one-off temporary surge in productivity, but this alternative view suggests this has not come at the expense of valuable investments in future productivity growth.

Lessons from Other Countries

In looking at what we have learned from the experiences of other countries, I am going to concentrate on Europe,[4] and the story for this region has been changing. There was a straightforward view a couple of years ago that said that productivity growth had not sped up in Europe after 1995, indeed, it may have slowed. At the same time, European businesses apparently had not invested in IT to the same extent as businesses in the US. These facts were very supportive of the hypothesis that IT investment had driven faster productivity growth in the US and suggested that Europe needed to increase its IT investment to get on the same bandwagon.

Then new results emerged suggesting that, in fact, Europe had invested rather heavily in IT. Previous studies had underestimated the extent of European IT investment partly because the structure of that investment is different—a lot of in-house software development in Europe was not being reflected in IT spending data. In addition, not all European countries use price deflators that are comparable to those used in the US, which again resulted in an understatement of IT investment. Even after allowing for these factors, IT capital stock in Europe still is lower than in the US, and certainly IT production is lower. But the gap in IT use is not nearly as large as had been thought.

It is possible that, with further study and revised measurement, the picture we have of Europe will change again. But, based on my assessment of the current state of knowledge, what has happened in Europe is that businesses have greatly increased their use of IT, unlike the US, however, the European economies have experienced continued slow productivity growth (with some exceptions).[5] These

4 See Baily and Kirkegaard (2004).

5 Recent work by the OECD (2003) has suggested that differences in measurement methods do not greatly change the standard results for aggregate labor productivity comparisons. These differences may change the industry distribution of growth.

findings indicate that rapid IT investment growth does not ensure rapid labor productivity growth.

Case studies of industries in France and Germany add to this picture.[6] If you look at the industry in these two economies, where productivity grew fastest, mobile telecommunications, the gains are indeed related to IT. The technology became available, it became cheap enough to spread, and the industry grew very rapidly. Indeed mobile telecom productivity grew much faster in France than in the US. For that sector, measured labor productivity in France in 2000 was twice as high as it was in the US. This is not because the technology in France is particularly better. It is because the regulation of mobile telecom is better in France, which is unusual. In France, they have had about the right amount of competition in mobile telecom. In the US in the 1990s there were too many small companies operating well below minimum efficient scale.

In most of the other case studies, IT did not play a major role in explaining differences in productivity growth among France, Germany, and the US. In retailing, productivity is not as high in Germany as it is in the US, even though many German retailers use IT in ways that are similar to businesses in the US. The difference in performance in retailing really has much more to do with the more limited access to land in Germany and the consequent inability to build big box stores.

Another example is where productivity in the automobile industry grew very fast in France, but not in Germany. That was because in France they were willing to undergo restructuring. In France, they decided to privatize the firms that had been state-owned, and this resulted in changes in management and an acceptance of the need for layoffs. Germany, in contrast, did not go through a similar restructuring; indeed, the German firms face restrictions on lay-offs. IT certainly is important to automobile manufacturers, whether in designing new cars or in using the computercontrolled assembly devices, but differences in the use of IT did not seem to account for differences in productivity growth between the countries in the 1990s.

---

6 See McKinsey (2002b).

Electric power is a case where Germany did pretty well in raising its productivity, though not necessarily through great investment in IT. Rather, it did so by privatizing the industry; and even before this occurred, the companies had been restructured in preparation for sale. Germany also changed the structure of regulation in the electricity industry. From the experience of California, we know that regulating electric power is not the easiest thing to do. However, if it is done correctly, there are tremendous gains from privatization and the right kind of regulation. That was the case in Germany, and it seems to have been the case for the United Kingdom also, after some false starts.

In summary, when industries are competitive and not overregulated in Europe, they use IT in ways that are similar to the same industries in the US. Differences in IT use came largely as a result of differences in industry structure and regulation, but were not, in any case, the main reason for productivity performance differences. I note that when these case studies were at an early stage, both the McKinsey consultants who did the research and I myself firmly believed that IT would explain much of the performance differences among the countries. As the work progressed, however, it became clear that the case study evidence would not support this view.

Conclusion

Let me bring the focus back to the acceleration of productivity in the US. Since the mid-1990s, the acceleration of productivity in the industries that produce IT hardware and the rapid investment in IT capital both contributed to the overall productivity acceleration. The need for businesses to build intangible capital to realize the potential from new technologies is important in understanding the pattern of productivity growth for the US in recent years. Nevertheless, reliance on growth accounting likely has led to an overstatement of the impact of IT.

Productivity is driven by innovation, which may be strongly related to IT use, but often is not. A high level of competitive intensity is important in encouraging leading companies to innovate and in forcing competitors either to adopt the same innovations or to find alternative innovations if they are to survive.

(Martin N Baily, Sr. fellow, Institute for International Economics.)

References

Baily, Martin N, and Jacob Kirkegaard. 2004. "A Radical Transformation of the European Economy". Washington, DC: Institute for International Economics.

Baily, Martin N, and Robert Z Lawrence. 2001. "Do We Have a New E-Conomy?" *American Economic Review* 91 (May) pp. 308–312.

Foster, Lucia, John Haltiwanger, and CJ Krizan. 2002. "The Link between Aggregate and Micro Productivity Growth: Evidence from Retail Trade." NBER Working Paper w9120 (August).

Gordon, Robert J 2000. "Does the 'New Economy' Measure Up to the Great Inventions of the Past?" *Journal of Economic Perspectives* 14(4) (Fall) pp. 49–74.

Jorgensen, Dale W, Man S Ho, and Kevin J. Stiroh. 2004. "Growth of US Industries and Investments in Information Technology and Higher Education." In Measuring Capital in a New Economy, eds. C Corrado, C Hulten, and D Sichel. Chicago: University of Chicago Press.

McKinsey Global Institute. 2001. "US Productivity Growth, 1995–2000." MGI Reports (October). *www.mckinsey.com/knowledge/mgi/productivity/*

McKinsey Global Institute. 2002a. "How IT Enables Productivity Growth." MGI Reports (November). *www.mckinsey.com/knowledge/mgi/IT/McKinsey* Global Institute. 2002b. "Reaching Higher Productivity Growth in France and Germany." MGI Reports (October). *www.mckinsey.com/knowledge/mgi/europe/*

OECD. 2003. The Sources of Economic Growth in OECD Countries. Paris: OECD.

Solow, Robert. 1987. New York Review of Books (July 12).

Stiroh, Kevin J 2002. "Information Technology and the US Productivity Revival: What Do the Industry Data Say?" *American Economic Review* 92(5) (December) pp. 1,559–1,576.

Triplett, Jack E, and Barry P Bosworth. Forthcoming. "Baumol's Disease Has Been Cured: IT and Multifactor Productivity in US Services Industries." The New Economy. How New? How Resilient? ed. Dennis W Jansen. Chicago: University of Chicago Press.

5

Does Electronic Business Create Value for Firms?

An Organizational Innovation Perspective

Youlong Zhuang

This study applies organizational innovation theory to one specific type of innovation—electronic business. It describes e-business innovation along seven dimensions – organizational focus, radicalness, centrality, adaptability, uncertainty, pervasiveness, and communicability. E-business is identified as both an administrative and technical innovation that satisfies the above dimensions. The study also links innovative use of e-business to firm performance. By analyzing data from InformationWeek and the Compustat Database, the study shows significant differences between the performance of e-business innovative firms versus the performance averages for their respective industries. The identification of e-business innovation attributes and the linkage between innovation and performance assists researchers in building ebusiness theories. The study also provides managers a basis for choosing the appropriate level of involvement in e-business.

Source: Journal of Electronic Commerce Research, Vol. 6, 2005. © Journal of Electronic Commerce. This article originally appeared in Journal of Electronic Commerce Research, Vol. 6, No. 2, 2005, pp 146-159. Reprinted with permission.

1. Introduction

The purpose of this study is to understand the role of e-business innovation in firm performance. It follows the lead of previous researchers on organizational innovation who suggests that it's more important to understand how innovation theory can explain one particular innovation instead of searching for a single unifying theory that could explain all innovations in general [Wolfe, 1994; Swanson, 1994; Damsgaard and Lyytinen, 1997]. Accordingly, the current research applies organizational innovation theory to a specific type of innovation—electronic business so that, first, the unique attributes of e-business innovation can be identified. This study then examines the attributes of e-business innovation and how they affect business success by linking early adoption and innovative use of ebusiness to firm performance.

The first research issue—understanding the important attributes of e-business innovation is valuable for both researchers and managers. Researchers report that innovation in general is critical to firm competitiveness and effectiveness [Wolfe, 1994] and, yet, any systematic study of e-business as an innovation is absent. Because e-business has been one of the most, if not the single most pervasive innovations for businesses in recent years, researchers want to know where e-business fits into the overall innovation classification in terms of its attributes [Wolfe, 1994]. Such a classification provides guidance to future researchers by laying a common ground for comparing findings and organizing the accumulation of knowledge of e-business [Wolfe, 1994]. Managers to understand e-business innovation attributes so that they can adjust their organizational process to facilitate e-business innovation and enhance firm performance [Zmud, 1984; Kettinger and Hackbarth, 2004].

The second issue of this study—understanding whether early adoption and innovative use of e-business contributes to firm performance is also valuable for researchers and managers. However, two shortcomings of previous researches limit their value for e-business application. One drawback in the study of general innovation is that it focus on antecedents of an organization's tendency to innovate (the dependent variable is typically organizational innovativeness), rather than studying the results of innovativeness [Wolfe, 1994]. Another shortcoming is a focus on e-commerce in general, rather than e-business, specifically [Lewis and Cockrill, 2002, Wang and Tsai, 2002].

E-business is defined in this study as "a broader definition of EC, not just the buying and selling of goods and services, but also servicing customers, collaborating with business partners, conducting e-learning, and conducting electronic transactions within an organization." [Turban *et al.*, 2004, p. 3]. Furthermore, while e-commerce studies address the factors that predict such adoptions, little is known about the effects of e-business adoption on firm performance. Managers want to know how some firms rather than others are able to establish leadership positions in the use of e-business.

As a step in overcoming the deficiencies described above, this study applies organizational innovation theory in the context of e-business. It first identifies seven e-business innovation attributes based on past research on organizational innovation [Wolfe, 1994; Downs and Mohr, 1976]. It then applies Schumpeterian [1934] innovation theory to link a firm's e-business innovativeness—early adoption and innovative use to its performance. The next section discusses organizational innovation theory in an e-business context. It includes a definition of innovation for e-business research and a review of e-business innovation attributes. Thereafter, the linkage between e-business innovation and firm performance is described and statistically tested. Finally, the concluding section provides discussion and implications.

2. Organizational Innovation Theory

Organizational innovation theory encompasses a broad range of research on innovation adoption and assimilation in organizations. It includes studies ranging from definitional issues to how innovation affects a firm's performance. Within this spectrum the current study focuses specifically on e-business innovation and how it affects firm performance.

Concepts from two previous organizational innovation studies are especially relevant for the current study. First, Damanpour's [1991] general definition of innovation is adopted for the e-business domain. Second, we argue that Wolfe's [1994] suggestions for specifying the attributes of innovation can be beneficially applied for understanding e-business performance.

2.1 Definition of Innovation for E-Business Research

Damanpour's [1991] general definition summarizes an innovation as "adoption of an internally generated or purchased device, system, policy, program, process, product, or service that is new to the adopting organization (p.556)." The elements of this definition are embedded in e-business technologies and, as such, e-business is an organizational innovation, it can be internally generated or purchased, either whole or in part. When it is introduced into a firm, e-business requires new devices such as computer hardware, software programs, and policies for using the computer networks and safeguarding confidential information. It stimulates changes in the business process such as customer's order-fulfillment to fit the new ways business is conducted. Thus, e-business innovation demonstrates the important characteristics of organizational innovations.

2.2 Attributes of E-Business Innovation

The current study follows one of the five research strategies suggested by Wolfe [1994]. He suggests that, "the attributes of the focal innovation can be well specified (p. 422)" because attributes affect the firm's adoption pattern, rate of innovation, and the antecedents and processes of the adoption. Other innovation researchers [Henderson and Clark, 1990; Meyer and Goes, 1988], too, assert that ignoring the classification of attributes is a major obstacle to generalizability of innovation research. Accordingly, we next elaborate those attributes for e-business.

Seven attributes for innovation derive from research by others in various innovation settings [Wolfe, 1994; Daft, 1978; Nord and Tucker, 1987; Downs and Mohr, 1976]: Organizational focus (technical vs. administrative), radicalness (radical vs. incremental), centrality (central vs. peripheral), adaptability (flexible vs. inflexible), uncertainty (high vs. low), pervasiveness (high vs. low), and communicability (high vs. low). The question for guiding e-business research is, "Where, along each bi-polar scale, do we expect e-business innovation to be positioned?"

Organizational focus reflects the areas of the firm to which innovation is most relevant [Wolfe, 1994]. Its original bipolar values—technical vs. administrative [Daft, 1978; Nord and Tucker, 1987; Kimberly and Evanisko, 1981] were later expanded by IS researchers to include IS innovations involving business partners that are strategically important for the innovating firms [Swanson, 1994]. Because the line between technical and administrative is easily blurred [Zmud, 1983], e-business often cannot be identified simply as either a technical or an administrative innovation. In some instances, however, e-business appears to be an administrative innovation because it arises from management needs. For example, managers seeking closer interaction with external business partners are more likely to adopt extranet and e-business. They scrutinize the environment, judge the fit of e-business to their own organization, and initiate innovations [Mehrtens, *et al.* 2001; Tan and Teo, 1998]. The adoption of intranet technologies for internal collaboration among geographically dispersed employees is a further example of administratively driven e-business innovation [Damanpour *et al.*, 1989]. At the same time, e-business is a technical-driven innovation arising from technological advantage residing within the firm's IS unit. For example, business transactions through public networks are feasible only after the implementation of encryption technology.

Swanson [1994], extended the two-core (technical vs. administrative) concept of organizational focus into a three-category construct to better classify IS innovations, which may enhance our understanding of the adoption and use of e-business technology. Type I is process innovation that enhances the efficiency or effectiveness of IS in a firm. Some examples are Computer Aided Software Engineering (CASE), relational database, and object-oriented technologies. These innovations may also support other business innovations more broadly in a "weak-order effects" (p. 1077). Software maintenance, for example, is a Type I innovation that is likely to have effects beyond the boundaries of the IS unit. Type II is innovations that enhance the administrative work processes of firms. Examples include automated financial accounting systems, payroll and personnel record systems, groupware, office productivity software, and decision support systems. This type is close to the administrative focus discussed above. Type III innovations are information technologies that have strategic relevance for enabling firms to gain competitive advantages. Enterprise resource planning systems, airline reservation systems, and computer integrated manufacturing solutions are examples for this type of innovations. Type III innovations focus on a firm's major business process, extend to its products and services, or facilitate the integration or coordination among business partners, particularly between suppliers and customers.

It should be noted that e-business innovation is a Type III innovation [Chatterjee *et al.*, 2002] that introduces a new way of doing business. It centers on a firm's major business processes and replaces traditional paper and physically-based business activities with digital information flows. Business activities such as order entry, order confirmation, shipping documentations, and others are conducted digitally with minimal human intervention. In fact, e-business introduces a new way of doing business.

Radicalness of an innovation is the degree of change it brings to the firms' systems and behaviors [Gopalakrishnan and Damanpour, 1997]. While technical innovation causes changes mainly within an IS unit, administrative innovation requires much broader changes [Zmud, 1982]. E-business innovation has high radicalness, because it is both a technical and administrative innovation. It significantly changes the way business is conducted by requiring greater integration of the firm's front end to its back-end systems [Sairamesh, *et al.* 2002]. It requires competing in real time instead of cycle time and often causes conflicts between new Internet-based distribution channels and the traditional supply chain when a firm uses both [Kalakota and Robinson, 2001]. It challenges the adopting firm on how to realize synergies in terms of inventory, transportation, and distribution [Swaminathan and Tayur, 2003].

Centrality indicates by how much e-business affects the major routine work of a firm. A central innovation dislodges and replaces major activities [Gatignon, *et al.*, 2002], while a peripheral innovation has no direct impact on its major day-to-day activities [Nord and Tucker, 1987]. To most firms, such impact of e-business is medium. A retailer with a grand opening of its Web store, for example, is unlikely to experience the severe disruptions in major routine that would accompany the closing of all its physical stores. On the other hand, the impact is not minor. The use of new media affects, among other activities, the adopter's supply chain and distribution channels, as when a supplier requires customers to place orders through its Website. Work skills required for employees may change, including more knowledge workers, because of new business processes introduced by e-business and physically-based work may be replaced with information flow and customer self-services [Straub, 2004; Rotchanakitumnuai and Speece, 2004].

Adaptability is about how much the adopter can refine, elaborate, and modify e-business innovation to fit its goals and objectives [Wolfe, 1994]. The fit, or compatibility, is a major factor in explaining technology innovation adoption behaviors [Cooper and Zmud, 1990]. An innovation may start with a simple prototype to which new features are added later to accommodate related innovations [Swanson, 1994]. In this view, e-business innovation is highly flexible, with uses in all major business activities or simply in a few. In many cases, the innovation begins with just a Website, adding new features to its front-end and gradually integrating to its back-end inventory and supply chain management systems to accommodate the diffusion of e-business [Wang, *et al.*, 2004]. In fact, firms often create new services or products to render new e-business technologies to be even more useful. E-business innovations may be tailored to the operations of a specific firm and be enhanced and extended to meet the demand of business functionality [Yang and Papazoglou, 2000].

Uncertainty is about the risk associated with e-business [Wolfe, 1994]. The risk is high for e-business as a new technology. For example, computer networks are less reliable than traditional phone lines, the investment of the first movers may be high compared to that of the followers, it is relatively easy for others to imitate a competitor's innovation, and protection of e-business innovation is hard, even with patent laws. For example, *Amazon.com* uses patented one-click checkout technology on its Website. But many other retailing sites have express checkout or similar functions. An additional source of higher risk is the falling price of computer and networking devices and increasing computing powers, following Moore's law -- doubling of transistors every couple of years. High risks also stem from dependence on the network effects [Oliva, *et al.* 2003; Rajgopal, *et al.* 2003]. For example, if only a few companies use the technology in business-to-business e-commerce, the benefits are limited. Further risk comes from firms' networks to its stakeholders which make them transparent to the outside world. As a result, e-business brings more risks to its adopters than many other technologies do.

Pervasiveness is about the involvement of the organization's employees in the innovation [Wolfe, 1994; Lyytinen and Rose, 2003]. This is high for e-business. Almost everyone in the firm could be affected. Each unit plays at least a supporting role of e-business. E-business is not the sole responsibility of one unit within an organization. The success of e-business depends on the endeavor of every employee. For example, if a firm decided to replace paper memos with intranet for its internal communications, every employee, from CEO to janitor, need to learn how to retrieve electronic information with some computer-type devices [Jacoby and Luai, 2005].

Finally, *Communicability* reflects the likelihood of communicating the aspects of an innovation to others [Rothman, 1974]. Communications promote innovative behaviors [Lind and Zmud, 1991]. Variations in the communicability of an innovation and cosmopolitan may affect the adoption of the innovation [Downs and Mohr, 1976]. E-business is a complex innovation. It requires coordination of several units within the firm and collaboration of many firms in the supply chain. The word of mouth effects are much different in the e-business environment [Singh and Kundu, 2002]. In traditional business, a consumer can spread his or her experiences with a company to a limited number of people. In e-business, the same person can easily tell thousands or even millions of people with online forum. Thus, communicability is high for e-business.

In summary, e-business is both an administrative and technical innovation that is flexible, has median centrality, high levels of radicalness, uncertainty, pervasiveness, and communicability. Table 1 summarizes the attributes of e-business innovations. It shows where e-business innovation stands at each bipolar dimension.

Table 1: Attributes of E-Business Innovation

Dimension	**Classification**		
Organizational focus	Technical	In-Between	Administrative
	✓		✓
Radicalness	Incremental		Radical
			✓
Centrality	Peripheral		Central
		✓	
Adaptability	Inflexible		Flexible
			✓
Uncertainty	Low		High
			✓
Pervasiveness	Low		High
			✓
Communicability	Low		High
			✓

3. E-Business Innovation and Firm Performance

The influential work of Joseph Schumpeter [1934] underscores the importance of innovation as the source of value creation. Schumpeterian innovation not only can change how an industry operates, but has even been called "creative destruction" because of its radical nature. Performance is, in effect, innovation-based [Mahoney and Pandian, 1992].

Schumpeterian innovation theory emphasizes the importance of technology and considers innovative use of technology as the foundation of new products and production methods. Examples include the introduction of a new good or of a new method of production, the opening of a new market, or the development of a new source of supply of raw materials or partly manufactured goods [Schumpeter, 1934].

With the attributes discussed in the previous section, e-business innovation is an example of Schumpeterian innovation. Its organizational-focus attribute suggests that such innovation crosses both technical and administrative boundaries, affects major business processes, and facilitates coordination among the business partners. Such innovation has strategic impacts on innovating firms [Mustonen-Ollila and Lyytinen, 2004].

The high radicalness attribute implies that e-business innovation brings profound changes to the adopting firm and its partners [Akkermans and Helden, 2002]. By moving one of its business processes to e-business, for example, the design and logistics of the adopter's remaining processes become much different. Its suppliers and customers, too, may be affected by those same innovations.

The high uncertainty attribute of e-business challenges the managers of e-business. It is the innovative use of the technology that differentiates a superior performer from a poor one. Such innovative use often accompanies introduction of a new good or of a new method of production as in Schumpeterian innovation.

Due to its high pervasiveness, e-business affects everything throughout the organizations. Employees need to be retrained to assume new responsibilities brought about by e-business. Firms reorganize its structure to fit e-business innovation which emphasizes the flow of information both within their boundary and among partners along the supply chain.

Typical of Schumpeterian innovation's creative destruction, e-business has been changing entire organizations and industries. Its diffusion often stimulates reconfiguration of the adopter's technology, strategy, and structure, and, for early adopters, sometimes provides a "dominant design" that gains initial competitive advantage [Mason, *et al.*, 1997]. Dell, for example, as one of the first firms to use the Internet to sell directly to businesses, governments, and consumers, gained significant advantages over its competitors [Metz, 1998; Menn, 1999].

Widespread adoption of e-business technology affects firm's performance by redefining the way firms compete. Among the most powerful sources of creative destruction in the last century is the introduction of the Internet for connecting millions of computers and other devices worldwide. Its commercial use, combined with the graphical user interface-based World Wide Web browser, is more than deployment of equipment and devices—it is also a social force. It has changed the way firms do business, including their product offerings, organizational boundaries and structures, value chains, and marketing channels.

E-business also affects firm performance by intensifying the competition. Towards the last few decades of the twentieth century, the competition among businesses is going global and becoming more severe. This global marketplace is characterized by intense social, economic, and technological changes. Innovation plays an important role in enhancing and sustaining the performance of firms to adapt to the change. [Gopalakrishnan and Damanpour, 1997]. E-business emerged as a critical business innovation. Managers become Schumpeterian entrepreneurs and adopt e-business to destroy the current organizational arrangements. This process resulted in some cannibalization of the firm's existing markets as the industry was launched on a new course [Mason *et al.* 1997]. Manufacturers often find e-business cannibalizing their existing distribution channels [Boyd and Bilegan, 2003]. E-business thus affects firm performance.

E-business influences a firm's performance by enabling organizational learning and knowledge management [Parker, 2003]. E-business innovation has provided new capabilities that produce values by creating more efficient markets, enabling easier access, making value and supply chains more efficient, disrupting current pricing power, enabling mass customization, and extending reach. Firms that adopt e-business early will cumulate more knowledge and thus can compete better in the new economy [Mustonen-Ollila and Lyytinen, 2004].

E-business also influences firm performance by changing business process [Wu, *et al*, 2003]. It changes business communications, order taking, and procurement processes. Better communications within and across corporate boundary enhances collaborative commerce and create values [Gibson and Edwards, 2004]. Online ordering and payment make transaction more accurate, timeliness, less expensive, and result in happier customers and more revenues for the firm [Laudon and Traver, 2004]. Automatic procurement allows a firm to search and locate potential suppliers in a larger pool and thus can find high quality suppliers [Rayport and Jaworski, 2004]

This leads us to two main hypothesis of this study:

H1: Superior e-business innovativeness will be associated with significantly higher profit ratios.

H2: Superior e-business innovativeness will be associated with significantly lower cost ratios.

4. Methodology

4.1 Sample Selection

Each year since 1989, InformationWeek has ranked companies on the basis of how they use IT innovatively. It awarded 500 firms that demonstrated a pattern of technological, procedural, and organizational innovation. During the period of 1998 through 2001, it also awarded gold citations to one third of the 500 firms for their early adoption and creative use of electronic commerce technologies. To identify firms with superior e-business innovativeness, this study uses the rankings provided by InformationWeek in its annual special issue during the period of 1998 through 2001. InformationWeek uses a rigor survey instrument. It has more than 10 years of experience in designing the instrument and collecting the data. The instrument is field-tested and the survey is not biased to company's prior financial performance [Shin, 2003]. Editors of InformationWeek prescreen the sample to examine if a firm demonstrates a pattern of technological, procedural, and organizational innovation and select firms with at least one billion dollar annual revenue. They then contact these firms through mail, phone, and fax. The subjects are IT executives of the firms [Weston, *et al.*, 2000].

According to these citations, a total of 417 companies are awarded gold citation for at least one of the four years, 163 companies are awarded gold for two or more years, and 62 are awarded gold for three or four years. The final sample of 62 firms contains companies with three or more gold awards. This provides a more robust sample of e-business technology innovators [Bharadwaj, 2000].

Our procedure next creates a matching set of control firms drawn from the Compustat database. The selection process utilizes the North American Industry Classification System (NAICS), a six-digit classification that identifies a firm based on its business activities. For each e-business technology innovator, instead of just one matching firm for each innovating firm, we select as matching firms all other having the same NAICS code. The average performance of same-code firms is used as the control group [Santhanam and Hartono, 2003]. The 62 innovator firms and the matching set of control firms are utilized to conduct the tests.

Data from sources such as InformationWeek and Compustat have been used in several researches [C F Bharadwaj 2000; Bharadwaj *et al.* 1999; Brynjolfsson and Hitt 1996; Hitt and Brynjolfsson 1996; Lichtenberg 1995; Santhanam and Hartono, 2003]. This research uses the method appeared in at least one of the above researches.

4.2. Dependent Variables

The dependent variables include two sets of measures. First, the profit ratios are five profit-based measures of net and operating income. The second set of the measures are three cost ratios. These same measures were used by Bharadwaj [2000] and Santhanam and Hartono [2003].

The profit ratios are the measures which are related to Return and Net Income. The return on assets (ROA) is the ratio of a firm's net income to its assets. The return on sales is the ratio of net income to sales. The operating income to assets (OI/A) is the ratio of operating income to assets. The Operating Income to Sales

(OI/S) is the ratio of operating income to sales. The Operating Income to Employee (OI/E) is the ratio of operating income to number of employees.

The second set of the measures are related to cost and expense. They are Cost of Goods Sold to Sales (COG/S), Selling and General Administrative Expenses to Sales (SGA/S), and total Operating Expenses to Sales (OEXP/S). The OEXP is calculated as the sum of COG and SGA.

5. Results

The results of statistical test for all the four years (1998 through 2001) are provided in Table 2. The performance data on some measures for a few innovator and control firms are not available in the Compustat database and hence have to be excluded. The actual sample size on each test is displayed in the table. The t-statistic from the t-test and the Z-statistic from the Wilcoxon test are reported. A significant negative test statistic for profit ratios and a significant positive test statistic for cost ratios indicate superior e-business performance for the innovative firms. Tests for financial performance halo effects and qualitative evidence of e-business innovativeness are provided as Appendix A and B respectively.

The findings strongly support the hypothesis with profit ratios significantly higher for the innovator sample and cost ratios significantly higher for the control sample in all tests except two. The two non-significant t-test statistics are for Return On Sales (ROS) in 1999 and Cost of Goods Sold to Sales (COG/S) in 2001. However, their corresponding Wilcoxon tests do support the hypothesis. Considering that a total of 64 tests are performed, it is not unreasonable to observe a few inconsistencies by chance.

6. Discussion

This study first explores the seven attributes of e-business innovation. It then tests the linkage between innovative use of e-business and firm performance by following Schumpeterian innovation theory. The statistical results strongly support the theory.

E-business innovation is characterized as both administrative and technical innovation in terms of organizational focus. This attribute indicates that the success

Table 2: Results

		N	Mean	Median	t	Z
				1998		
ROA	Innovator	62	0.046	0.042	-4.940***	-5.154***
	Control	62	-0.107	-0.062		
ROS	Innovator	62	0.054	0.050	-3.374***	-5.369***
	Control	62	-1.266	-0.084		
OI/A	Innovator	62	0.111	0.105	-5.258***	-6.037***
	Control	62	-0.036	0.014		
OI/S	Innovator	62	0.131	0.108	-3.487***	-6.533***
	Control	62	-1.190	-0.010		
OI/E	Innovator	62	43.422	27.557	-4.037***	-4.884***
	Control	62	12.885	10.487		
COG/S	Innovator	62	0.638	0.687	2.976**	4.134***
	Control	62	1.551	0.788		
SGA/S	Innovator	53	0.213	0.203	3.572***	5.157***
	Control	61	0.705	.301		
OPEXP/S	Innovator	53	0.826	0.844	3.308**	5.892***
	Control	61	1.511	0.955		
				1999		
ROA	Innovator	62	0.049	0.054	-4.903***	-6.047***
	Control	62	-1.879	-0.053		
ROS	Innovator	62	0.064	0.056	-0.273	-4.827***
	Control	62	-2.596	-0.041		
OI/A	Innovator	62	0.104	0.090	-5.111***	-5.928***
	Control	62	-0.128	-0.017		
OI/S	Innovator	62	0.134	0.100	-3.188**	-6.412***
	Control	62	-3.932	0.009		
OI/E	Innovator	62	47.959	29.020	-3.664***	-5.218***
	Control	62	10.920	10.716		
COG/S	Innovator	62	0.637	0.682	2.753**	4.147***
	Control	62	3.967	0.789		
SGA/S	Innovator	53	0.210	0.197	3.674***	4.927***
	Control	61	0.869	0.278		

Contd...

Contd...

OPEXP/S	Innovator	53	0.821	0.841	3.603**	5.812***
	Control	61	1.526	0.960		
				2000		
ROA	Innovator	62	0.037	0.042	-2.708**	-5.847***
	Control	62	-0.458	-0.096		
ROS	Innovator	62	0.057	0.056	-3.269**	-5.360***
	Control	62	-1.896	-0.059		
OI/A	Innovator	62	0.108	0.098	-4.059***	-6.313***
	Control	62	-0.232	-0.022		
OI/S	Innovator	62	0.135	0.103	-3.407***	-6.222***
	Control	62	-1.472	-0.004		
OI/E	Innovator	61	54.342	34.993	-4.993***	-5.565***
	Control	62	-3.621	5.146		
COG/S	Innovator	62	0.641	0.695	2.636*	4.042***
	Control	62	2.060	0.785		
SGA/S	Innovator	53	0.208	0.183	3.691***	5.104***
	Control	61	0.707	0.293		
OPEXP/S	Innovator	53	0.823	0.848	3.796***	6.139***
	Control	61	1.365	0.959		
				2001		
ROA	Innovator	58	0.014	0.019	-2.556*	-5.264***
	Control	62	-0.496	-0.062		
ROS	Innovator	58	0.018	0.028	-2.468*	-5.017***
	Control	62	-3.930	-0.061		
OI/A	Innovator	58	0.077	0.075	-2.639*	-5.311***
	Control	62	-0.283	0.017		
OI/S	Innovator	58	0.103	0.070	-3.003**	-5.462***
	Control	62	-1.738	-0.017		
OI/E	Innovator	57	33.963	21.598	-3.705***	-4.495***
	Control	62	-5.349	2.895		
COG/S	Innovator	58	0.639	0.699	1.764	-3.055***
	Control	62	1.215	0.722		
SGA/S	Innovator	50	0.228	0.220	2.506*	-4.107***
	Control	61	1.790	0.312		
OPEXP/S	Innovator	50	0.844	0.873	2.620*	-5.111***
	Control	61	2.466	0.960		

*p<0.05, **p<0.01, ***p<0.001

of e-business depends on more than the effort of a single business unit within the firm. Factors both inside and outside of the organization can impact e-business performance.

E-business innovation brings high radical changes to the way firms conduct business. The radical changes favor organizations that adopt e-business early. One example is the changes occurred in the stock trading. No stock exchange firms today ignore online trading. However, early adopters claim large customer base.

The medium centrality suggests that firms could not change everything to e-business overnight, because of the continuity of business and the involvement of many parties. The business continuity requires a thorough testing of a new system before widespread adoption of it. A firm may want all of its business processes to be electronic. Yet, other firms may not be ready to do so, or the corresponding laws and regulations may not be in place. Firms that carefully plan their migration to e-business without impair to their overall business would win.

The flexibility of e-business allows a firm to adopt the technology to the extent it desires. Firms can start using e-business to conduct their non-strategic activities and later extends it to more critical business processes. For example, a firm can begin with a simple content dominated Website providing information about the company and its products and services to publicize the firm and promote its products before a full version of online business transaction is carried out. Or a firm can start with an intranet to test how it works before extending it to the business partners.

The high uncertainty of e-business gives rise to the need of a well planned flexible e-business strategy. A flexible strategy allows a firm to adjust its e-business investment according to the environmental and technological changes and it becomes more agile in competition. New technologies in e-business come and go faster than any other technologies preceding it. As a result, business purposes dominate the use of e-business.

The high pervasiveness implies that e-business affects everyone in the organization. Education and training are important for e-business organizations.

For example, if a firm decides to distribute its internal announcement through e-mail, the firm should train its employees not only how to use e-mail but also how to use it correctly following an e-mail usage policy. The effectiveness of the system depends on how employees utilize it.

The high communicability of e-business innovation requires team of individual unit within a firm and collaboration of firms along the supply chain. Powerful firms may demand their business partners to conduct business electronically. It is to the benefit of the firm to participate actively in e-business.

This study supports the hypothesis that e-business innovativeness enhances firm's performance by increasing profit ratios and lowering cost ratios. E-business innovativeness is based on a panel of experts' judgment of early and innovative use of e-business. The results confirm that e-business as Schumpeterian innovation affects firm performance. E-business provides more efficient sales channels than the traditional ones. It reaches more customers with less cost. It allows collaboration among business partners adding values to consumers.

The support of the hypothesis encourages firms to make more innovative use of e-business. The technology has provided equal opportunities for all firms. However, only organizations that can learn from their own and others' experiences and use the technology innovatively will gain competitive advantages.

7. Implications for Managers

Managers can benefit from the findings of the attributes of e-business innovation and the relationship between innovative uses of e-business and firm performance. The findings can assist them choosing appropriate level of participation in e-business that match their own organization's infrastructure and business objectives. They can thus better plan their e-business strategy.

The finding of linkage between e-business innovation and firm's performance is interesting to managers. It helps them to understand the importance of e-business. Early adoption and creative use of e-business enhance firm performance. Early adopters can establish brand images and gain large customer base. Early's adopters will also be able to accumulate knowledge on e-business and reap more benefits. Innovative use of e-business makes a firm one step ahead of the competition.

In order to use e-business innovatively, managers need to understand the attributes of e-business. Organizational focus, for example, is important when assigning the responsibility of e-business. E-business is more than a technical issue. Delivering all responsibilities to one single unit within the firm will not bring the success of e-business. E-business is more than an administrative issue. It is a business issue. It is related to a firm's everyday business activities and future development. Thus, both the suppliers and customers play important roles in the forming and implementing of e-business strategy. The success requires the coordination of many partners. Firms will collaborate while competing with rivals.

8. Limitations

The study uses external rankings of e-business innovators and thus could have some inherent potential biases. The rankings may be based on subjective evaluations of a firm's innovativeness. The criteria used in the selection process are determined by InformationWeek editors and may thus lack academic rigor. For example, to be selected, a firm must have at least one billion dollar annual revenue. Thus the result may be biased with only large firms in the sample. Future research should focus on developing more objective metrics for evaluating e-business innovativeness. Another limitation of the study is the sample size of only 62 firms. Future research may include larger samples and have more robust statistical tests.

The study applied Schumpeterian innovation theory to explain the differences between the performance of e-business innovative firms versus the performance averages for their respective industries. However, the underlying mechanisms of how e-business affects firm's performance are by no means clear. Additional systematic research is needed to identify the full chain of variables linking e-business innovativeness to firm performance.

9. Conclusion

This study helps both researchers and practitioners better understand e-business. It identifies the attributes of e-business innovation and examines its value in firm performance. It provides researchers with attributes of e-business and enables them to compare findings of e-business performance. It helps managers decide to what extent their organizations should invest in e-business by matching the e-business attributes to their own organization's characteristics.

(Youlong Zhuang is associated with College of Business, University of Missouri-Columbia.)

References

Akkermans, H and K Helden, "Vicious and Virtuous Cycles in ERP Implementation: A Case Study of Interrelations between Critical Success Factors," *European Journal of Information Systems*, Vol. 11, No. 1: 35-46, March 2002.

Anonymous, "Office Depot is Ranked No.1 On PC Computing's Business E-Shopping List for – Office Supplies," *Business Wire*, Vol. 12: 11:34, January 2000.

Anonymous, "Mellon Bank's Automated Payments Service Leads To Reengineering Award At Carnegie Mellon University," *PR Newswire*, Vol. 12: 14-24, January 1998.

Anonymous, "Mellon Global Cash Management Systems Achieves CMM Level 2," *PR Newswire*, Vol. 5: 9-48, April 2001.

Bharadwaj, A S "A Resource-Based Perspective on Information Technology Capability and Firm Performance: An Empirical Investigation," *MIS Quarterly*, Vol. 24, No. 1: 169-196, 2000.

Bharadwaj, A, S Bharadwaj, and B Konsynski, "Information Technology Effects on Firm Performance as Measured by Tobin's q," *Management Science*, Vol. 45,.No. 7: 1008-1024, 1999.

Boyd, E A and I C Bilegan, "Revenue Management and E-Commerce," *Management Science*, Vol. 49, No. 10: 1363-1386, October 2003.

Brown, B and S Perry, "Removing the Financial Performance Halo from Fortune's Most Admired Companies," *Academy of Management Journal*, Vol. 37, No. 5: 1347-1359, 1994.

Brynjolfsson, E, and L Hitt, "Paradox Lost? Firm-Level Evidence on the Returns to Information Systems Spending," *Management Science*, Vol. 42, No. 4: 541-558, 1996.

Chatterjee, D, R Grewal, and V Sambamurthy, "Shaping Up for E-Commerce: Institutional Enablers of the Organizational Assimilation of Web Technologies," *MIS Quarterly*, Vol. 26, No. 2: 65-89, June 2002.

Cooper, R B and R W Zmud, "Information Technology Implementation Research: A Technological Diffusion Approach," *Management Science*, Vol. 36, No. 2: 123-139, Feb. 1990.

Daft, R L "A Dual-Core Model of Organizational Innovation," *Academy of Management Journal*, Vol. 21, No. 2: 193-210, June 1978.

Damanpour, F "Organizational Innovation: A Meta Analysis of Effects of Determinants and Moderators," *Academy of Management Journal*, Vol. 34: 555-590, 1991.

Damanpour, F, K A Szabat, and W M Evan, "The Relationship between Types of Innovation and Organizational Performance," *Journal of Management Studies,* Vol. 26: 587-601, 1989.

Damsgaard, J and K Lyytinen, "Hong Kong's EDI Bandwagon Derailed or on the Right Track," in McMaster, T, Mumford, E, Swanson, E, Warboys, B, and Wastel, D (Eds.), Facilitating Technology Transfer Through Partnership: Learning from Practice and Research, Chapman and Hall, London, 1997.

Downs, G W and L B Mohr, "Conceptual Issues in the Study of Innovation," *Administrative Science Quarterly,* Vol. 21: 700-714, 1976.

Gatignon, H, M L Tushman, W Smith, and P Anderson, "A Structural Approach to Assessing Innovation: Construct Development of Innovation Locus, Type, and Characteristics," *Management Science,* Vol. 48, No. 9: 1103:1122, September. 2002.

Gibson, P R and J Edwards, "The Strategic Importance of E-Commerce in Modern Supply Chains," *Journal of Electronic Commerce in Organizations,* Vol. 2, No. 3: 59-76, July-Sep, 2004.

Gilbert, A "Profile 3M Co.—Take My Post-It, Please-And Electronic Paper, Too," *InformationWeek,* Vol. 803: 316, September 11, 2000.

Gopalakrishnan, S and F Damanpour, "A Review of Innovation Research in Economics, Sociology and Technology Management," Omega, *International Journal of Management Science,* Vol. 25, No. 1: 15-28, 1997.

Henderson, R M and K B Clark, "Architectural innovation: The Reconfiguration of Existing Product Technologies and the Failure of Established Firms," *Administrative Science Quarterly,* Vol. 35, No. 1: 9-30, 1990.

Hitt, L and E Brynjolfsson, "Productivity, Business Profitability, and Consumer Surplus: Three Different Measures of Information Technology Value," *MIS Quarterly,* Vol. 20, No. 2: 121-142, 1996.

Jacoby, G A and Luai, "Critical Business Requirements Model and Metrics for Intranet ROI," *Journal of Electronic Commerce Research,* Vol. 6, No. 1: 1-30, 2005.

Kalakota, R and M Robinson, e-Business 2.0: Roadmap for Success, 2001.

Kettinger, W J and G Hackbarth, "Integration of Electronic Commerce Networks into the Sales Processes of Samll Firms," *Journal of Electronic Commerce Research,* Vol. 5, No. 3: 153-171, 2004.

Kimberly, J R and M J Evanjsko, "Organizational Innovation: The Influence of Individual, Organizational, and Contextual Factors on Hospital Adoption of Technological and Administrative Innovations," *Academy of Management Journal,* Vol. 24, No. 4: 689-713, 1981.

Laudon, K C and C G Traver, *E-Commerce: Business*, Technology, Society. 2nd Edition, Addison Wesley, Boston, 2004.

Lewis, R and A Cockrill, "Going Global - Remaining Local: The Impact of E-Commerce on Small Retail Firms in Wales," *International Journal of Information Management*, Vol. 22, No. 3: 195-209, June 2002.

Lichtenberg, F R "The Output Contribution of Computer Equipment and Personnel: A Firm Level Analysis," *Journal of Economic Innovation and New Technologies*, Vol. 3: 201-217, 1995.

Lind, M R and R W Zmud, "The Influence of a Convergence in Understanding between Technology Providers and Users on Information Technology Innovativeness," *Organization Science*, Vol. 2, No. 2: 195-217, May 1991.

Lyytinen, K and G M Rose, "The Disruptive Nature of Information Technology Innovations: The Case of Internet Computing in Systems Development Organizations," *MIS Quarterly*, Vol. 27, No. 4: 557-595, December 2003.

Mahoney, J T and J P K Pandian, "The Resource-Based View within the Conversation of Strategic Management", *Strategic Management Journal*, Vol. 13: 363-380, 1992.

Mason, R O, J L McKenney, and D G Copeland, "Developing an Historical Tradition in MIS Research," *MIS Quarterly*, Vol. 21, No. 3: 257-278, September 1997.

McDermott, M J "Scaling New Heights," *Chief Executive*, 30-35, February 1, 2001.

Mehrtens, J, P B Cragg, and A M Mills, "A Model of Internet Adoption by SMEs," *Information and Management*, Vol. 39: 165-176, 2001.

Menn, J "Strategies straight from Dell: Fifteen Years After He Spun $1,000 into One of the Biggest Success Stories in the Computer Industry, Michael Dell takes a look at the state of today's industry and the future of the PC," *Los Angeles Times*, C14, March 11, 1999.

Meyer, A D and J B Goes, "Organizational Assimilation of Innovations: A Multilevel Contextual Analysis," *Academy of Management Journal*, Vol. 31: 897-923, 1988.

Metz, P "Innovation in a Wired World," *Journal of Business Strategy*, Vol. 19, No. 6: 7-12, November-December 1998.

Mustonen-Ollila, E and K Lyytinen, "How Organizations Adopt Information System Process Innovations: A Longitudinal Analysis," *European Journal of Information Systems*, Vol. 13: 35-51, 2004.

Neter, J, M H Kuther, C J Nachtsheim, and W Wasserman, *Applied Linear Statistical Models* (4th Ed.), Irwin, Chicago, 1996.

Nord, W R and S Tucker, Implementing Routine and Radical Innovations. Lexington, D C Heath and Company, 1987.

Oliva, R, J D Sterman, and M Giese, "Limits to Growth in the New Economy: Exploring the 'Get Big Fast' Strategy in E-Commerce," *System Dynamics Review*, Vol. 19, No. 2: 83-117, Summer 2003.

Parker, D "SME Clusters within Community-Portal Constellations," *Management Science*, Vol. 47, No. 2: 14-18, Feb. 2003.

Rajgopal, S, M Venkatachalam, and S Kotha, "The Value Relevance of Network Advantages: The Case of ECommerce Firms," *Journal of Accounting Research*, Vol. 41, No. 1: 135-162, March 2003.

Rayport, J F and B J Jaworski, "Introduction to E-commerce 2nd Edition", McGraw-Hill/ Irwin, Boston, 2004.

Ricadela, A "Priorities Shift," *InformationWeek*, pp. 26-35, Sep. 17, 2001.

Rotchanakitumnuai, S. and M. Speece, "Corporate Customer Perspectives on Business Value of Thai Internet Banking," *Journal of Electronic Commerce Research*, Vol. 5, No. 4: 270-286, 2004.

Rothman, J Planning and Organizing for Social Change: Action Principles from Social Science Research, New York, Columbia University Press, 1974.

Sairamesh, J, R Mohan, M Kumar, L Hasson, and C Bender, "A Platform for Business-to-Business Sell-side, Private Exchanges and Marketplaces," *IBM Systems Journal*, Vol. 41, No. 2: 242-252, 2002.

Santhanam, R and E I Iartono, "Issues in Linking Information Technology Capability to Firm Performance," *MIS Quarterly*, Vol. 27, No. 1: 125-153, March 2003.

Schumpeter, "J A Theory of Economic Development", Harvard University Press, Cambridge, MA (first published in 1911; republished 1968), 1934.

Shin, N "An Empirical Investigation of Economic Payoffs of E-business and CRM Innovations," *Proceedings of the Ninth Americas Conference on Information Systems*, pp. 175-182, 2003.

Singh, N and S Kundu, "Explaining the Growth of E-Commerce Corporations (ECCs): An Extension and Application of the Eclectic Paradigm," *Journal of International Business Studies*, Vol. 33, No. 4: 679-697, 2002.

Straub, D "Foundations of Net-Enhanced Organizations", John Wiley & Sons, Inc., Hoboken, New Jersey, 2004.

Swaminathan, J M and S R Tayur, "Models for Supply Chains in E-Business," *Management Science*, Vol. 49, No. 10: 1387-1406, October 2003.

Swanson, E B "Information Systems Innovation among Organizations," *Management Science*, Vol. 40, No. 9: 1069-1092, September 1994.

Tan, M and T S H Teo, "Factors Influencing the Adoption of the Internet," *International Journal of Electronic Commerce*, Vol. 2, No. 3: 5-18, 1998.

Turban, E, D King, J Lee, and D Viehland, "Electronic Commerce: A Managerial Perspective", Prentice Hall, Upper Saddle River, New Jersey, USA, 2004.

Wang, J and K Tsai, "Factors in Taiwanese Firms' Decisions to Adopt Electronic Commerce: An Empirical Study," *The World Economy*, Vol. 25, No. 8: 1145-1167, Aug 2002.

Wang, Y C W, C Chang, and M S H Heng, "The Levels of Information Technology Adoption, Business Network, and a Strategic Position Model for Evaluating Supply Chain Integration," *Journal of Electronic Commerce Research*, Vol. 5, No. 2: 85-98, 2004.

Weston, R, H D'Antoni, and L Boomer, "Methodology: Results Are Deeper Than Money," *Information Week*, Vol. 803: 75, September 11, 2000.

Wolfe, R A "Organizational Innovation: Review, Critique and Suggested Research Directions," *Journal of Management Studies*, Vol. 31, No. 3: 405-431, May 1994.

Wu, F, V Mahajan, and S Balasubramanian, "An Analysis of E-Business Adoption and Its Impact on Business Performance," *Journal of the Academy of Marketing Science*, Vol. 31, No.4: 425-447, Fall 2003.

Yang, J and M P Papazoglou, "Interoperation Support for Electronic Business," *Communications of the ACM*, Vol. 43, No. 6: 39-47, Jun 2000.

Zmud, R W "Diffusion of Modern Software Practices: Influence of Centralization and Formalization," *Management Science*, Vol. 28, No. 12: 1421-1431, Dec. 1982.

Zmud, R W "The Effectiveness of External Information Channels in Facilitating Innovation within Software Development Groups," *MIS Quarterly*, Vol. 7, No. 2: 43-58, June 1983.

Zmud, R W "An Examination of 'Push-Pull' Theory Applied to Process Innovation in Knowledge Work," Management Science, Vol. 30, No. 6: 727-738, June 1984.

APPENDIX A

Testing for Financial Performance Halo

The gold citations of InformationWeek 500 firms were selected by a panel of experts who did "an extensive mail, phone, and fax study" (Ricadela, 2001, p. 32). These types of ratings are often influenced by the past performance of the firm. It is called "halo effect" by Brown and Perry (1994). In this appendix, we test whether such an effect exists. We also test the effects of e-business innovation. We use the method of Santhanam and Hartono (2003). The method is similar to those of Brown and Perry (1994), Neter *et al.* (1996), and Bharadwaj (2000).

The test uses two sets of regression analysis. The first set of analysis regress prior year's performance (profit or cost ratios) on current year's performance. The second set extends the first one with a dummy variable added. The dummy variable is a binary indicator coded as 1 for innovative firms and 0 for firms in the control group. The formulas of the two models are:

$$FP_t = \beta_0 + \beta_1 FP_{(t-1)}$$

$$FP_t = \alpha_0 + \alpha_1 FP_{(t-1)} + \alpha_2 D$$

Where FP_t is performance measure at year t, β_0 and α_0 are intercepts, β_1, α_1, and α_2 are regression coefficients, and D is the (0,1) binary variable.

The results of the regression analysis are shown in Table A1. It includes the R-square changes by adding the dummy variable and respective regression coefficients. Model 1, indicates that 21 of the 24 performance measures were significantly predicted by prior year's measures.

What is more interesting is that the significance of coefficient of dummy demonstrates the e-business innovation effect on firm performance. The coefficients of profit measures are expected to be positive while the coefficients of cost measures are expected to be negative. Model 2 indicates eighteen of the 24 coefficients are significant with the right sign. Thus, the halo effects may not be a major concern in this study because of the significant e-business innovativeness effect on firm performance.

Table A1: Regression Analysis of Financial Performance Halo Effects

	1999				
	Model	N	R-Square Change Performance	1998 Financial	Dummy
ROA	1	124	0.196***	0.443***	
	2		0.057***	0.326***	0.265***
ROS	1	124	0.010	0.099·	
	2		0.000	0.100	-0.005
OI/A	1	124	0.280***	0.529***	
	2		0.037**	0.419***	0.222**
OI/S	1	124	0.174***	0.417***	
	2		0.025*	0.367***	0.166*
OI/E	1	124	0.710***	0.843***	
	2		0.002	0.830***	0.041
COG/S	1	124	0.130***	0.360***	
	2		0.023*	0.319***	-0.157*

Contd...

Contd...

SGA/S	1	114	0.385***	0.620***	
	2		0.020*	0.575***	-0.147*
OPEXP/S	1	114	0.101***	0.318***	
	2		0.50***	0.243***	-0.235***
				2000	
ROA	1	124	0.034***	0.185***	
	2		0.066***	0.105	0.196**
ROS	1	124	0.111***	0.333***	
	2		0.077***	0.326***	0.278***
OI/A	1	124	0.097***	0.311***	
	2		1.453***	0.196**	0.267***
OI/S	1	124	0.111***	0.334***	
	2		0.045**	0.273***	0.221**
OI/E	1	122	0.656***	0.810***	
	2		0.024***	0.763***	0.161***
COG/S	1	124	0.056***	0.236***	
	2		0.034**	0.190**	-0.191**
SGA/S	1	114	0.389***	0.624***	
	2		0.016*	0.581***	-0.133*
OPEXP/S	1	114	0.648***	0.805***	
	2		0.005	0.782***	-0.072
				2001	
ROA	1	120	0.025*	0.158*	
	2		0.040**	0.109	0.206**
ROS	1	120	0.021	0.145	
	2		0.034**	0.090	0.194**
OI/A	1	120	0.117***	0.343***	
	2		0.016	0.294***	0.137
OI/S	1	120	0.160***	0.400***	
	2		0.025*	0.351***	0.165*
OI/E	1	118	0.612***	0.782***	
	2		0.000	0.792***	-0.024
COG/S	1	120	0.191***	0.437***	
	2		0.005	0.420***	-0.071
SGA/S	1	111	0.041***	0.202**	
	2		0.030*	0.144	-0.184*
OPEXP/S	1	111	0.014***	0.119	
	2		0.050**	0.044	-0.235**

*p<0.10, **p<0.05, ***p<0.01

APPENDIX B

Qualitative Evidence of E-Business Innovativeness

To further validate the sample of e-business innovators and to understand the nature of their innovation capabilities, a search of the Dow Jones business database *(Factiva.com)* is conducted for articles describing the e-business innovations undertaken by the sample of innovators in this study during the period 1998 through 2001 [Bharadwaj, 2000].

Specifically, we search the Dow Jones business database to understand how some firms are able to establish leadership positions in the use of e-business while others are not. We study those firms that are identified by experts as innovative adopters of e-business and look for explanations to the results of their uses of e-business and the managerial processes they use [Mason *et al.*, 1997].

Evidences from five innovative firms are collected and summarized in Table B1 [Bharadwaj, 2000]. Evidences of strategic investment rationale for e-business are collected. Firms and articles about their e-business innovation are listed in Column One of Table B1. Column Two shows the innovative use of e-business of the exemplar firms.

Column Three demonstrates the advantages of such innovative use of e-business. The impact on competition is illustrated in Column Four.

Table B1: Case Exemplars of E-Business Innovators

Case Exemplars	Innovative Use of E-Business	Advantages	Effects on Competition
Dell Computer's online direct sales model [Metz, 1998; Menn, 1999]	Early and innovative use of Web as a sales medium. Collect information that would otherwise be difficult to get.	Benefits includes cost reduction, product development improvement, supply chain efficiencies enhancement. Information about customer preferences and demand is accurate and instantaneous. Dell uses the information of consumers' click stream to guide intensive multi-year planning with key vendors. Its mass-customization delivers products that address the specific requirements of individual customers.	Dell's competitors have to pay an 8% to 10% distribution premium for their value added reseller channel. They have to hold larger inventory because of lacking accurate and instantaneous customer information. They have to carry 80 days' worth of inventory vs. Dell's 11 days. A conventional firm would be difficult to sell online without alienating an existing network of dealers and re-sellers.
3M Co. [Gilbert, 2000]	DealerHut – An extranet to manage relationships with unauthorized distribution channels.	It helps small unauthorized distributors order directly from 3M. It gathers valuable customer data through online showrooms. It provides electronic communications, a means of collaborative product development via the Internet to lower inventory and reduce the production cycle.	3M connected all its business partners, large and small, into a very efficient virtual organization. Competitors would be hard to establish similar relationships with these same firms.

Contd...

Contd...

Office Depot [Anonymous, 2000]	Early and innovative use of Website	The Website has an innovative "Office Solutions" section. It has thousands of pages of information and services for business and linked to leading technology solutions providers. The Contract Business Unit is dedicated to creating innovative solutions for its larger customers that enable employees to conveniently purchase from their desktop.	Office Depot was ranked above both the Officemax and Staples Internet sites in terms of shopping convenience, usability, performance, technology innovation, value, and next day service.
FedEx Corp. [McDermott, 2001]	Customer Relationship Management (CRM)	FedEx Corp. is one of the first firms in the industry deploying an innovative CRM strategy. It developed a multimillion-dollar CRM program to cut costs and optimize its existing customer data in efforts to cross-sell and up-sell services to existing and new customers. It provides its sales force a comprehensive view of every customer.	Knowing the customers is the prerequisite for serving the customers better. Only innovating firms that know customers well will survive the e-business competition.
Mellon Financial Corporation [Anonymous, 1998; Anonymous, 2001]	Global Cash Management's Automated Payments (AP) RemEDI (SM) service	It is a knowledge-based system that totally automates the receipt, analysis, payment and reporting of gas and electric utility bills. It reviews and validates the invoices and pays the bills based on a number of user preset "rules". It also helps users manage utility usage more effective by having a digital format of usage in a database. It enables users to focus on issues that need their attention. It can reduce bill payment processing costs by at least 50 percent. It lowers costs for processing bill payments, and using EDI capabilities without the cost of employing EDI.	Mellon Bank Corporation is one of the nation's largest bank holding companies in market capitalization. Mellon Global Cash Management is an industry leader. It designs complete solutions through its comprehensive line of cash management services. The innovation made it one step ahead of its competitors.

Section II

Emerging Trends

6

E-Business Driving Innovation

Niels Bjørn-Andersen

Investment in information and communications technologies is frequently cited as a key factor in improving firms' competitiveness and fostering innovation. Even if ICT is seen as a basic business tool today, there are clear opportunities for high-growth SMEs to prosper using e-business. But they require commitment beyond simple investment. ICT also needs to be accompanied by changes in processes and working methods if a firm is to embrace e-business fully.

The take-up of Information and Communications Technologies (ICT) has, for many years, been seen as a key driver of innovation and competitiveness. For example, many commentators have put the USA's higher growth rates (in comparison to the EU) in recent years down to higher investment in ICT and faster and wider diffusion of ICT tools throughout the economy. (In fact, recent data from the European Innovation Scoreboard shows that ICT investment in the USA is now at a similar level to that in the EU-15, so the related competitive advantage should be diminishing.)

But what is ICT investment in aid of? What are companies spending their money on and how are they using the tools they purchase? Not all ICT investment by firms contributes to the development of e-business, however. For example, an internal system for managing personnel may represent a considerable investment in ICT for a large firm, but would not have an impact on the firm's key business processes.

In short, e-business is about trading and about using ICT tools to manage a firm's relationships with its customers and suppliers. The popular image of e-business – also called e-commerce is of consumer goods (books, DVDs, airline tickets, food shopping, etc.) being traded over the internet. Many internet sales and auction – sites have been set up, some by existing traders, others by new start-ups. The so-called *dot.com* boom saw the majority come and go, and the ease with which an internet 'shop' may be set up means many more try to get off the ground every week. But this type of B2C (Business-To-Consumer) trade represents only one-tenth of the total volume of e-business. B2B (Business-To-Business) trade is by far the more significant area of e-business.

Today, more than one-quarter of world trade is conducted using ICT tools, representing turnover of over €2 trillion (i.e. million million). "But in just a short time, perhaps in five years, that will go up to one-third of global trade," predicts Professor Niels Bjørn-Andersen of Copenhagen Business School, one of the contributors to a global survey of e-commerce undertaken by the Centre for Research on Information Technology and Organisations of the University of California at Irvine (CRITO)(1).

Impact

The CRITO survey talked to senior managers from both large and small firms in ten countries. It found that practically all firms surveyed used e-mail, and three-quarters have a website (see Table 1). Intranet was used by almost two-thirds of the firms, whereas extranet taking restricted information outside the walls of the company was used by only one-third. Other tools, such as electronic funds transfer and call centres, were used by fewer than half of the surveyed firms, but these tools are particularly relevant only in certain business sectors, for example banking and finance.

Table 1

% of firms using...	USA	Mexico	Denmark	France	Germany	China	Singapore	Global
E-mail	99.6	98.3	100.0	97.7	100.0	95.9	99.9	98.5
Website	79.8	79.0	96.3	54.5	91.8	69.5	83.0	74.1
Intranet	56.2	50.9	83.7	68.0	84.4	60.8	67.0	63.6
Extranet	28.7	31.1	39.8	15.2	22.3	36.3	31.5	32.7
– Accessible by Suppliers/ Business Partners	16.9	22.6	30.0	11.6	14.0	28.7	23.8	20.9
– Accessible by Customers	15.6	16.2	23.1	11.4	11.8	21.9	20.0	17.8
Electronic Data Interchange of Some Type	42.5	58.4	69.1	44.6	67.7	25.0	32.8	44.3
– Over Private Net Only	17.1	19.7	16.5	29.9	30.8	9.7	16.6	19.4
– Over Internet Only	8.4	28.5	20.3	4.6	10.1	3.9	9.7	8.4
– Over Both	16.1	10.1	31.5	8.3	26.6	10.4	6.0	15.9
Electronic Funds Transfer	62.7	70.6	73.5	30.3	86.6	25.7	42.8	43.4
Call Centre	40.5	44.5	27.4	22.4	30.3	20.8	24.5	32.3

Source: Niels Bjørn-Andersen/CRITO.

Table 2

% of firms using the internet for:	USA	Mexico	Denmark	France	Germany	China	Singapore	Global
Advertising and Marketing Purposes	64.3	72.9	88.8	26.4	77.7	52.1	61.0	57.6
Making Sales On-line	43.2	11.8	47.2	12.1	57.3	23.0	29.6	29.9
After-sales Customer Service and Support	55.6	40.2	56.9	16.3	53.3	55.4	38.9	43.7
Making Purchases On-line	73.2	64.8	67.5	24.1	60.8	31.3	28.6	46.8
Exchanging Operational Data with Suppliers	42.8	50.1	55.8	35.7	59.7	47.0	44.9	48.1
Exchanging Operational Data with Business Customers	53.8	46.7	40.5	39.7	51.9	52.1	50.5	50.7
Formally Integrating the Same Business Processes with Suppliers/Partners	35.5	54.8	44.4	24.0	47.6	30.1	40.9	33.9

Source: Niels Bjørn-Andersen/CRITO

But when it comes to the uses that firms make of these tools, the most common use is for advertising and marketing. Companies use the internet to promote their services, but once a potential customer wants to deal with the firm, less than one-third have facilities to conclude a sale on-line (see Table 2). In fact, the proportion of the firms buying on-line is larger than that selling. The only other application used by a majority of firms is the exchange of data with existing customers. These findings indicate that, whilst most firms have access to the basic tools required for e-business, only a minority have gone so far as to integrate them into their central business processes.

Looking at the impact of ICT on their businesses, one third of firms in the survey at most saw a high impact from their tools in any of the areas suggested (see Table 3). The greatest impact was seen in improving efficiency internally and in improving customer service. Overall, less than 30% felt that their competitive position had improved as a result of their take-up of ICT tools. "This is clearly not satisfactory," Bjørn-Andersen underlines.

In the Market

Behind these survey results, it is clear that developing e-business methods, and therefore potential impacts on innovation and competitiveness, requires much more than simply buying and installing ICT tools. To derive major benefits from ICT tools means they have to be integrated into the company's key processes, and not just used passively, as with a promotional website. For example, a new order-processing system may free up time for the sales department to do more selling, but if it is not integrated effectively with the stock-control system in the warehouse, the gain in sales may be offset by additional non-value-adding activities elsewhere.

So what sort of tools does e-business depend on? Perhaps the most crucial business process is buying and selling, and much development in e-business methods and tools addresses this. Here, multinational firms have often set the framework in which their suppliers operate.

"If your firm only processes a couple of orders a day, the system you use does not really matter. But for a large company, their system is vital to the smooth running of the business," explains Bjørn-Andersen. "But multinational firms will

Table 3

% of Firms indicating high impact...	USA	Mexico	Denmark	France	Germany	China	Singapore	Global
Internal processes More Efficient	28.0	53.5	39.4	37.9	41.8	31.0	35.1	33.9
Staff Productivity Increased	30.8	37.5	16.5	26.2	18.6	23.9	39.9	27.2
Sales Increased	24.1	36.2	24.6	9.3	19.1	25.6	30.6	20.5
Sales Area Widened	35.9	25.4	19.6	19.1	31.5	48.5	47.0	31.4
Customer Service Improved	40.2	54.9	44.6	24.1	35.5	36.9	44.6	34.8
International Sales Increased	9.0	19.7	3.8	13.0	28.1	32.8	42.3	19.5
Procurement Costs Decreased	12.5	20.0	17.7	6.7	11.2	29.7	32.4	17.7
Inventory Costs Decreased	10.8	13.8	11.8	3.8	6.2	21.1	20.7	14.0
Coordination with Suppliers Improved	29.2	50.7	27	24.3	14.5	29.4	43.6	29.8
Competitive Position Improved	33.3	45.1	29.7	12.5	23.1	41.2	49.5	29.8

Source: Niels Bjørn-Andersen/CRITO

never have entirely compatible systems. This means that small companies which supply to more than one big firm have to be able to adapt to the different systems of their major customers." And their own systems have to be able to cope with electronic documents in these different formats.

Even quite large companies have to adapt their systems to the requirements of major customers. "For example, Novozymes, a Danish-based supplier of industrial enzymes, employs around 4,000 people and deals with some 20,000 customers. They have their own order forms and processing system." "But when it comes to the 16 largest customers, they have to employ different solutions to integrate with each of them."

Behind the Scenes

"But small firms want to do much more than wait for orders to come in," he underlines. There are some productivity gains to be had in more efficient order processing, but they are not enough to transform a business, or gain a significant competitive advantage. Gaining a privileged relationship with a key customer allows the supplier to increase the efficiency of production.

"Once a smaller firm seals an agreement of this nature with a major customer, they are able to plan their production schedule more efficiently, and need not maintain as large stocks. That is particularly important for producers of perishable goods, such as enzymes." "Besides their production schedule, they can also optimise their logistics, and other processes. Through better advance planning of this sort, rather than waiting for orders to come in, a company can reduce its costs by as much as 25%."

Collaborative planning gives suppliers access to accurate, updated forecasts of the demand for a given product from their major customers. Within such a relationship, the supplier could also have access to the real-time inventory of their customer, so that they can see for themselves when the customer will require replenishment. And the supplier can also optimise its relations with its own suppliers.

"Take a company supplying cushions for a car manufacturer like Volkswagen. If they have access to VW's production schedule, they can not only tailor their production schedule, but also optimise their batch sizes." If they know in advance that they will have to produce 1,000 seats in a specific pattern, they can order the right quantity of cloth and other components from their suppliers, as well as organise their production line, and even staffing levels, to meet that order more efficiently.

Hardship

The privileged relationship between supplier and customer inherent in collaborative planning allows SMEs, in particular, to become more efficient and grow. But another facet of e-business makes the trading environment for the small firm much more demanding: e-auctions put the customer in the driving seat, forcing down prices when they seek bids from suppliers for a given quantity of a particular product.

"Suppliers can be squeezed very heavily in e-auctions; it is a process they fear, particularly when they are in danger of losing out to a competitor they did not know of beforehand," Bjørn-Andersen says. "E-auctions are only suitable for commodities where the price is the only factor that matters. In these cases, a buyer can reduce the cost of a particular product by as much as 10-20% using e-auctions."

By E-Design

Another area of e-business where SMEs get a better deal is in collaborative design. ICT tools mean that designers can share their work much more easily than in the past. Drawings, shapes, colours, and music can all be transmitted and shared now. "For instance, design work on the Boeing 777 was carried out around the clock in offices in different parts of the world," Bjørn-Andersen notes. "And it was also the first large aircraft to fly without first testing in a wind tunnel, as electronic testing was used instead."

The textile and clothing industry comes low on the 'e-maturity' index developed by e-business watch(2), coming in 15th out of 17 industrial sectors in the survey. This shows that, in general, take-up of e-business tools in the industry is low. Furthermore, the survey found that companies' short-term objectives do not suggest major advances in e-business adoption. The one e-business application which has been widely taken up is collaborative design, building on long-standing practices of sharing product data in the industry, and early adoption of computer-aided design tools.

Driving Innovation?

The adoption of e-business tools and methods presents opportunities for business, but these are limited without changes in the way firms operate. Small firms are no worse prepared for e-business than their larger counterparts, according to the CRITO survey. Whilst SMEs are more adaptable, they inevitably face a greater threat from changes in business methods than larger companies.

"SMEs put themselves in a stronger position if they become integrated into a supply chain." "To do that, they need to offer something different, or special, and need to be willing to integrate with their customers' systems. It is problematic that companies outside Europe are more prepared to integrate with customers' systems – it is vital for small companies that want to grow to get into longer-term relationships with their customers, if they are to remain stable." E-business tools may not be a panacea for European innovators, but for an SME that integrates them into its business, they can certainly provide a major fillip to efficiency.

(Niels Bjørn-Andersen Professor, PhD Department of Informatics and Center for Electronic Commerce Howitzvej 60, 2000 Frederiksberg.)

Reference

(1) *http://www.crito.uci.edu/2/prGEC3.asp*

(2) *http://www.ebusiness-watch.org/*

7

Business Case Modelling for E-Services

Wil Janssen, René van Buuren and Jaap Gordijn

In this paper we show how business value modelling and enterprise architecture can blend into an integral approach for modelling e-services business cases. The approach, building upon e^{3}value and ArchiMate, allows to link revenues and cost in a single model. The approach is illustrated on by the business case model of a virtual laboratory in the process industry. First experiences have shown significant value in the approach for different stakeholders (managers and engineers).

1. Introduction

Advances in ICT offer companies opportunities to improve their operational efficiency and to differentiate themselves among competitors by providing innovative ICT-based services. To exploit these opportunities companies need to develop new services, build computer networks, buy software licenses and more. Since most industry players currently lack the resources and capabilities to do so, ICT-based services are increasingly being developed and provided by networks of cooperating organizations. Various studies (see, e.g., Levine & Byrne, 1986; Bleeke & Ernst, 1993) indicate, however, that companies encounter serious difficulties

Source: 18th Bled eConference, eIntegration in Action, Bled, Slovenia, June 6-8, 2005.

in achieving the anticipated benefits from cooperation. These studies indicate that 40 to as many as 60 percent of all business cooperations fail. Designing innovative ICT-supported services seems to be a daunting task. Given the disappointing success rates of inter-firm cooperations and the risks and cost involved in the introduction of new ICT supported services, it is not surprising that practitioners and academics pay a great deal of attention to the concept of business models and business networks.

Traditionally, there has been a substantial gap between business models and business strategy on the one hand, and business architecting on the other hand. Systems' design barely touches upon the business model questions, such as organisational and financial aspects, business modelling and business model analysis, on the other hand, only incidentally moves beyond the save borders of discussion and analysis to actual design and architecting. Moreover, the role of business modelling as a means to bridge the gap between strategy/business on the one hand, and design on the other hand is controversial (Grey *et al.* 2003, Osterwalder & Pigneur 2003, Winter 2003).

Business model research became popular during the dot.com bubble during which venture capitalists needed concepts to judge and understand the viability of new ICT-based business initiatives. Gradually the scientific community adopted this concept. The research field has developed over the past few years from defining business models, via exploring business model components and classifying business models into categories, to developing descriptive models (see Pateli & and Giaglis, 2003, for an overview). The emphasis in more recent literature is shifting away from classifications to representations or descriptive models of business models. The majority of researchers (see, e.g., Tapscott *et al.*, 2000; Gordijn & Akkermans, 2001; and Weill & Vitale, 2001) focus on the actors, relationships, and value objects exchanged.

One of the main issues today is that business models do not stand on itself, but relate to many other perspectives, such as an inter-organizational business processes and supporting ICT. How to relate these perspectives is still a matter of debate. Therefore, an enterprise can be viewed as a complex "system" with multiple domains (business value, process, ICT) that may influence each other. In general, architectures are used to describe components, relations and underlying design principles of a system (IEEE 2000). Constructing architectures for an enterprise may help to increase insight and overview required to successfully aligning the business and ICT.

Although the value of architecture has been recognized by many organizations, mostly separate architectures are constructed for various organizational domains, such as business processes, applications, information and technical infrastructure. The relations between these architectures often remain unspecified or implicit. Enterprise architecture focuses on establishing a coherent view of an enterprise.

In the end it is all about service offering and realization. This is where enterprise architecture and business modeling methodologies meet. In general, business models focus on the service value generated by a business, whereas enterprise architecture models show how a business realizes these services. Linking these approaches results in a powerful modeling tool that couples the value exchange between businesses and the costs that are required to realize these services.

In this paper, we study the research question of how to bridge the gap between strategy and design using a model-based approach? In doing so, we integrate methods for business model analysis, such as e^{3}value (Gordijn & Akkermans, 2001), and enterprise architecture and design (Janssen & Steen 2000; Jonkers *et al.* 2003; Lankhorst 2005). We argue that business architecture and business value can be seen as different views (IEEE, 2000) on the same object, being the service under construction. This can be deduced from a conceptual analysis of the domain of business models and enterprise architecture, where a substantial coincidence in concepts can be found. Therefore, a joint business network ontology forms a solid basis for an integral approach. The paper is primarily a conceptualisation of the idea, more than a proven concept. First validations have been done, and are illustrated in the paper. A more thorough validation is forthcoming.

We use a running example of an innovative service to illustrate our ideas. The service is a virtual laboratory, allowing analysts in the process industry to access advances analysis instruments in a controlled way over the Internet. The example is introduced as follows.

1.1 Running Example: A Virtual Laboratory

In the *Collaboratory.nl project*[1], industry and research partners cooperate in the design of a virtual lab for material analysis that is suitable for commercial exploitation. The idea is that partners can make their equipment and expertise remotely available through the virtual lab and/or can remotely use the equipment and expertise of others. The industrial setting enforces strict requirements on security and trust between partners. From a business perspective, it also requires satisfactory accounting/billing and management support. From a user perspective, the virtual lab involves multiple actors working at multiple locations, using an instrument such as an electron microscope or a mass spectrometer. Operators operate the instruments, researchers and experts determine and discuss experiments, and the work is done for a customer with a specific purpose. In the present working practice, this involves collaboration with people that might be geographically dispersed. The virtual lab facilitates collaborations and may even improve or simplify the way of working. It should support the daily work of an industry material analyst, who forms part of the primary production process.

The user-interface of a virtual laboratory is presented in Figure 1. At the left hand side we have implemented a selection of possible collaborative tooling. The

Figure 1: User-Interface of a Virtual Laboratory

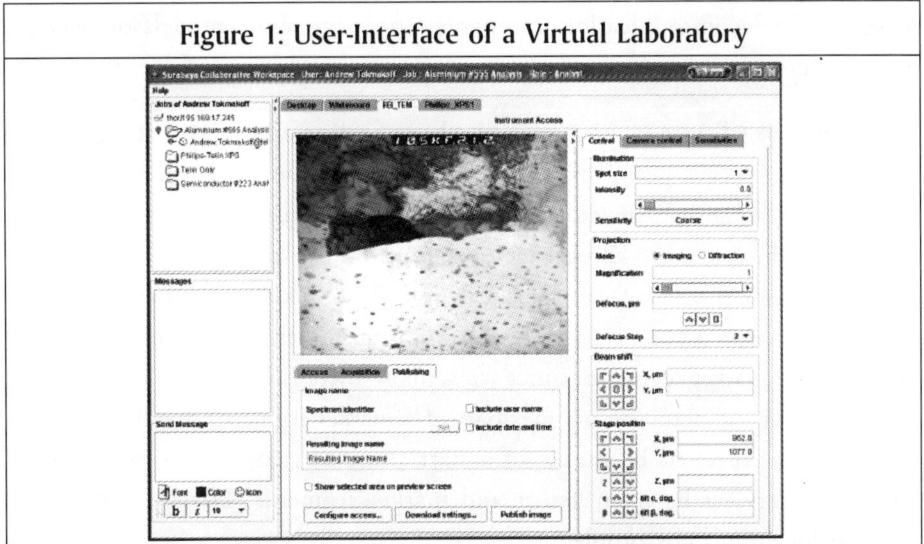

1 *www.collaboratory.nl*

folders present different jobs. At the top-middle the shared resources and shared workspaces are represented by tabs. In this example, there is a desktop, white board and remote control tab. The centre of the example user-interface shows the selected remote control interface of an instrument.

In the following two sections we introduce the modelling methods e³value and ArchiMate, for business models and enterprise architecture, respectively. Both take the virtual laboratory to illustrate the concepts. In section 4, we introduce the integral business case model, and illustrate this with the actual business case analysis for an instance of the virtual lab. Section 5 concludes with the main findings and research steps to be taken.

2. E³value Modelling

The first step in developing an Internet-enabled service is to develop its business model. Such a model states the actor (enterprises) involved as well as the object of value these actors generate, distribute and consume. We summarize the e³value modelling constructs below for describing a business model only briefly (for more details, see Gordijn & Akkermans 2003, Gordijn & Akkermans 2002). The methodology has been previously applied for analysing business scenarios in a series of case studies including media, news, banking and insurance, electricity power, and telecommunication companies to design value models of network organisation.

The virtual lab case consists of a number of actors and market segments. An actor is entity that is perceived by its environment as an independent economic (and often legal) entity. An actor makes a profit or increases its utility. In a sound, sustainable, business model each actor should be capable of making profit. A market segment is a set of similar actors, for which we suppose that they assign economic value in a same way. In Figure 2, the customer, analyst and instrument owner all are market segments. Since we suppose there is only one virtual lab, the lab is an actor. An actor (sometimes part of a market segment) may have a need. This need is expressed by means of a start stimulus that triggers exchanges of goods and services between actors and market segments. Here, the need is a solution for an analysis problem.

Figure 2: Value Model for the Virtual Lab

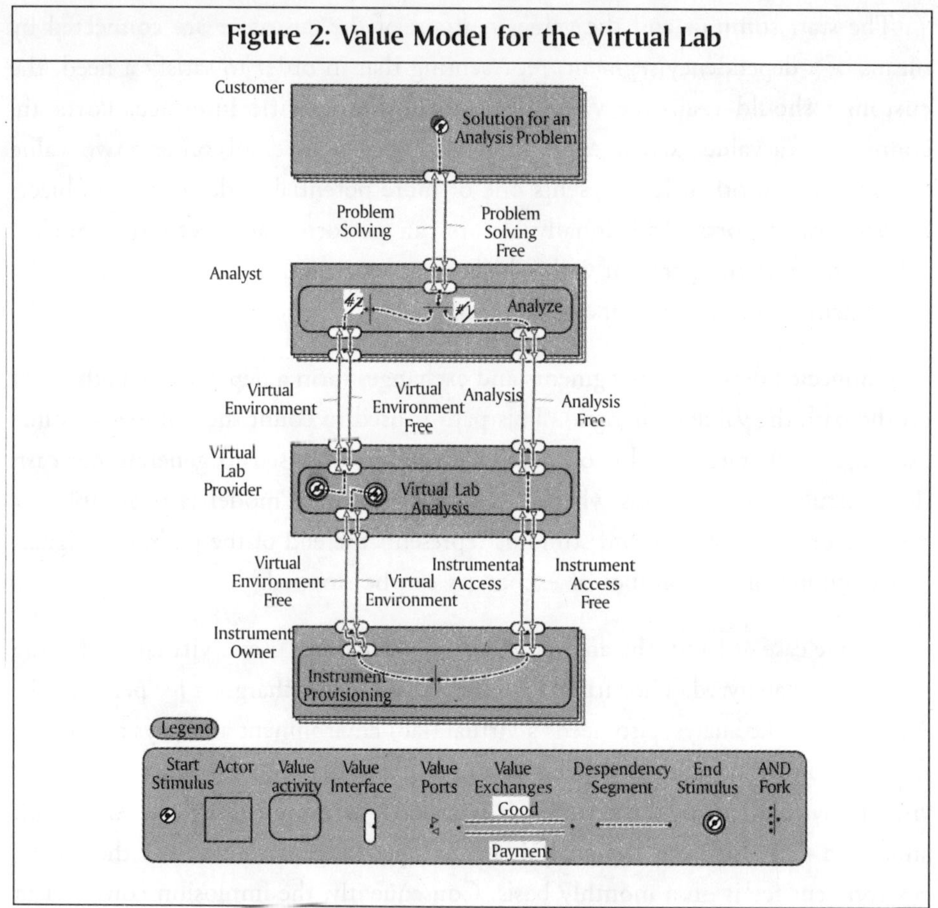

In order to satisfy the need, an actor exchanges objects of economic value with other actors (or market segments). The value objects are services, products, money, or even consumer experiences. The important point here is that a value object is of value for one or more actors. In the case at hand, problem solving as well as the fee to paid are both examples of value objects. These value objects are offered/requested via value ports of an actor. The concept of port enables to abstract away from the internal business processes and to focus only on how external actors and other components of the business model can be 'plugged in'. Ports are grouped into a value interface, expressing that all objects via ports in the interface should be exchanged or none at all. This models economic reciprocity and bundling. So, a customer can only obtain a solution for the problem if he pays for it, and vice versa.

The start stimulus and the value interface of the customer are connected by means of a dependency segment, representing that in order to satisfy a need, the customer should exchange value objects via that specific interface. Ports are connected via value exchanges. A value exchange is used to connect two value ports with each other. It represents one or more potential trades of value objects between value ports. Additionally, actors can perform value activities. Such a value activity is an operation with which an actor creates profit. In this case, the instrument owner earns money with instrument provisioning.

Connected dependency segments and exchanges form a dependency path (with on the path the value exchanges). This path is used to count the number of value exchanges as a start stimulus occurs. These counts are used to generate net cash flow calculations, to assess whether the business value model is profitable for every actor involved. The end stimulus represents the end of the path, and signals that counting of the number of exchanges can be stopped.

For the case at hand, the analyst will do his work and uses a virtual lab for the sample to be analyzed. The virtual lab offers analysis and charges a fee per analysis. Additionally, the analyst also needs a virtual (lab) environment and pays a monthly fee for it. For the problem solving task of the analyst, both the analysis and the virtual environment of the virtual lab is needed, as expressed by the AND fork annotated #1. Moreover, the analysis fee is a per usage basis whereas the virtual environment fee is on a monthly basis. Consequently, the implosion construct (a special case of an AND fork, and annotated #2) models that for N analyses, only one virtual environment fee has to be paid. To provide analysis, the virtual lab provider obtains from an instrument owner (remote) access to instruments and pays a fee for doing so. The instrument owner needs for this instrument access also access to the virtual environment and pays a monthly fee. We use a similar implosion construct here, as discussed earlier, to model that for N times instrument access, only one virtual environment (per month) needs to be paid.

Typical in the current business model it is the fact that the Virtual Lab Provider shields the customer from the Instrument time provider. In this case, this means that for further analysis the customer can be left out.

3. Enterprise Architecture

A coherent description of the enterprise architecture provides insight, enables communication among stakeholders and guides complicated change processes. In the ArchiMate project (Lankhorst 2005) an integrated language was developed and validated. It identifies concepts that relate architectural domains.

In ArchiMate concepts for describing the relationships between architecture descriptions at the business, application, and technology levels play a central role, related to the ubiquitous problem of business–ICT alignment. For each architectural domain ArchiMate conforms to existing languages or standards, such as UML. In particular, usage of services offered by one layer to another plays an important role in relating the behaviour aspects of the layers (see Figure 3 for

Figure 3: An Ontology for Enterprise Architecture

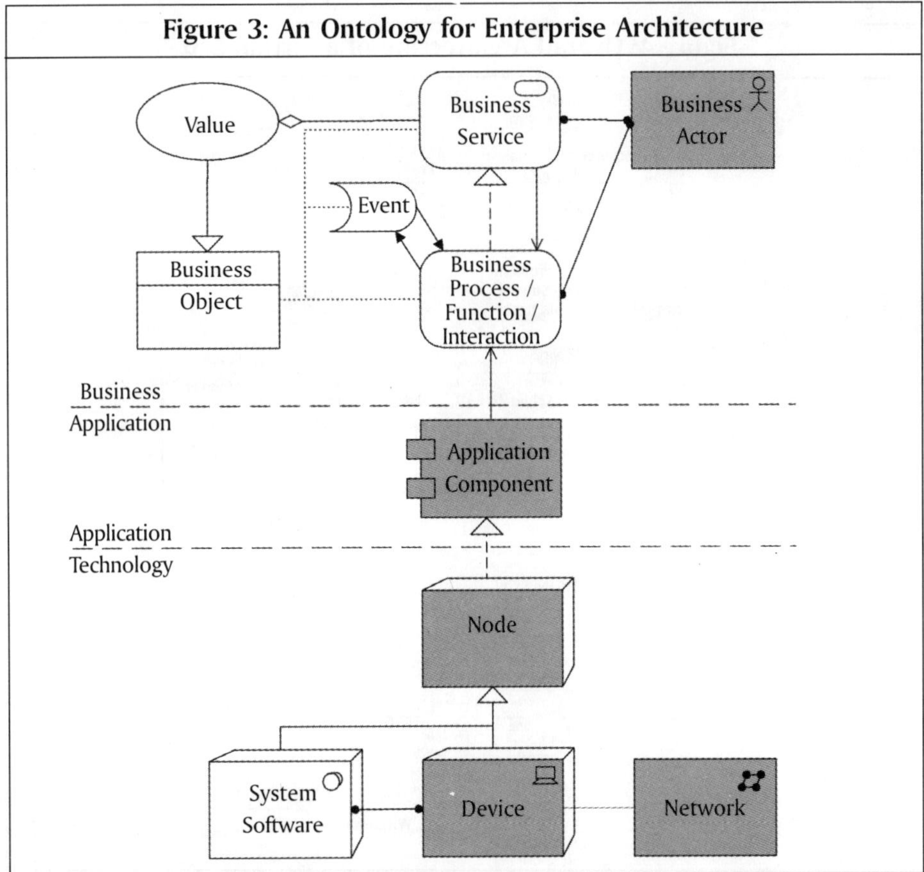

a subset of the concepts in ArchiMate, used in the context of this paper). This enterprise architecture ontology builds upon the work that has been done in systems' analysis and design, notably UML, as well as business process modelling and e-business modelling (de Vos *et al.* 2000, Janssen & Steen 2000).

Using enterprise architecture modelling, a holistic approach to enterprise can be taken, as enterprise architecture covers all different relevant domains. We illustrate this using the running virtual lab example. We have already described the main organization roles and services. This can be expanded towards the technology domain, by identifying the services and components that implement the services delivered. These components, in their turn, build upon a technological infrastructure, consisting of servers and analytical instruments. This is illustrated in Figure 4.

Figure 4: Overall Architecture of a Virtual Lab

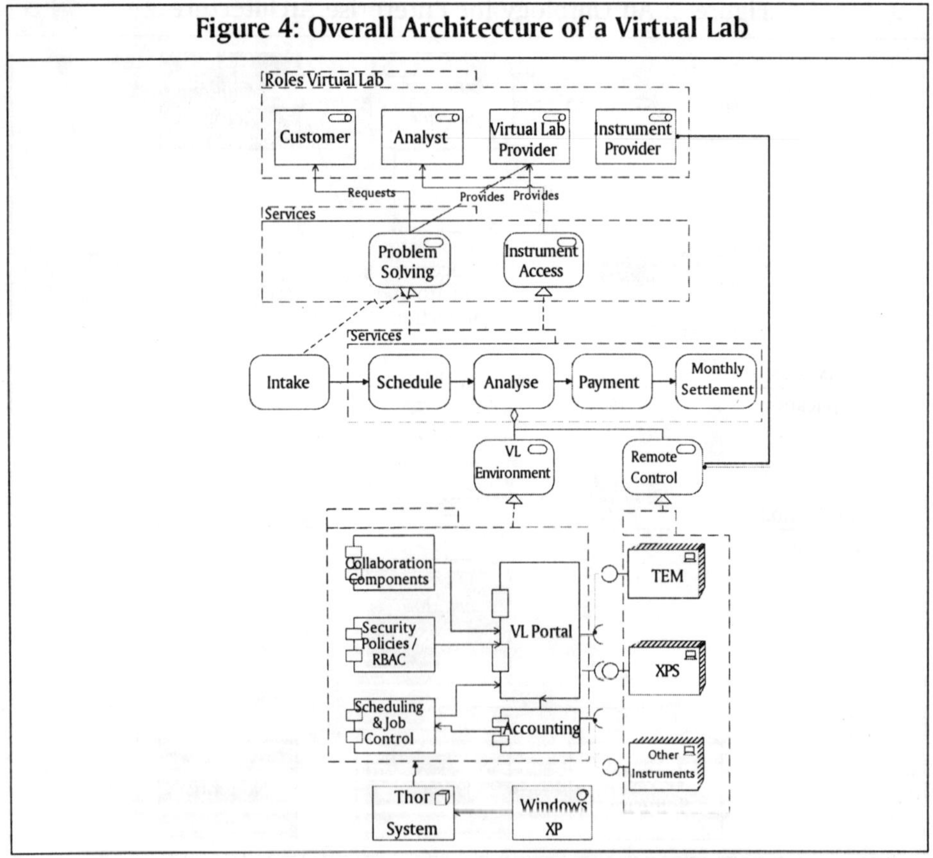

The upper part of the model describes the services delivered externally to the actors or roles involved. The middle part identifies the steps in the analysis process, in relation to those services. The lower part, finally, shows what application services and components and systems have been used to implement the services delivered. This includes the analytical machines, such as X-ray Photoelectronic spectroscopy (XPS) and Transmission Electron Microscopy (TEM). It thereby closes the gap between the value model and the ICT implementation.

4. From Business Model Analysis to Service Design

When we compare the meta-models of e³value and ArchiMate, we see a striking similarity on the business level. This can be exploited to combine both approaches to allow for an integral approach to model e-services, stretching from revenue to implementation aspects, as is illustrated in Figure 5. The idea now is to link the

Figure 5: Combined Conceptual Model

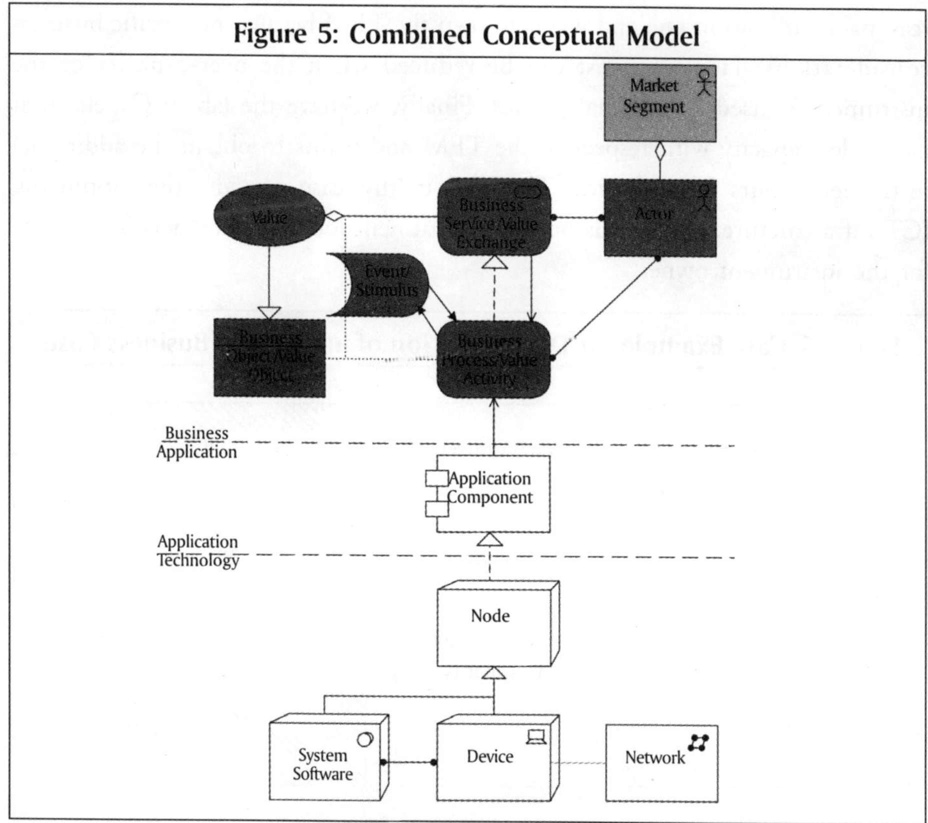

revenue defined in the business part and analysed in e^{3}value, to the cost defined in the application and technology layers. For the enterprise architecture we can use the business processes and supporting applications and technical infrastructure to determine the cost of the service offering. In this way, the cost for each actor in the value chain can be unambiguously determined, or the savings when outsourcing of current activities is taken into account. In the ArchiMate language a value concept is coupled to the ultimate service offering, which provides the link with the e^{3}value models.

In order to show the possibilities of the presented combination of modelling approaches, we consider an example business case for the virtual lab, depicted in Figure 6. In this example, there are three labs that work with a specific analytical instrument – a TEM. The lab in Arnhem has a very low utilisation rate and wants to outsource the ownership of the instrument. The lab in Bilthoven has a reasonable utilisation rate and wants to own the TEM because of specific business considerations. However, cost can be reduced when the over-capacity of the instrument is used by external parties. Finally, we have the lab in Capelle that has under-capacity with respect to the TEM and wants to obtain the additional instrument hours from outside. The VLP in this case provides the supporting ICT infrastructure, has the customer of instrument locked-in and acts as a broker for the instrument owner.

Figure 6: Case Example for Determination of an Integral Business Case

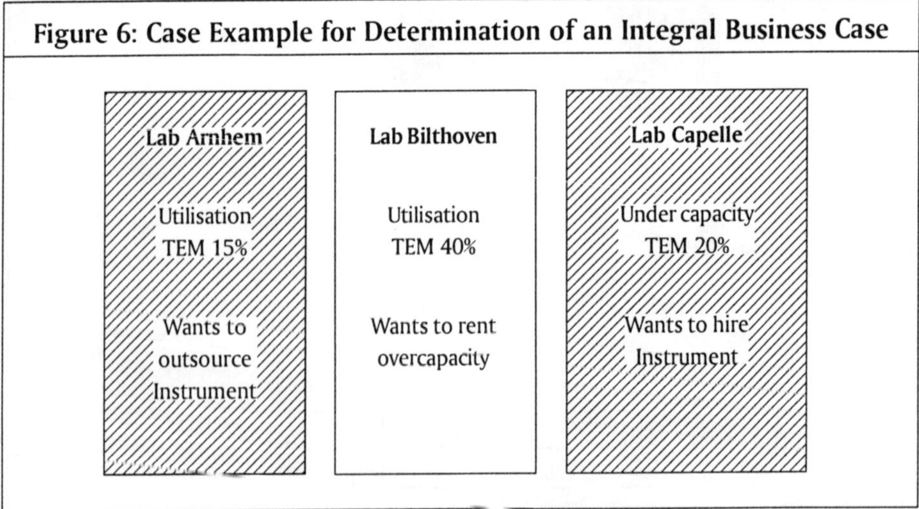

By means of the overall architecture in Figure 4, we can now determine the cost which are involved in the specific service offerings and demands. The cost for owning a TEM is around €3,54.000 per year. This includes, among others, interest, depreciation, and infrastructure. This is the basis to determine the value of the remote control service in Figure 4. Equally, we can determine the costs of maintaining and building the software required for the virtual laboratory. For this purpose we have assumed a relatively small VLP enterprise, arriving at a total cost of around €577.000 for the VLP (calculation details omitted). This relates to costs of the virtual environment service in Figure 4, supported by the specific applications components and required hardware. Furthermore we assume that the cost for owning a TEM are equal for all three labs.

Next to the cost infrastructure, we require a settlement schema to couple the revenues to the costs. In this case we assume that the parties add 10% to the cost for services involving the instrument. This means that the instrument owner adds 10% to its hourly cost rate for the VLP, and the VLP in its turn, adds 10% to this amount for the analyst of a certain lab. For the virtual environment services we assume that the total cost for the virtual environment are 20% of the total costs/revenues involved for instrument. Taking this costs and settlement schema's into account we arrive at the figures in Table 1. The table shows that lab Arnhem can save a lot of money by hiring a instrument, instead of buying a new one. This conclusion is not very surprising, as lab Arnhem now only pays for the small amount of time it really uses the instrument. Exploiting its overcapacity pays off for lab Bilthoven. The only additional cost lab Bilthoven has to pay is the contribution to the virtual lab.

Of course, in real life there will be variable costs, which have to be taken in consideration. From the table we conclude that it is not profitable for lab Capelle to hire instrument time for its under-capacity: Lab Capelle offers a fixed price to its customers. In this example, where each party applies the same margin, it pays more than it receives. When lab Capelle has to deliver all requested instrument time to its mother company, it might take the loss: the loss is still far less than the cost of a new instrument.

Table 1: Cost and Revenues for the Example Case		
Lab Arnhem	Savings	274.350
Lab Bilthoven	Additional revenues	102.218
Lab Capelle	Additional revenues	–28.320
Virtual Lab	Virtual environment revenues	71.242
	Instrument mediation revenues	12.390

For the current situation the business case is not positive for the lab Capelle and the VLP. We argued that for this settlement schema it will never become attractive for the lab Capelle. So, when is there an overall positive business case for the lab Arnhem, lab Bilthoven and the VLP?

The costs of the VLP are €577.000 a year and the yearly maximal (based on a 100% TEM) income for the VLP on a TEM is €238.950. Therefore, the VLP needs to rent 3 full TEMs a year to make ends meet. When we assume that lab B is representative for all providers, we need 5 providing labs to reach 5 x 60% = 300 % TEM time. When we assume that the demand of lab A is representative for all customer labs, we need 20 customer labs to reach 20 x 15% = 300% TEM time.

5. Concluding Remarks and Tentative Research Agenda

In this paper we indicated that there are strong conceptual analogies between value modelling as in e^3value, and enterprise architecture modelling as in ArchiMate. This analogy can be exploited in order to come to an integral business case modelling framework for e-services. In doing so, business cases can move from high-level strategic analysis to analysis rooted in the actual process and systems architectures. Thus, the business case can be substantiated, and on the other hand, the consequences of architectural choices can be translated to the business case level.

First applications of this approach in our research have shown added value of this integral approach, and we seek a more extensive validation of the route taken in other cases. At this stage, it is too early to conclude under what circumstances this approach proves its value best, and what type of support is needed. Our experiences, however, already indicate that there is substantial value in the approach, allowing to bridge the gap between engineers and managers to a certain extent – making managers aware of the technological consequences, and have engineers think in terms of business cases. In doing so, we move way beyond informal approaches, such as Grey *et al.* (2003), and Patelli & Giaglis (2003).

As a next step, the conceptual correspondance should be formalised, and integrated into the tool environments that have been defined for both modelling language (Obelix and ArchiMate workbench). Also, the right viewpoints for stakeholders involved in the analysis must be identified (Lankhorst 2005, IEEE 2000). On the basis thereof, and by performing additional cases, a well-supported methodology will be developed, that has a solid scientific basis on the one hand, and is applicable in practice as well.

(Wil Janssen, René van Buuren, Telematica Instituut, P.O. Box 589, 7500 AN Enschede; Jaap Gordijn, Vrije Universiteit Amsterdam, Faculty of Sciences, de Boelelaan 1081a, 1081 HV Amsterdam.)

References

Franken, H, Bal, R, Berg, H van den, Janssen, W & Vos, H de (2000). "Architectural Design Support for Business Process and Business Network Engineering". *International Journal of Services Technology and Management*, 1(1), 1-14.

Gordijn, J & Akkermans, J M (2003), "Value-Based Requirements Engineering: Exploring Innovative E-Commerce Ideas", *Requirements Engineering Journal*, vol. 8, no. 2, pp 114-135, Springer Verlag, Berlin, D

Gordijn, J & H Akkermans (2001), "Designing and Evaluating E-business Models", IEEE Intelligent Systems, July/August: 11-17.

Grey, W, Katircloglu, K, Bagchi, S, Shi, D, Gallego, G, Seybold, D, & Stefanis, S, An Analytic Approach for Quantifying the Value of E-Business Initiatives. *IBM Systems Journal*, Vol. 42, No. 3, pp. 484-497.

Haaker, T, E Faber & H Bouwman (2004), "Customer and Network Value of Mobile Services: Balancing Requirements and Strategic Interests". In: proceedings ICIS conference 2004.

IEEE Computer Society (2000), IEEE Std 1471-2000: "IEEE Recommended Practice for Architectural Description of Software-Intensive Systems", IEEE, New York.

Janssen, W, & Steen, M (2000). "Rapid Service Development: An Integral Approach to E-Business Engineering". In S Murugesan & Y Deshpande (Eds.), Web Engineering – Managing Diversity and Complexity of Web Application Development. LNCS 2016, pp. 119-132, Berlin/Heidelberg: Springer-Verlag.

Jonkers, H, *et al.* (2003), "Towards a Language for Coherent Enterprise Architecture Descriptions". In Proc. 7th IEEE International Enterprise Distributed Object Computing Conference (EDOC'03), Brisbane, Australia, pp. 28-37. IEEE Computer Society.

Lankhorst, M. (ed., 2005), "Enterprise Architecture at Work – Modelling", Communication and Analysis. Springer-Verlag. Forthcoming.

Magretta, J (2002). "Why Business Models Matter", *Havard Business Review*, May: 86-91.

Osterwalder, A & Y Pigneur (2003), "Towards Strategy and Information Systems Alignment through a Business Model Ontology", In: proceedings of the 23rd Annual International Conference of the Strategic Management Society (SMS), Baltimore.

Pateli, A G, Giaglis, G M (2003), "A Methodology for Business Model Evolution: Application in the Mobile Exhibition Industry", paper presented at the M-business conference 2003.

Porter, M E (2001), "Strategy and the Internet", *Havard Business Review* (March) 62-78.

Tapscott, D (2001), "Rethinking Strategy in a Networked World (or why Michael Porter is Wrong about the Internet", *Strategy + Business*, Issue 24, Third Quarter: 1-8.

Winter, R (2003), Conceptual Modelling of Business Networks and Business Strategies. In: proceedings 16th Bled Electronic Commerce Conference eTransformation, Bled, Slovenia.

8

ATM: Innovative Vehicle of Tomorrow's E-Banking

C Rama Gopal

ATMs could be the best way to teach e-Banking to customers at minimal cost. It would help banks to reduce the cost and offer hassle-free services.

Bankers claim that recent times have shown the virtual shift in banking from traditional brick and mortar model to e-Banking, with no human intervention, operating across time zones, geographic locations and contact points. Are the claims indeed true in their full perspective? What deliverables the ordinary man looks for, without much fanfare? "No more waiting in long queues. Just log on to your account and log out with cash. With this card, there is no need to carry cash in your wallet and you need not fear of overspending on your credit card! You can now withdraw cash and make purchases anytime you wish to." These are the words that best describe how the present day banking is moving forward in the country. If this is the only wish of e-Banking, this has been amply fulfilled with the pace of growth, ATMs have shown in recent times. However, the real potentialities of e-Banking are not exploited as a certain basic facility and it is not yet within the reach of the common man.

Source: Professional Banker, March 2006. This article was originally published as "ATM: Potential Vehicle of E-Banking".

Why ATMs are Popular?

To the common man who does not have much knowledge of technology, ATM is a great hit with him. He may not know how to operate the computer, but it does not stand in the way of transactions. However, to use an ATM, a customer doesn't need a computer of his own. At the same time operating an ATM is easy and there are no intricacies involved. This is the reason behind the popularity of ATM, even with the aged.

Banks are constantly in the process of upgrading themselves for newer ways of doing transactions. From plastic to virtual money, these banks are adopting technology to offer the latest modes for transacting business. Internet banking, or e-Banking as it is popularly called, offers banks and customers a huge opportunity by way of convenience and reach. ATM is the right place in terms of accessibility. But, extension of technology and required infrastructure still are to take place at ATM level to make the numerous facilities of e-Banking easily accessible to the public. Banks need to adopt required technology, primarily, in this area to improve customer satisfaction as they are forced to remain competitive while reducing costs.

Greater Challenges

In order to attract and retain customers, banks need to market new products and increase delivery channels. The need of the hour is to identify the basic needs of customers and find ways to fulfill them. The grassroot level needs do not seem to be gaining the attention, adequately. Speed of response to customer needs is critical and first-mover advantage is significant. Traditional business planning and evaluation processes can hamper the response time. Thus, for banks, technology has come to play a decisive role in considerably reducing time to market new products. However, understanding the real requirements in simple terms has not yet gone with the banking in the real spirit. To understand the requirements, whether any survey has been made how much the advertised products of e-Banking are really used by the public and what impediments stand in their way to use? The much publicized concept "anywhere, anyhow and anytime banking" that fits in with their simple and existing lifestyle is what consumers are looking at today. Technology allows this to become a reality, if the requirements of public are really understood.

What E-Banking can Do?

Other than instantaneous withdrawal of cash, irrespective of location, the primary requirement of a common man, is to make routine payments for electricity, water and telephone bills and insurance premium payment every month, without going to the concerned office and waiting in the long queue to deposit, alternatively draw the cheque, put it in an envelop and post, not knowing for sure whether it would reach or miss in transit, thanks to the crowded postal service. All these facilities are not possible to avail without a computer and the knowledge, of Internet after becoming a net banking customer. For making payments to public utility services, the only information that the system should demand is the number code of client to whom payment is to be made, which should consist of the digital code for bank, branch and account number, amount to be remitted and option to type details of payment made.

Real Solution

In the ATM structure, the customer is guided step-by-step and driven to move for the fulfillment of his needs. The customer does not experience any difficulty to operate an ATM in order to know the account balance or withdrawal of cash. The same and simple approach is required to be adopted to avail the range of services e-Banking offers. ATMs are already located in almost every corner. Yet, we do not take advantage of their presence fully. The reason is that many ATMs do not have the upgraded software solutions to provide the full range of services.

Banks advertise that they are moving towards paperless banking and the customer need not write the cheques and prepare the cover and post them for making payments to telephone or electricity departments. This would be possible when present ATMs have the facilities in the form of infrastructure and technology to take the benefits of e-Banking.

Plethora of ATMs

Every bank is more concerned about opening its own ATM unit. In the process, the fixed and operational costs are going up and have become a reason for dwindling profit margins. We have several private airlines but every airline does not own an independent airport. Infrastructure facilities existing at a common airport are shared and competition is confined to the area of services and fares. Banks have to adopt the same approach. The idea of opening new ATMs has to be discarded and the existing ATMs have to be shared. ATMs should be a public restroom and the concerned bank has to pay to the owner of ATM for the services utilized by the customers of its bank. Emphasis should be on the provision of service areas rather than opening ATMs. This releases funds. Additionally, operational costs go down as consumption of cheques and their processing get reduced. So, banks can bear the incidental cost without passing it on to their respective customers. A comprehensive networking system has to be developed, whereby any customer of any bank can avail ATM of any bank to operate his account without paying any additional service charges that is presently collected for using other bank's ATM. We have many places in the country where ATMs of major banks do not exist. A great inconvenience is caused to the public as many possess ATM cards of one or two banks at best. If ATM of that bank is not available, virtually, the customer cannot withdraw cash. He has to run to the adjoining town where an ATM of his bank is located. The concept of "Anywhere Banking" is not to be limited to a particular bank, but should be extended to the universal banking, as a whole, at least within the country. Once this common pool facility is available, it would open doors to share revenues, while providing services to the common man on a universal platform. Banks should consider ATM as a window for them to improve their revenue earning ability. Each ATM owner bank can display its name for popularity and advertising while projecting names of banks whose cards are accepted. In this way, each bank can retain its independent image of publicity by showing its own identity, but can extend them to other banks to share their infrastructure as a means of making money.

E-Seva

The Andhra Pradesh State Government has taken a remarkable initiative in introducing e-Seva in Hyderabad and Secunderabad, where people can make payments like water tax, property tax, telephone and electricity bills apart from securing even birth and death certificates, learners' driving license, sales tax registration and many more facilities, all under one roof. The idea behind the introduction of e-Seva is that the common man should not be made to run from pillar to post, searching and visiting various departments for his activities connected with day-to-day life. Definitely, life has become more comfortable to those living in the twin cities after the introduction of this unique concept. There are 46 e-Seva centers in the twin cities itself. No doubt, it is a good service to the public, but the only inconvenience is distance. The ready access of ATM card, definitely, has an edge over e-Seva, as ATM is more conveniently located at almost every corner of the area. Andhra Bank provides all these e-Seva services through its ATM card at its 81 centers in the twin cities.

Awareness

Application of sophisticated technology, no doubt, has been growing in banking. Some banks like HDFC, who have a tie up arrangement for making payments through ATM, have made some beginning in this regard. But, the sad part is even its own customers do not know the services provided by the banks and therefore their actual benefit is not derived by them. A recent survey in Bhopal has revealed that the majority of ATM cardholders of HDFC Bank do not know that they can make payment of Airtel bills through their ATM card. What is the real reason for this state of affairs? Is it the apathy of the bank or its customers? A visit to an ATM center of HDFC Bank shows that there is no advertisement regarding what its ATM offers to its cardholders in the ATM room, which really affords all the scope to advertise its product. Majority of their customers know that their ATM card is meant for facilitating cash withdrawal only! A simple poster showing that their ATM cardholder can take the benefit of services for making payment to Airtel, with a beautiful picture presentation could have educated their customers. Family members accompanying the person who comes to withdraw money is a common sight. They have the opportunity to learn what further uses their existing ATM card can be put to. Awareness has to be passed on to customers in the right atmosphere and at the right place. Banks do not appear to be taking full advantage of their own premises, where the service is provided.

Future Focus

The transactions through brick and mortar banking costs around $1.1, while through ATM it costs around $0.27, according to an international report. Statistics such as these have woken up the Indian Banking Industry, but not adequately. Global trends and practices cannot be adopted totally. They have to be Indianised to suit the local constraints and conditions. Technology is the root of this change that can be brought. The Indian banking system can bring about a fabulous change in the quality of service that can be provided to the customers who are not so sound financially and technologically, making ATM as the window and vehicle for future e-Banking operations.

Security Fears

Surprisingly, security fears that deter Internet Banking operations do not exist with ATM. Customers feel ATM 'reads' only identity, does not store it permanently, and gives access for conducting required transaction. People are afraid that Internet Banking 'stores' that personal identity information, which may later be fraudulently abused by unscrupulous elements. ATM as a tool scores a psychological edge over the Internet Banking set up. Progress in e-Banking would be visible to the common man, if the focus were redirected towards ATMs rather than towards Internet Banking for achieving the goals of e-Banking. Is it not advantageous for the banking industry to strengthen the existing ATM structure with a little extra cost through empowered solutions, where customer's confidence and e-Banking can be taken to greater heights?

(C Rama Gopal is Professor at VNS Institute of Management, Bhopal. He can be reached at sandhyaramagopal@yahoo.com).

Trade Related 'E-Banking'

Today, e-banking has become imperative to the basic existence and success of banks worldwide. In modern times, new dimensions like trade related e-banking is taking it to greater heights.

When we talk of trade related e-banking and other e-finance, we have an array of things to discuss, ranging from e-payments and trade to bank-based e-trade finance platforms.

1. E-Payments and Trade

The Internet has become an important platform through which the consumers can shop, bank and invest online. While most consumers use credit or debit cards to make online payments, other methods like 'e-wallets' are also becoming prevalent.

As banks continue to play a crucial role in the trade-related payments and finance, there is a clear indication that it will maintain a similar role in the emerging world of e-payments and e-finance. When deciding matters like extension of trade credit to an enterprise, banks are the prime users of credit information and credit insurance products. While, credit information deals with information on the financial state and payment record of the borrowers, credit insurance policy of the borrower enables a bank to transfer the risk to the credit insurer. Thus, credit information assists the creditors to assess the borrower's risks. Recent studies reveal that owing to the lack of adequate credit reporting systems in most of the developing countries, they lack a modern credit-based economy. Today, the rapid dissemination of the Internet and innovative Information and Communication Technologies (ICTs) are ensuring the transparency in communication, while improving the asymmetries in creditor-borrower relations.

Agreeing to a recent study by the Boston Consulting Group (2004), there is competition amongst banks and between the banking and non-banking institutions to capture both domestic and international payment traffic. This will further reduce transaction margins and force innovations that promise the spread of online payments. As these payments are expected to become more customer-focused, in order to stay competitive, the banks will need to take active participation in multi bank e-payment models like SWIFTnet (Society for Worldwide Interbank Financial Telecommunication – based on the Internet). SWIFTnet, the biggest inter-bank payment system, is a network – based payment system where all the participating banks can address each other directly and make payments to one another without a centralized processing and routing site. A new paradigm introduced by Internet communications, SWIFTnet ensures direct communication between all the participating banks and they can also operate independently. At present, 95 percent of banks initially connected through SWIFT have upgraded to SWIFTNet.

2. Bank-Based E-Trade Finance Platforms

Both the bank based e-trade finance platforms and the integrated trade finance platforms are competing models. An understanding of the former is possible by looking at examples of leading banks in trade finance like ABN AMRO, BNP Paribas, Citibank, JP Morgan and Standard Chartered, among others who have their own electronic platforms for documentary credit[1] and open account[2] e-payments to match emerging needs of their corporate clients. However, in order to match their client's desire to work with multiple banks, these banks, besides, developing their own e-trade finance platforms, have entered into collaboration with other banks in an endeavor to offer multi-bank platforms to the clients. This is where the latter model sets in. It provides services to the major clients who prefer working with multiple banks. The major banks also provide technical support to other banks or to the banks of their major clients in order to overcome the limitations of the mono-bank model.

Ideally, these bank-based e-trade finance platforms, regardless of whether they belong to the mono-bank or multi-bank model, carry out the following functions – documentary and

Contd...

Contd...

open-account e-trade finance and payments, e-credit protection, e-discounting, among others. The Internet-based solutions entail transaction initiation, supply chain e-financing, etc. Some banks also provide e-credit protection.

An example of the bank-based e-trade finance platform is JPMorgan Chase. It is one of the leaders in the banking industry, especially in trade finance. This bank provides e-payments and e-finance services to other banks, besides its traders in order to overcome the drawbacks of the mono-bank solution.

ICICI bank is one such advanced bank in terms of online financial services in Asia. It renders efficient e-trade finance services to corporate, with a special set of services for Small Medium and Micro Enterprises (SMEs). The E-Business suite of this bank includes internet banking, bill payment features, trade services, cash management, etc.

In conclusion, it can be reiterated that innovative ICTs and the internet are potential tools for enhancing trade-related e-banking services.

Reference

Information Economy Report 2005, UNCTAD

[1] "A documentary credit can be defined as a conditional undertaking of payment given by a bank. Expressed more fully, it is a written conditional undertaking issued on behalf of the importer (applicant) by the issuing bank to the exporter of goods (beneficiary) to pay for the goods or services, provided the documents submitted conform strictly to terms and conditions of the credit." V.Krishnamurthy, (Nov 12, 2001). *The Hindu Business Line*.

[2] "Credit extended by a business to a customer." *www.thefreedictionary.com*

9

RFID and the Innovation Cycle

Yossi Sheffi

This paper looks at several "disruptive" technologies. It traces the path they have taken from the early innovation phase to full implementation. The technologies discussed include refrigeration; the automobile and highway system; incandescent lighting; the television and the personal computer. The paper first traces each technology through several steps leading from the early innovation to wide adoption. Then the same steps are applied to RFID, placing it in this historical context and speculating on the possible future adoption and impact of this technology.

A lot has been written about the implications of RFID technology to supply chain management. In fact there was hardly a scientific or professional conference in logistics and supply chain management during 2003 and 2004 without a session on the topic. As depicted in Figure 1,[1] the topic has also become prevalent in the general news and business media.[1]

---

[1] Figure 1 is based on Factiva, a database of 8,000 news and business publications, by Dow Jones & Reuters. The 2004 figure is annualized, based on the first two months of the year.

Source: The International Journal of Logistics Management, Vol. 15, 2004. www.emeraldinsight.com.

Figure 1: Number of RFID Publications

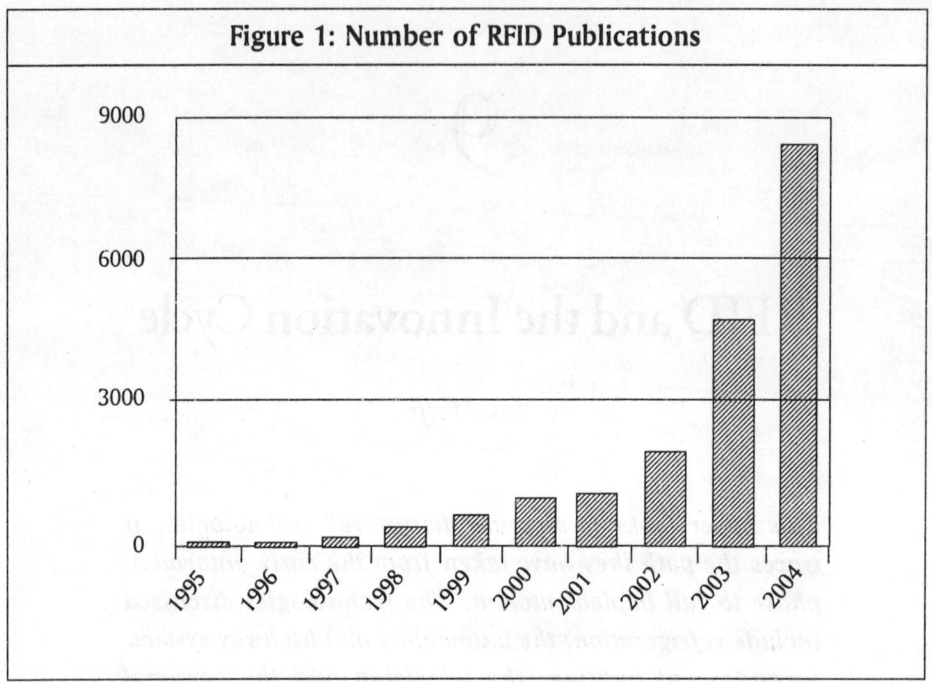

The technology aims to replace the barcode system to track items as they move through supply chains.[2] Finkenzeller [2] provides a general overview of RFID technology, while Sarma [3] describes the specific technology for supply chain management (see also McFarlane and Sheffi [4, 5]). An RFID-based system generally comprises the following elements:

1. A unique standard identification number assigned to a particular item.
2. Low cost identity tag which is attached to the item.
3. Networked RFID readers and data processing systems.
4. Networked data bases that store the information and enable information exchange.

---

2 For the most part, the discussion of RFID in the context of supply chain management looks at passive RFID tags, which are excited by the reader. Unlike passive tags, much more powerful active RFID tags contain their own power source. They can be read over longer distances and can even communicate with the satellite-based global positioning system.

The advantages of RFID systems over barcode systems include the following:

- Ability to have continuous information rather than at discrete points in time.
- Potentially more accurate than the bar code combination of humans and readers.
- Many tags can be read simultaneously into a computer, increasing the reading speed.
- The content of various conveyances (such as trailers, cases, pallets, shopping carts) can be read automatically without opening and sorting the content.
- More data can be stored on the tag, leading possibly to item-level information.
- RFID tags offer future possibilities for recording other data such as temperature exposure and location[3].

RFID hardware is now very much in active development around the world. For example, Figure 2 depicts a glove-based reader, originally developed by Intel Inc. and then further developed at the MIT Center for Transportation and Logistics.[6]

Figure 2: The "iGlove"

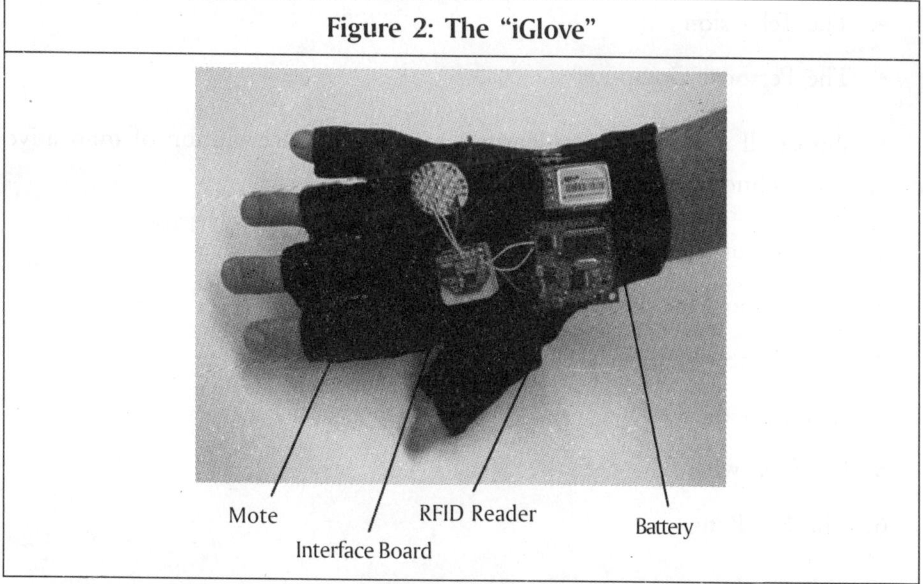

[3] For example, by pulsing the readers in a known sequence and measuring the time of a reading.

Despite the advantages offered by RFID-based systems, it is unclear to what extent they will replace barcodes, given the benefits offered by the existing barcode technology and its ubiquity. In addition, a number of challenges associated with the widespread adoption of RFID remain. These include the cost/benefit for some applications and interference issues for metallic products and liquids. Consequently, a number of supply chain professionals are not sure whether current RFID systems are destined to narrow "special applications" adoption or a technology that will fundamentally change supply chain management.

Path of Innovation

To take a historical perspective on the development of RFID and conjecture about the future of this technology, one can look at the path of other technological breakthroughs and try to deduce where RFID is in terms of its life cycle as an innovation. The following sections discuss five technological innovations:

- Refrigeration Technology
- The Automobile and Highway System
- Incandescent Lighting
- The Television
- The Personal Computer

In almost all cases, one can identify six stages in the evolution of innovative disruptive technologies:

1. The Fog of Innovation.
2. Life Support for Existing Technologies.
3. The Stamp of Approval.
4. Out with the Old.
5. It's Everywhere.
6. The Big Bang.

Not every innovation goes through all these stages. Furthermore, in most cases these stages are not followed in a clean chronological order. Instead, they are intermingled, sometimes skipped, and in many cases are difficult to identify. Yet, such somewhat anecdotal evidence may suggest where RFID is heading.

The last section places the development of RFID in the context of the six steps above, trying to assess where we are today in the innovation cycle and what can be expected in the future.

The Fog of Innovation

At this stage the innovation is young. There may be numerous companies developing many variants of the future product; the technology is adopted at this stage by small market segments where it has a clear advantage or by "early adopters." Many established players do not understand the new technology and ignore it.[4] Other established players may try to discredit the technology and may attempt to erect legal and regulatory barriers to impede its progress. And indeed, the current new product or process may be too expensive and "buggy."[5]

When ice-making machines started replacing the process of harvesting ice blocks from ponds (mainly in New England), it was difficult for ice-makers to break into the market for ice.[6] The reason was that the cost of harvesting ice in New England ponds in the middle of the 19th century was quite low and the quality of the harvested ice was superior. (The harvested ice was clearer, since the mechanical process used to make ice caused air to be trapped in the ice blocks produced.) Thus, the machine-made ice took hold first in the South, where the cost of transported ice was very high, providing a natural segment for the machine-made product. Interestingly, this only seems to have expanded the

---

4 The following may illustrate the point: • A Western Union internal memo noted in 1876: "This 'telephone' has too many shortcomings to be seriously considered as a means of communication. The device is inherently of no value to us." • A Yale University management professor remarked "The concept is interesting and well-formed, but in order to earn better than a 'C', the idea must be feasible", in response to Fred Smith's paper proposing reliable overnight delivery service.

5 A similar description of the first stage of disruptive technology is given by Beaumont in the context of mobile phone technology in general and 3G in particular [7]

6 The first modern ice-making machine, was patented in Britain by Perkins in 1834 (Jones [8]) The first US patent for manufacturing ice was awarded to Dr. John Gorrie of Florida in 1851, who developed the process to help cool malaria victims. The first factories were built in the South in the 1860s.

market; in 1886 the ice harvest was the biggest ever [9] at 25 million tons, while the new technology continued spreading throughout the South.

Both the current system of automobile and modern roads is the result of many years of development. When the internal combustion engine was being developed in the middle of the 19th century, horse- drawn carriages were still the preferred mode of transportation. Driving an automobile required a high degree of technical dexterity and mechanical skill, as well as special clothing including hat, gloves, duster coat, goggles and boots. Tires were notoriously unreliable at the time, and changing one was an excruciating experience. Fuel was a problem, since gasoline was in short supply. Consequently the automobile was not seen as a general means of transportation but rather as a hobbyists' curiosity.

After Edison invented basic incandescent lighting technology in 1879, the gas industry sprung into action to thwart his progress. The dangers of electric lighting were exaggerated and its cost inflated. In addition, regulatory barriers to electricity distribution were introduced with the help of friendly legislators. Interestingly, after Edison established his lighting company, he in turn fought bitterly against the Alternating Current (AC) technology used today, which was developed and championed by the Thompson-Houston Arc Light Company and George Westinghouse. The latter moved successfully into the lighting business while the former was able to take over Edison's company in 1892 and became known as General Electric [10].

Television

Early television systems were mechanical devices, generating very crude images. In 1927, Philo Farnsworth applied for patent for the first electrical television system.[7] His system included both a transmitter and a receiver. David Sarnoff, chairman of the Radio Corporation of America (RCA) understood the potential of this invention and tried to buy him out, but Farnsworth insisted on a royalty arrangement. RCA, who was used to collecting royalties rather than paying for them [11], tried to discredit the device and the inventor, and at the same time challenged Farnsworth's patent as infringing on work carried out at RCA.

---

[7] The patent was granted in 1930. Farnsworth was 24 at the time.

PCS

In the early days the technology was either scoffed at or ignored. Ken Olsen, founder, chairman and CEO of Digital Equipment Corporation, quipped in 1977 "there is no reason anyone would want a computer in their home..."[8] IBM believed the concept to be insignificant and saw no reason to fight it. The company even decided that it could make some money manufacturing the new-fangled machines. Developing the operating system, however, was not worth its while (the system could be bought from a small company named Microsoft) and neither was developing the integrated circuit which was the electronic heart of the machine (which could be bought from Intel).[9] The other major supplier of personal computers, Apple, was hardly a threat to the incumbents. At the time Apple computers could process words in capital letters only, and no secretary would swap her slick IBM electric typewriter for one of these troublesome machines.

Thus, in the early days of these innovations the fledgling technologies were generally inferior to what was already available. As a result the established leaders either did not recognize the commercial potential of these new ideas, or fought to bury them if they perceived a genuine threat.

Life Support for Exiting Technologies

At this stage two processes take place – market incumbents perceive the threat and are trying to improve the old technology in order to increase its competitiveness, while at the same time adopting some aspects of the new technology to help them sell and develop the established products (thereby prolonging their lives).

Refrigeration

As the ice-making technology improved and took hold in Southern US, ice harvesters in the North found that they could harness it to make their industry more competitive. Using refrigeration technologies, they were able to move the harvested ice over long distances and increase their markets in the Far East and

---

8 For completeness, note that Thomas Watson, chairman of IBM, remarked in 1943 "I think there is a world market for maybe five computers."

9 One can only imagine the size of IBM, today if it had controlled both the chip and the operating system of the PC, rather than merely produce the casings...

southern US. Thus, they were increasing their sales by using the technology that eventually replaced them.

In addition, the ice harvesters improved their processes by investing in new automation, thus cutting costs and increasing their competitive reach. These advances prolonged the existence of the ice harvesting industry by a few years.

While there do not seem to be cases in which engine technology was used to advance the cause of the horse and carriage, one of the main uses of early internal combustion engines was to help cyclists peddle their bikes. In fact, the Duryea Brothers, who were bicycle manufacturers, were the first manufacturers of gasoline powered engines[10] and are generally recognized as the first American automobile manufacturers.[11] Furthermore, while the automobile itself did not help the technology it replaced, many of the innovations that would make the automobile-and highway system the dominant form of transportation were originally introduced to help its rival – the horse-drawn carriage. Shock absorbers, rubber tires and roads with drainage systems, were all introduced long before the automobile, to serve the needs of the carriage business.[12]

In response to the invention of the incandescent lighting (which was based on a filament of carbon heated by electricity), the gas industry adopted a technology developed by Austrian inventor Carl von Welsbach that involved hitting a metal oxide filament with a gas flame. The resulting gas mantle, first introduced in 1883, increased gas lighting efficiency five-fold. Ten years later, continuous improvements reduced the costs of gas lighting by two thirds [13]. While boosting sales for gas lighting at the end of the 19th century, this invention did not prevent the ascendancy of electric lighting which finally took over at the beginning of the 20th century.[13]

---

10 The Duryea Motor Wagon Company was founded in 1896

11 Even though their Duryea Motor Wagon Company made only 13 cars.

12 Thomas Telford John Loudon McAdam improved the design of roads in the beginning of the 19th century by introducing geometric design and pavement design principles. Asphalt roads were introduced in France in 1824 while the first modern asphalt road in the US was in Battery Park and on Fifth Avenue in New York City in 1872 [12].

13 The gas industry did not collapse, since it found a market in space heating and a few related areas.

Interestingly, one of the first uses of electrical energy was to help the technology it eventually replaced. In 1852 the City of Boston installed electric fire alarm boxes throughout the city; they were needed to mitigate the fire hazard presented by gas and candle lighting.

Television

In 1923, David Sarnoff predicted, in an RCA board meeting, that some day each American household would be equipped with a television that "will make it possible for those at home to see as well as hear what is going on at the broadcast station." [14]. While television did not drive radio out of existence, it certainly replaced it as the main mode mass communications and entertainment. Sarnoff's comment demonstrates the thinking at the time, that television will basically help increase the appeal of radio broadcasting by allowing the audience to watch the broadcasters as they deliver.

PCS

Early PC technology was basically used as a terminal to connect with a mainframe computer. In fact 'terminal emulation' programs are still being built into operating systems today. Furthermore, companies like Digital Equipment Corporation used the technology which eventually fueled the modern PC to develop departmental computers (such as their venerable PDP 11), not realizing that they may be sowing the seeds for their own demise.

These examples demonstrate how old technology players responded initially to upstart competitors by improving their existing offerings or products. Some actually used the new technology to bolster their market positions and fend off the competitors that eventually usurped them.

The Stamp of Approval

In many cases, new technologies cannot break through until an established player decides to adopt the technology, thus giving it a "stamp of approval." This creates a marketing "buzz" and in many cases leads to the emergence of a dominant design or standard. Marketing executives refer to this as the "verification" of the new technology. In most of the cases it is a positive development for the new entrants even if a competitor adopts the technology since it helps to convince potential customers of the need for the new product or service.

Cars

In the case of the automobile, the stamp of approval probably came from the government's push to build roads, thereby not only supporting the new automobile technology, but building an important component of the system. Well before the Interstate Highway System project, in the Model T days, the US Congress and many state legislatures funded the building of roads under the slogan "get the farmers out of the mud."[14]

Light

Edison's reputation as an inventor and businessman was so well-entrenched in the public mind in the late 19th century, that the mere fact that the new innovation came from him ensured that his company was successful in selling electric lighting equipment to businesses and homes.

Television

After fighting Farnsworth for a decade, RCA acquiesced and agreed to Farnsworth's royalties arrangement for the television technology. "The RCA attorney is said to have had tears in his eyes as he signed the contract."[14] RCA then started to push the technology, exhibiting it in the 1939 New York World's Fair. Importantly, in 1941 the US Federal Communications Commission established the standard of 525 lines per frame and 30 frames per second.

PCS

The entrance of IBM into the market for personal computers legitimized the new product for business users. The presence of Big Blue also brought competition for Apple and initially validated the new product category, helping many PC manufacturers that sprung up in the early days of the industry to sell more products (even though many of these firms were later driven out of business).

---

[14] For example, in 1920, the Minnesota constitution was changed to enable the funding of a system of paved trunk highways, plus helping the building of county and city roads. It was to be funded by a gasoline tax and a vehicle registration fee. [15]

Out with the Old

As the new technology becomes accepted, it replaces the old technology for many of the same applications.

Refrigeration

Ice harvesting continued as a viable business until the beginning of the 20th century, even though manufactured ice was taking over. The old industry finally died when ice boxes at homes and businesses gave way to the electric refrigerator.

Cars

The most significant impetus to the wide adoption of the automobile was probably the development of the assembly line by Ford Motor Company. This innovation was launched in 1908, and by 1927 the price of a Model T dropped from $1,000 to $300 per unit, even as the product improved.

Light

In 1881, Edison demonstrated his vision by lighting large parts of lower Manhattan from a central generating station. After that, incandescent lighting took hold in homes, stores and offices all over the world.

Television

After World War II, television broadcasts of news started replacing radio news as the main source of news for American households. The price of television sets were dropped dramatically and the quality improved with the addition of color and larger sets.

The spreadsheet by VisiCalc was the first major "killer-application" that caused many accountants to buy a computer. The machines became more and more popular as they became easier to use with the addition of graphical user interface and many more applications.

It's Everywhere and Beyond

The last stage in the innovation life cycle marks the replacement of the old technology by the new one. In many cases, the new technology then inspires new applications which were impossible with the old technology.

Refrigeration

The wide adoption of refrigeration technology led to the development of the frozen food industry, by enabling a much wider variety of fresh foods to be traded and consumed out-of-season.

Cars

There were 204 million cars in the US in 2001, or almost two cars per household.[16] The automobile and highway system has changed travel and vacation patterns, leading to the development of roadside motels and drive-through restaurants.

Light

Inexpensive and reliable lighting systems extended human activities into the night on a scale impossible with gas lighting. Examples include night sports, night construction activities, night driving, etc.

Television

In 2001 there were 248 million television sets in the US, almost one per person and significantly more than one per household. It became the main source of entertainment for a growing part of the population, leading to "couch potatoes" and TV dinners.

PCS

The availability of easy-to-use applications played a key role in the widespread adoption of personal computers. These included word processing and spreadsheet programs, presentation packages and games. The expansion of the PC market also led to declining prices and accelerating market growth for these machines.

Structural Changes: The Big Bang

Many important technological innovations had their most dramatic impacts in ways that were never envisioned by the original inventors. In many cases these latent changes were orders of magnitude larger and more profound than the immediate impact.

Refrigeration

The adoption of refrigeration meant that not only could food be stored and handled for longer periods without spoilage, but houses and workplaces could be cooled as well. The structural results of these changes were, for example: (i) the industrialization of agriculture, by allowing out of season consumption and long distance shipments, making it easier to achieve economies of scale in production, and (ii) the development of the US South (as well as many other southern regions around the world), which would not have been possible without airconditioning.

Cars

The adoption of the automobile as the main mode of transportation led to the decline of urban centers as populations moved to the suburbs. In business, the flexibility and relatively low cost of truck transportation paved the way for new approaches to manufacturing, such as just-in-time. On a global level the spread of automobiles has raised air pollution levels and with it respitory diseases.

Light

Modern lighting has encouraged the entry of other electrical appliances into the home, such as washing machines and televisions. This has promoted important social changes, since household chores have become less onerous, releasing women to pursue roles outside of domestic work. It also brought the era of the television.

Television

Television did not only add another dimension to news reporting, but changed the face of news and the involvement of people in the political process. By bringing pictures of the Vietnam War, the 2001 World Trade Center attack, or the 2004 prisoners' abuse at Abu Ghuraib prison in Iraq to the world's living rooms, television images have been changing world politics. In addition, television is responsible for the rise of professional sports, the adoption of a multitude of products through advertisement, and the homogenization of the world fashion and culture.

PCS

Personal computers are responsible for the large increase in business productivity. The ease of using many PC applications (word processing, filing, presentations, etc.)

meant not only an increase in productivity; office responsibilities changed, and with it the role of office workers. Performing work on a PC has led to the rise in knowledge workers and, with it, new forms of eneterprise organizations. Such organizations rely on the ability of kowledge workers to have access to information everywhere, perform the work anywhere, and communicate with their colleagues from anyplace. It also enabled the use of the World Wide Web, online shopping, e-mail and instant messaging communications.

RFID Innovation

At this early stage of RFID innovation, it is very difficult to assess the significance of the technology. In fact, many consulting firms are advising their clients to wait rather than jump on the RFID bandwagon. This section focuses on RFID technology for supply chain management, trying to evaluate where it is in the innovation cycle in light of the examples analyzed above.

1. The Fog of Innovation

In the first stage of an innovation there may be several competing standards, multiple enterprises jostling for market position, and substantial doubt about the value of the new technology. Clearly, many see RFID as still in this stage. Proponents of bar codes argue that RFID does not provide significant incremental benefits, and on this basis it is difficult to justify investments in the new technology. There are still several standards competing in different regions of the world, the costs of RFID are still higher than the five cents per tag that many in the industry consider the threshold for wide-spread adoption, and there are still some technical challenges to overcome, such as interference issues when reading through metals and liquids.

In addition, the technology has raised fears of privacy intrusion, slowing down the adoption of the RFID at Benetton and others.[15] Such privacy concerns are, by and large, stemming from lack of understanding of the technology, yet it caused some retail chains to investigate "kill tag" devices at their checkout counters, as well as to focus their efforts on upstream supply chain activities.

15 For example, *The Guardian* wrote on July 13, 2003 that "One potential problem with RFID tags is that they can still work long after the product has been bought. If the tags become as ubiquitous as the manufacturers would like, people could be bristling with the chips in clothes and possessions. Anyone from police to potential thieves could work out exactly what they carry."

2. Life Support for Existing Technologies

As the debate goes on, certain forms of automatic identification (much more powerful than RFID tags, it should be noted) are being used to enhance the value of the information collected with barcodes. For example, conveyances such as trucks are being traced using satellite-based GPS systems, while (mostly active) RFID-based readers are used to locate containers, trailers and rail cars in ports and yards. The conveyance location information is then correlated with details of the goods being carried (collected using barcodes) to complete the tracking picture.

3. Stamp of Approval

In June 2003 the world's largest retailer, Wal-Mart, announced that it will require its top 100 suppliers to install RFID tags in the goods sent to its distribution centers starting in January 2005. A few months later Sun Microsystems, Inc. announced that it will open an RFID test center where Wal-Mart suppliers can test their RFID solutions to guarantee compliance with the Wal-Mart standard. Another huge operator, the US Department of Defense, announced in September 2003 that it too will require its suppliers to put passive RFID tags on the lowest possible shipping element for which this makes sense (piece/ part/case/pallet/ packaging) by January 2005. The statements by these enterprises – especially Wal-Mart, which is widely recognized as a technology leader created significant momentum in the field.

At the beginning of 2003, Gillette Inc. announced the purchase of 500 million RFID tags from Alien Technology. Gillette said it was planning to use the tags with smart shelf technology to avoid pilferage, as well as for inventory management. The company has been testing the technology throughout 2003 and 2004, and this work has contributed to the buzz about the future of RFID.

However, some supporters of the technology have had to make some adjustments as their ambitious plans clashed with the reality of unstable technology and untested processes. For instance, Wal-Mart retreated from its aggressive development schedule, delaying the implementation of RFID in some pharmaceutical products which should have preceded the January 2005 implementation. The giant retailer also reduced the scope of the January 2005 top 100 suppliers' implementation, deciding instead to limit the roll-out to its distribution centers in Texas.

Still, Wal-Mart's announcement has ensured that RFID technology will figure largely in the future of supply chain management, not-withstanding premature announcements on its readiness for system-wide implementation and certain technological shortcomings.

4. Out with the Old

As RFID gradually replaces bar codes, it will appear first in applications where the benefits justify the costs. These include the following:

- **Sub-Conveyance Tracking:** The management of these sub-conveyances is where the impact of RFID-based systems can be felt immediately. Being able to track individual pallets automatically and accurately would enable material handling companies to reduce the number of pallets in circulation, charge customers appropriately for their use on an individual pallet basis, and better maintain the pallets. Similarly, transportation and logistics companies will be able to track returnable containers and racks, thereby improving the utilization of these items. Other examples of current use of RFID in sub-conveyances tracking include the following [17]:

  a. Scottish Courage Brewing tracks a UK inventory of 10 million beer kegs with RFID, reducing shrinkage, improving operations (shipping, receiving, payments, etc.) and providing an immediate audit trail.

  b. Marks & Spencer, the UK retailer, is using RFID to track food trays and rolling cages, cutting down the time required to read and identify these sub-conveyances by a factor of five.

  c. The military has been using (active) RFID tags to track containers during the second Gulf war.

- **Tracking High Value Items:** The cost of the tags is, obviously, less significant when tracking high value items and/or when accurate tracking is particularly important. For example, expensive items will benefit from better inventory control more than low value items. In addition, the technology has already been undergoing tests (by Gillette Inc. and Tesco Plc.) aimed at reducing theft of razor blades in retail stores. Such an application is obviously relevant to high value products at locations throughout the supply chain. Finally, RFID tags can help to reduce counterfeiting of such products.

For particular industries, such as pharmaceuticals, RFID offers additional potential benefit of reducing the ability to tamper with products. In addition these products are subject to recalls which can be carried out very effectively and accurately using RFID technology. Thus,. the pharmaceutical industry is likely to be one of the early adopters.[16]

5. It's Everywhere

Widespread implementation is likely to take until the end of the decade. And even at that point, it is unlikely that a complete item-level RFID code will be available on every product.

The original vision of the MIT Auto ID Center, was founded in 1999 to develop an open architecture for a seamless network of physical objects, called for storing the information about all moving and stored items in a database, accessible from anywhere around the globe through the Internet. This is unlikely to take place any time soon, since it is not clear that such vast amounts of information are needed. Additionally, data ownership issues may prevent complete sharing, and there are privacy concerns that may impede the free flow of information.

But even without a complete item-level implementation it is clear that the technology can still yield major efficiency and productivity gains. RFID can lead to more accurate information gathering – what is shipped and received and what is in the warehouse and the store. It can reduce the need for manual counting at shipping/receiving docks and throughout warehouses and retail locations, as well as at checkout counters.

6. Structural Changes

At this point, while the technology is still nascent, it is difficult to imagine the structural changes that might unfold. By definition, these changes are not part of the current vision. Some will come into being because RFID will provide some unknown value in conjunction with others, yet-to-be invented technologies. (E-mail, for example, required both personal computers and the Internet).

---

16 Accenture, one of the leading management consultants, has organized a group of pharmaceutical industry leaders, associations and government agencies as part of its "Jump Start" program to coordinate the implementation of RFID.

On its own, one can think about RFID providing quantum leaps in the design of inventory management methods. Existing warehouses are geared for human 'put away' and pick up operations. For example, most modern warehouses use "pick to light" techniques for directing the pickers to the right bin. With RFID systems, put away locations can be determined by new, optimized trade-offs using criteria such as the efficiency of put away and picking operations, minimizing space requirements, or a combination of these criteria. Under any of these scenarios, the typical warehouse design will change drastically. No longer will items need to be stored in specific locations, so to the naked eye the warehouses will appear chaotic. However, to the electronic eye these facilities will appear well organized and efficiently run.

Experiments at Cambridge University show the potential of re-designing manufacturing operations [4]. In the lab, robots can read the content of partly-assembled product recipes, and change them quickly and efficiently, responding to changing requirements with little or no set-up times, thus allowing for more efficient mass customization.

Future retail operations could also change substantially. Continuous shelf inventory checking and more frequent replenishments mean that shelf space for each item can be reduced considerably, while increasing the level of service and avoiding out-of-stock situations. The result may be smaller supermarkets and other retail outlets while the number of SKUs offered remains constant. Thus, the trend towards suburban large malls may be reversed by offering all the variety of suburban supermarkets in a corner store.

Possible future interactions between personal readers (built into personal digital assistants or mobile phones) and the items in a retail location may change the way shoppers interact with retail outlets. In these futuristic stores, shoppers actually may not need to see items before purchasing them.

As of this writing, in the middle of 2004, we are still somewhere between the first stage and the third stage of the innovation cycle of RFID. It is still not out of the Fog of innovation – the benefits of the technology are not entirely clear, especially in terms of its advantages over bar code technology. RFID does not have an assigned frequency and it interferes with some existing UHF frequencies (such as the wireless 802.11b). New communications technologies often run into standards issues and RFID is no exception, with different regions of the world using different standards. In addition, there are still questions of security, privacy and a lack of protocol for information sharing. None of these challenges seem insurmountable, but they are indicative of a technology in its infancy.

Despite these hurdles Wal-Mart and most other large retailers, as well as many other organizations, including the US Department of Defense expressed their support for RFID and are going ahead with implementation plans.

Beyond Supply Chains

While it seems that RFID systems will eventually replace the barcode as the main tool for tracking products and managing inventory, the most intriguing possibilities lie in the structural changes which the technology may bring, possibly in combination with other emerging technologies. Some of the relevant related technologies include ZigBee and WiMax [18]. ZigBee is a technology that coordinates communications among thousands of tiny sensors. These sensors can detect and transmit information about heat, moisture, particle content, forces exerted and other environmental variables from one to another and finally to a computer. WiMax is a more potent version of WiFi – it can transmit digital information at an order of magnitude faster than WiFi over distances of 25–30 miles instead of the 100 feet or so of WiFi – thus creating "city-size" "hot spots." Like RFID these technologies work in the radio spectrum, which is free, thus promising low-cost information movement.

One of the aspects common to all the cases mentioned in this paper is that the Big Bang – the move from invention to innovation, took place when consumers adopted the technology in large numbers.

RFID, in combination with the technologies mentioned in this section, as well as and other technologies, still in the laboratory, may transform the way humans experience the world. They may lead to a sixth "digital sense" of the human environment and all the innate objects in it. Thus, one may not have to see, hear, smell, feel or taste the presence of some items, but rather sense digitally their location and condition. Such sensing may be subject to the owner's permission, creating a new social etiquette and a new way in which we all interact with each other and our environment.

(Yossi Sheffi Prof, M.I.T & Director, MIT Center for Transportation and Logistics, Cambridge.)

References

[1] Guitton, A, "The Value of RFID in Transportation: From Greater Operational Efficiency to Collaborative Transportation Management", unpublished Master of Engineering in Logistics Thesis, MIT, Cambridge, MA, 02139.

[2] Finkenzeller, Klaus, "RFID Handbook: Fundamentals and Applications in Contact-less Smart Cards and Identification", John Wiley & Sons, 1999.

[3] Sarma, S, "Towards the 5c Tag, Auto ID Center" White Paper, CAM-AUTOIDWH01, *www.autoidcenter.org*, 2002.

[4] McFarlane, D and Y Sheffi, "Impact of Automatic Identification on Supply Chain Operations", *International Journal of Logistics Management,* Vol. 14, No.1, pp. 1-17, 2003.

[5] McFarlane, D and Y Sheffi, "Speeding the Supply Chain", *Information Economic Journal,* December 2003, pp 26–27.

[6] Cassett, D and C Hopeman, "Radio Frequency Identification (RFID) in Semi-conductor. Manufacturing", unpublished Master of Engineering in Logistics Thesis, Massachusetts Institute of Technology, Cambridge, MA, 2004.

[7] Beaumont, M, 3G: "Another Technology Cycle", Ericsson, Australia, 2002.

[8] Jones, J America's "Ice Men: An Illustrative History of the United States Natural Ice Industry", 1665–1925. Humble, Texas: Jobeco Books, 1984.

[9] Utterback, J, "Mastering the Dynamic of Innovation", Harvard Business School Press, Boston, MA, 1994.

[10] Mack, Pamela, Thomas Edison, *http://people.clemson.edu/~pammack/lec122/edison.htm*

[11] Barnouw, "E Tube of Plenty: The Evolution of American Television", Oxford University Press, New York, NY 1990.

[12] Bellis, Mary, "The History of Roads and Asphalt", *http://inventors.about.com/library/inventors/blasphalt.htm*

[13] Bright, Arthur, Jr., "The Electric Lamp Industry: Technological Change and Economic Development from 1800 to 1947", McMillan, NY, New York, 1949.

[14] Flatow, I., "They All Laughed", Harper Collins, New York, NY, 1992.

[15] Erik Hare: "Think Drivers Pay the Cost of Roads? It's a Myth", Minneapolis/St. Paul StarTribune, September 7, 2003.

[16] Miller, Leslie. "Cars, Trucks now Outnumber Drivers". Salon, August 29th, 2003.

[17] Ericson, J (2003) "RFID Rising", Line56, February 13th, 2003.

[18] Green, Heather, No Wires, No Rules, *BusinessWeek*, April 26th, 2004.

10

SUMMARY

The European E-Business Report 2005

Hannes Selhofer

E-Business continues to develop dynamically in the EU and in other advanced economies of the world. The article portrays the relevance of ICT and e-business in 10 sectors of EU in 2005 and explores emerging trends. It states that the rapidity and direction of e-business developments differ considerably between industries. Furthermore, within sectors, the opportunities and challenges are different for small, medium-sized and large firms. Besides, regional disparities in enterprise's ICT use and their readiness for innovation exist within the EU, especially among smaller companies. In conclusion, the article presents the various policy implications of e-business.

E-Business continues to develop dynamically in the EU and in other advanced economies of the world. Rapid technological progress, for example in wireless technology, and the increasing competitive pressure on companies in the global economy have been important drivers for e-business adoption in the past 2 years. However, the pace and the direction of related developments differ considerably between industries. Within sectors, opportunities and challenges are different for

Source: e-Business W@tch 2005: The European e-Business, Report, 2005 edition. A portrait of e-business in 10 sectors of the European economy. Luxembourg: Office for Official Publications of the European Communities. ISBN 92-894-9405-0. © European Commission, 2005. Reprinted with permission.

small firms and for medium-sized and large ones. Moreover, regional disparities in enterprise's ICT use and in their readiness for innovation can still be found within the EU, mainly among smaller companies.

The Statistics – Trends in 2005

- **ICT Infrastructure**: further migration towards broadband internet connections: about a third of firms* had adopted broadband in 2005.
- **ICT Solutions for E-Commerce**: About 19% of firms* use ICT solutions for e-procurement, about 17%* to support marketing or sales processes.
- **Digital Divide** between small and medium sized enterprises: for many E-Business applications, medium firms (50-249) appear to have the 'critical size' for adoption. For instance, e-standards adoption by micro and small firms generally trails behind.
- **Alignment in International Development**: EU companies are, on average, on a similar stage in E-Business adoption as their international counterparts. Differences are more pronounced between individual countries within the EU.

W@tch Out: New Developments Ahead

- **Breakthrough of RFID?** RFID solutions promise substantial improvements in tracking and tracing products along the supply chain, for example in the food industry. Opportunities for combating counterfeiting activities could be a key driver for RFID adoption in the pharmaceutical and the textile industries.
- **E-Invoicing**: Triggered by policy initiatives, e-invoicing could drive the digital integration and e-standards development in B2B transactions.
- **Focus on Marketing and Sales**: As it has been the case in procurement, increasing cost pressure could now become a driver for E-Business in marketing and sales. Specific solutions, such as CRM systems and new mobile applications, promise a high potential to increase the efficiency of related processes.

* in % of employment

Sectoral E-Business Differences – Manufacturing, Construction, Services

Results of the e-business Survey 2005 and sector studies confirm that the nature, intensity and impact of electronic business activity still differs between sectors, particularly between manufacturing and service sectors. The e-business Index (see Exhibit 1.1-1) is a compound indicator for the intensity of ICT use in the 10 industries studied in 2005, enabling relative comparisons of sectors to each other.

The Relevance of ICT and E-Business in 10 Sectors in 2005

(Overall Assessment Based on Survey Results, Desk Research and Case Studies)

Application Sector	Broadband Adoption	ICT for Innovation	ERP/SCM	Sourcing & Procurement	Marketing and Sales	Overall Significance
Food & Beverage	•	•	••★	••	•	•★
Textile	•	•★	••	•	•	•
Publishing	•••	••••	•	••	•••	••★
Pharmaceutical	•••	••	••••	•••	••	•••
Machinery	••	••	•••	••	•★	••
Automotive	•••	••	••••	•••	•★	•••
Aerospace	•••	••	•••	••••	•	•••
Construction	•	•	•	•	•	•
Tourism••	••	•	••	•••★	••★	
T I services	••••	••••	•••	•••★	•••★	••••

• = low relevance/diffusion; •• = average relevance/diffusion; ••• = above average relevance/diffusion •••• = high relevance/diffusion; ★= applies only for some sub-sectors/applications

Source: E-Business W@tch (2005) – based on analysis from the respective Sector Studies.

Exhibit 1.1-1: E-Business Index 2005 for 10 Sectors (EU-7 data)[1]

Benchmark Based on Employment-Weighted Data* (Indexed Values: Highest Score = 100)

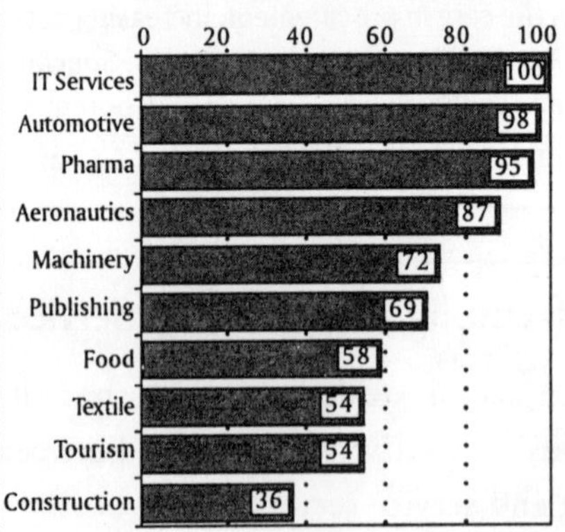

*) Employment-weighted data express E-Business adoption as "activity in firms comprising ...% of employment in a sector", thus emphasizing the situation in larger firms.

Benchmark Based on Firm-Weighted Data (Indexed Values: Highest Score = 100)**

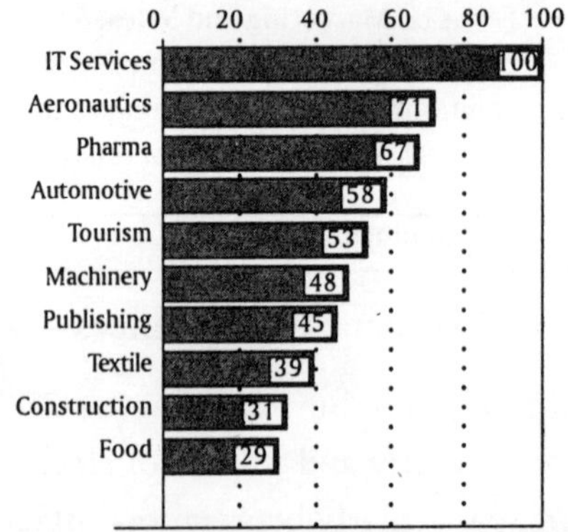

**) Firm-weighted data express E-Business adoption as "of firms in a sectorwith a certain activity", irrespective of the size of the firms (i.e. small companies and large ones count equally). Results are mainly determined by the situation in smaller firms, as there are many more small companies than large ones.

Source: E-Business W@tch (2005).

[1] For background information about the construction of the index, see Annex III (Methodology Report).

Manufacturing

- Among the 7 manufacturing sectors surveyed in 2005, electronic business activity has reached the highest level of intensity in the automotive, pharmaceutical and aeronautics industries. The rapid development in these sectors is mostly driven by the large international companies.
- Supply-chain integration and the streamlining of procurement processes are common objectives in these industries for which e-business solutions are attractive. Online procurement has become a part of everyday business and belongs to the most frequently adopted e-business applications.
- In the pharmaceutical industry, the use of ICT and e-business plays an important role for the process of discovery and development of new drugs and pharmaceutical treatments. Thus, ICT have an impact on R&D efficiency and, thereby, on lowering the competitive pressure.
- In the machinery and equipment industry, electronic business activity has not yet reached the same level of intensity. At first sight, this confirms the findings of the Survey 2003. However, developments in this sector have been quite dynamic since then. For example, e-business is increasingly recognized as a useful means of providing customer service.
- The publishing and printing industry has a different e-business profile, as major segments of this sector operate in B2C markets. ICT has a considerable impact on production and internal work processes. Furthermore, customer-facing activities (online publishing, marketing, advertising) are critical. On the other hand, processes with a high e-business potential such as inventory and supply-chain-management are less critical in this sector.
- The food and beverages sector, and the textile and clothing industry, are late adopters of ICT compared to the other manufacturing sectors studied.
- However, in the food and beverages industry, there are signs of increasing e-business activity, mainly in response to structural changes and new regulatory requirements. Important issues that promote e-business are food safety and the digital integration of the value chain. RFID (Radio Frequency Identification) based technologies could play an important role in these areas.

- In the textile and clothing industry, and this is new evidence compared to the previous sector studies of 2004, there are signs that the use of advanced ICT systems in large companies is quite in line with adoption rates among large firms from the most advanced manufacturing sectors. Examples are Enterprise Resource Planning (ERP) and Supply Chain Management (SCM) systems. It appears that a significant share of large textile firms have taken the lead towards supply chain integration and online trading with business partners.

Construction

- ICT adoption and e-business activity in construction companies appears to be very limited compared to all other sectors studied by the e-business w@tch. The structure of the industry, which includes many small craft companies, cannot fully explain this gap.
- Construction is an industry with a multitude of standards, technical specifications, labels, and certification marks. This is not an optimal environment for drawing benefits from electronic business. However, e-business tools have the potential to benefit complex construction projects where there is a need to coordinate a large number of sub-contractors.

Service Sectors

- The IT services sector is a special case with regard to e-business. Although companies in this sector have Information Technology and e-business as their end product, ICT also plays a significant role in the way that this product is produced, promoted and provided. This specific way of using ICT distinguishes the IT services industry from the other sectors analysed by e-business w@tch. Here, the use of ICT and the production of related services are difficult to separate from each other.
- The IT services sector shares a common feature with tourism – in both industries, online channels have become key tools for marketing, communication and interaction with customers. Online tourism, online booking and reservation services have been widely accepted among consumers and business travellers, and "e-tourism" has truly taken off. However, the great importance of ICT in this sector is not properly reflected

in the e-business Index. The main reason is that e-business normally does not have the same significance in supply-side activities and internal work processes (for example in hotels), as in manufacturing sectors.

Geographic Disparities in ICT Use for Business

In international comparisons, EU enterprises are (on average) head-to-head with their counterparts in other advanced economies in terms of electronic business activity.[2] However, gaps are more pronounced within the European Union (i.e., between Member States) than on the aggregate level in international benchmarks. The same observation could be made for other large economies, notably for the USA, where digital divides between states or regions also exist. The e-business Index 2005 shows differences in the ICT adoption and use between firms from 7 EU countries.

Exhibit 1.1-2: E-Business Index 2005 for 7 EU Countries[3]

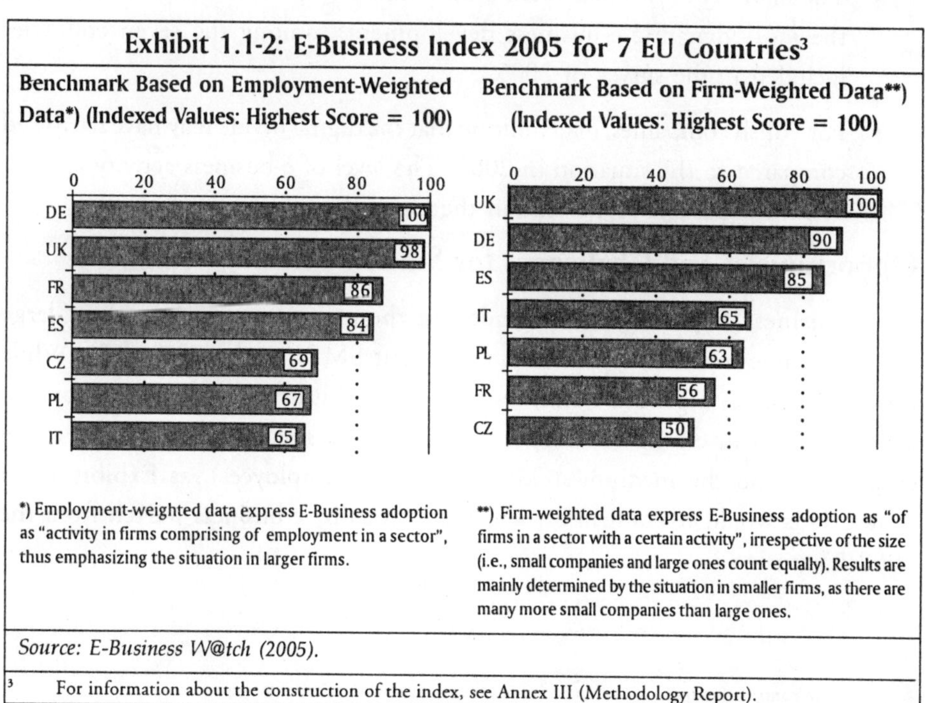

*) Employment-weighted data express E-Business adoption as "activity in firms comprising of employment in a sector", thus emphasizing the situation in larger firms.

**) Firm-weighted data express E-Business adoption as "of firms in a sector with a certain activity", irrespective of the size (i.e., small companies and large ones count equally). Results are mainly determined by the situation in smaller firms, as there are many more small companies than large ones.

Source: E-Business W@tch (2005).

3 For information about the construction of the index, see Annex III (Methodology Report).

2 See E-Business W@tch Special Report "Overview of International E-Business Developments", July 2005.

- Country comparisons, however, should be taken with a pinch of salt, as they partly reflect industry structure. In Italy, for example, sectors dominated by small firms are much more prevalent than in other countries. Since large firms are more advanced in electronic business, aggregate employment-weighted data consequently point at a comparatively lower level of e-business activity in Italy. This reflects, at least to some extent, the structure of the economy rather than the overall e-maturity of firms.

- In general, firms from the UK and Germany tend to be most advanced in e-business among the 7 countries. Among larger companies, companies from France and Spain are close behind.

- Firms from the Nordic countries, which were not covered by the e-business Survey 2005, are likely still to be leaders within the EU. Eurostat data mostly confirm this assessment.

- The survey confirms that Spain is the country where firms have demonstrated the most dynamic e-business development[4], among the seven countries included in the survey of 2005.

- For Polish companies, data indicate that the digital divide may have narrowed compared to the situation in 2003. The level of e-business activity appears to be comparable to the one in the Czech Republic.

Opportunities and Challenges for Smaller Firms

The e-business Report 2004 concluded in the executive summary that "large firms continue to drive the development – but SMEs catch up" (p. 12). While this holds true as a general trend, results of the e-business Survey 2005 point at a peculiar gap in e-business adoption between the small firms (with up to 49 employees) and the medium-sized ones (50-249 employees), as Exhibit 1.1-3 shows. This would re-confirm earlier observations by e-business w@tch from the 2002/03 period.[5]

4 See also contribution by Jesus Galvan on "E-Business in Spain" in Part 3 of the report.

5 A presentation of E-Business W@tch findings at the IST Conference 2003 in Milan (4th Oct. 2003), for example, was titled "SMEs or MLEs?", indicating that E-Business activity in medium-sized and large enterprises ('MLEs') could have more in common than activities of small and medium ones ('SMEs')-

Exhibit 1.1-3: The E-Business Index 2005 by Firm Size

	A	B	C	D
Micro (0-9)	35	23	41	45
Small (10-49)	44	29	42	50
Medium (50-249)	72	63	68	82
Large (250+)	100	100	100	100

A = Sub-Index "ICT Infrastructure" B = Sub-Index "Internal Processes" C = Sub-Index "Procurement and Supply Chain Integration" D = Sub-Index "Marketing and Sales"

Overall Index (Based on Firm-Weighted Data*)

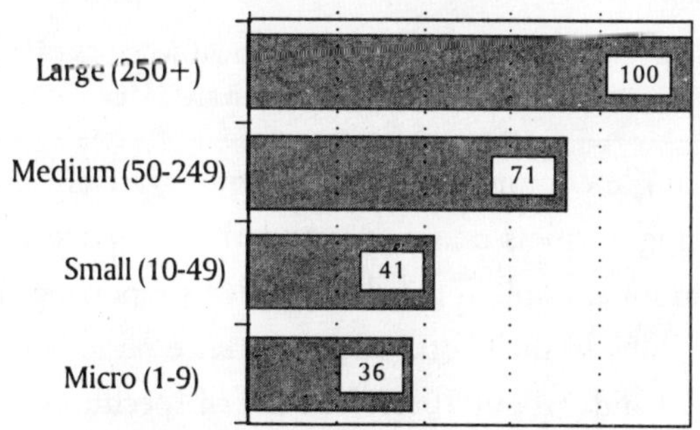

* Firm-weighted data express E-Business adoption as "% of firms within a size-band with a certain activity".

Source: E-Business W@tch (2005).

In general, ICT systems of large companies obviously tend to be more powerful and sophisticated than those of small firms. This translates into more intensive and advanced electronic business practices, and a greater potential for exploiting cost-saving opportunities.

However, research by e-business w@tch conducted in 2005 on the automotive industry indicates that the relationship between innovative activities and firm performance is independent of company size.[6] Consequently, ICT-based innovations are attractive for both large and small enterprises. This should hold true for other sectors as well, and lead to further ICT adoption among smaller firms in the medium and long run.

[6] See E-Business Sector Study on the Automotive Industry (July 2005), p. 75.

E-Business Opportunities for Small Firms

- **Flexibility**: SMEs can be more flexible in decision-making and implementing organisational changes than larger firms.
- **Internal Communication** processes are often 'smoother' in smaller organisations.
- **Used to Cooperation**: Out of necessity, SMEs tend to be used to cooperating with other companies, for example in tendering. E-cooperation can further enhance this attitude.

E-Business Challenges for Small Firms

- **Lack of ICT Strategy and Skills**: Smaller firms often lack a coherent ICT investment strategy or the related skills.
- **Standards**: The lack of e-standards and inter-operability increases risk in technology decisions and investments.
- **Pressure on Prices and Margins**: Sophisticated e-procurement schemes of large buyers increase the pressure on supply companies, many of which are SMEs.

As regards customer-facing e-commerce activities, comparatively many small firms have specialised in doing business online, particularly in service sectors. The tourism industry can serve as an example – the share of firms reporting that online sales account for more than 25% of their total sales (reference period: 2004) is the same across all company size-bands (about 10%). The use of specific ICT solutions for e-marketing and sales, on the other hand, increases with company size.

Trends from 2003-2005: The Base for 'Next-Level' E-Business has Matured

The deployment of Enterprise Resource Planning (ERP) systems is a good indicator for the overall e-business maturity in many sectors. ERP is the technical backbone for various e-business applications, including systems for product planning, purchasing, inventory management, order tracking and finance. A comparison of results to earlier surveys by e-business w@tch shows that ERP adoption has significantly increased in the EU since 2002/03. Thus, companies can now implement new and more advanced e-business solutions than 2-3 years ago. This should also facilitate productivity growth.

Further Growth in E-Commerce, in Particular in B2B Online Trading

B2B online trade has reached a significant level in all industries. Companies are eagerly exploiting cost saving opportunities of e-procurement and e-sourcing. In any of the 10 sectors studied, 40-60% of firms (by their employment share) are

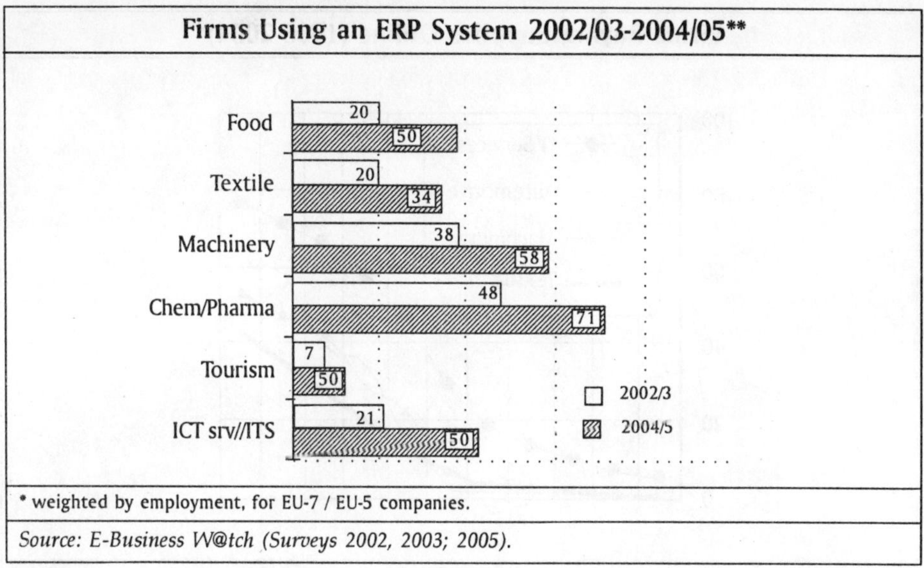

Firms Using an ERP System 2002/03-2004/05**

* weighted by employment, for EU-7 / EU-5 companies.

Source: E-Business W@tch (Surveys 2002, 2003; 2005).

purchasing at least some of their supplies online, for example from their suppliers' websites, on internet trading platforms or via dedicated firm-to-firm connections. Among IT services companies, e-procurement is even more common. It is used by close to 80% of firms and accounted for about 15-18% of their total purchasing volume in 2004 (estimate by e-business w@tch for the EU-7). In most other sectors, the share is estimated at 3-8%.

Sector profiles differ widely in terms of customer facing e-commerce activities. In publishing and in tourism, for example, the internet has a profound impact on how companies communicate with their customers. Close to 40% of companies in these sectors (by employment) enable customers to buy products online (e.g., by downloading articles, or making online reservations). In most manufacturing sectors, online marketing and sales show only moderate growth. However, Sector Studies of 2005 demonstrate that activity in this area is not fully grasped by the concept of 'online selling'. For example, online channels are of growing importance for the delivery of after sales services.

Policy Implications of E-Business

E-business developments can have implications for several policy areas. Relevant considerations made in this context can be grouped around two overall objectives which are paradoxically, to some extent, antagonistic:

Firms Buying Supplies Online (1995-2004)*

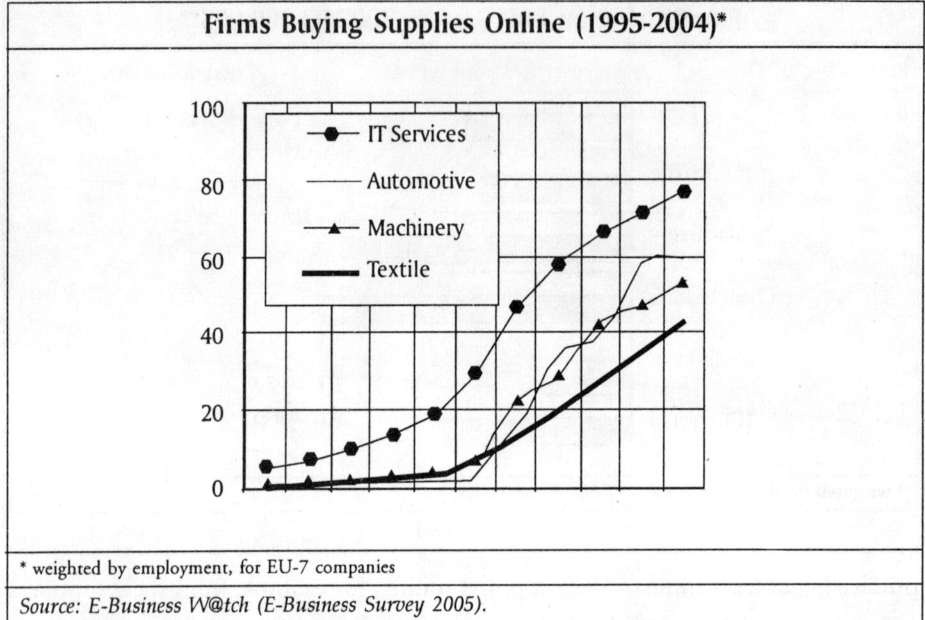

* weighted by employment, for EU-7 companies

Source: E-Business W@tch (E-Business Survey 2005).

- **Promote ICT Adoption:** Policy may have an interest in accelerating the adoption of ICT and e-business activity among companies, particularly among SMEs. This is based on the assumption that ICT is a driver of productivity and competitiveness.
- **Counteract ICT Induced Market Failure:** At the same time, policy will have to consider intervention if e-business activity causes undesirable effects on the aggregate level, i.e., market failure.

The following exhibit summarises the most frequently stated policy objectives, and suggested actions, from the e-business w@tch Sector Studies of 2005. These objectives should be regarded as relevant for most sectors. Two objectives were seen as particularly important in 2005 – the improvement of e-skills among smaller companies, and the advancement of inter-operability and standards.

Exhibit: Policy Implications Arising from e-business

Policy Objective	Suggested Actions	Possible Initiators
Improve e-skills in SMEs	• Counteract E-Business skill-shortages in the market, e.g. by offering opportunities for vocational training and for ICT product demonstrations to companies. • Facilitate knowledge transfer between research centres and enterprises • Provide information on how to assess cost-benefits of E-Business • Provide incentives for conducting ICT training • Help SMEs to better understand organisational aspects of E-Business, not just focused on technology • Identify good practices and communicate their benefits to SMEs • Stimulate the use of e-learning • Create opportunities for dialogue between SMEs and ICT service providers	• Business support agencies • Competence centres • Chambers of commerce • Other intermediaries • Member States (via their E-Business programmes)
Promote interoperability and standardisation	• Grant support for research projects, e.g. targeting standardised internet-based systems • Support for related industry initiatives • Promote adequate representation of SMEs in standardisation processes • Policy can act as a neutral coordinator and promoter of standardisation initiatives	International/national standardisation bodies EU Member States • Industry associations
Encourage cooperation among SMEs	• Encourage initiatives for networking and cooperation, e.g. through competence centres	Sector associations • Business intermediaries • Competence centres

Contd...

Contd...		
	• Stimulate the participation of SMEs in business networks	
Promote a positive climate for innovation	• Create incentives for innovation activity in SMEs • Emphasise the innovative potential of E-Business • Promote cooperation between companies and fair benefit sharing practices	Member States • Regional governments • Associations
Ensure fair competition, address barriers in the legal environment	• Address intellectual property rights issues • Protect relationship-specific investments • Monitor implications of E-Business on concentration of ownership • Consider harmonization of taxation (e.g. VAT)	EU Member States

(This article is based on the "European e-business Report 2005", the 4th Annual Synthesis Report by the e-business w@tch of the European Commission, Enterprise and Industry Directorate General. e-business w@tch was launched by the European Commission in late 2001 to monitor the growing maturity of electronic business across different sectors of the economy in the European Union. The observatory has analysed ebusiness developments and impacts in about 20 manufacturing, financial and service sectors since. All publications are available on the internet at www.ebusiness-watch.org. e-business w@tch is implemented by an international research team which is coordinated by empirica GmbH, Germany (www.empirica.com). Editor of the "European e-business Report 2005": Hannes Selhofer, empirica GmbH., Germany (www.empirica.com).)

11

International E-Business Developments

Hannes Selhofer

The article compares the status–quo of e-business monitoring activities in major economies of the world. It further identifies the major national monitoring initiatives and their institutional set-up, and features the main results. Five countries outside Europe have been selected for this purpose: Australia, Canada, Japan, Korea and the USA. The findings for these countries are compared to equivalent activities in the European Union. The study concludes with some policy recommendations for international e-business monitoring in the future.

Introduction

This chapter summarises the main results of the special report "Overview of International e-business Developments", published by e-business w@tch in July 2005.[1] This report compares the status–quo of e-business monitoring activities in major economies of the world. It identifies the major national monitoring

1 Available at *www.ebusiness-watch.org* ('resources')

Source: e-Business W@tch 2005: The European e-Business, Report, 2005 edition. A portrait of e-business in 10 sectors of the European economy. Luxembourg: Office for Official Publications of the European Communities. ISBN 92-894-9405-0.

initiatives and their institutional set-up, and features the main results as far as they have been accessible. Five countries outside Europe have been selected for this purpose: Australia, Canada, Japan, Korea and the USA. The findings for these countries are compared to equivalent activities in the European Union. The selection considers the economic importance of these countries in the global economy, access to sources on e-business development, and the objective to include economies from different continents. The study concludes with some policy recommendations for international e-business monitoring in the future.

E-Business Monitoring in Australia

Institutional Background and Main Surveys

The Australian Bureau of Statistics (ABS – *www.abs.aov.au*) is Australia's official statistical organisation. The ABS collects a range of information technology data as part of its innovation and technology statistics programme of work.

In this context, the ABS also collects e-commerce related data by one dedicated survey measuring the "Business Use of Information Technology" (BUIT). The survey uses the narrow OECD definition of an internet commerce transaction and focuses on income (revenues) resulting from internet orders for goods and services. Further information is collected on barriers to internet sales. Measuring units are enterprises of any size covered by the ANZSIC (Australian and New Zealand Standard Industrial Classification). BUIT has been conducted annually since 1999-2000, while before 1999 it was conducted biennially.

Main Results

Based on the BUIT surveys, the ABS reports that Australian companies continue to embrace information technology. The proportion of businesses which reported placing orders via the internet was 31% for 2003/04, an increase of 3 percentage points from the previous year (see Exhibit 1). This growth is a continuation of the trend seen over recent cycles for this business practice. Over the same period, the proportion of companies selling via the internet slightly decreased from 13% to 12% of all businesses.

Electronic commerce represented approximately 2% of total income for all businesses surveyed, and approximately 7.2% of total income reported by those businesses surveyed who received orders via the internet or web during the period.

Exhibit 1: Orders for Goods and Services Via the Internet of Web (Australia)				
	2000/01	2001/02	2002/03	2003/04
Businesses which placed orders via the internet or Web (%)	20	25	2S	31
Businesses which received orders via the internet or Web (%)	9	6	13	12
Internet income (m AUD (€) billion)	9 (5.2)	11 (6.3)	24(13.8)	33(19.6)
Source: ABS-BUIT 2003/4 {doc. 8129.0)				

In comparison, for the year 2003, internet income was approximately 1.4% of total income for all businesses surveyed, and approximately 4.9% of total income reported by those businesses surveyed who received orders via the internet or web during the period. Of the 34,000 businesses estimated to be receiving internet income in 2003-04, 44% generated 5% or more of their total income in this manner.

A good deal of e-commerce activity, however, still appears to be conducted by rather simple means. Businesses which received orders via the internet or web were asked to identify ways in which these orders were received. Businesses could identify more than one way of receiving orders. E-mail not linked to a website was the most common method (81% of businesses received orders in this way). Orders received via an e-mail linked to a website was reported by 30% of businesses, 15% of businesses received orders through a website online order form and only 6% received orders through a web site shopping-cart facility.

Of these businesses that accept online orders, 86% indicated that their systems which are used to receive orders did not have automated links to any other business system.

E-Business Monitoring in Canada

Institutional Background and Main Surveys

Statistics Canada (*www.statcan.ca*) has been active in monitoring developments in ICT-induced transformations and e-business adoption and usage by Canadian enterprises. Its research in several aspects of ICT-related phenomena include the size, growth and significance of the ICT sector, the penetration and use of ICT by households and individuals, business and government connectivity and engagement in e-commerce. Much of Statistics Canada's work in this area is shared internationally, in a quest for common knowledge and learning.

Additionally, the Canadian e-Business Initiative (CeBI), a private sector-led partnership located within the Electronic Commerce Branch of Industry Canada, aims to foster Canada's e-business success by focusing on productivity, leadership and innovation issues (*www.cebi.cal*).

The main survey dedicated to the collection of e-commerce related data in Canada is SECT (Survey of Electronic Commerce and Technology). SECT is based on the narrow OECD definition of internet commerce transactions and measures the income resulting from internet orders for goods and services, with or without online payment. Included is the value of orders received over the internet. Sales using electronic data interchange over proprietary networks and transactions conducted on automatic teller machines are excluded. Businesses are stratified by type of activity. Statistics Canada has conducted annual surveys to measure ICT use by business since 1999 (and since 2000 under the name of SECT).

Main Results

Online sales by Canadian companies and government departments grew substantially for the fifth consecutive year in 2004, but e-commerce still accounted for less than 1% of total operating revenues for private businesses.[2]

Sales from B2B amounted to CAD 19.8 (€12.3) billion, which represented about 75% of total e-commerce by private firms, up from only 68% the year before. The value of business-to-consumer (B2C) sales in 2004 amounted to CAD 6.6 (€4.1) billion.

Findings confirm the importance of firm size in conjunction with the sector of activity – Sales from one business to another are still concentrated in large, private

2 Data reported are taken from several issues of The Daily. Statistics Canada's official release bulletin. Some additional data are taken from reports of the Canadian Business Initiative's (CEBI) Net Impact Study IV of 2004.

sector companies. In 2004 these large firms accounted for 63% of business-to-business sales. Smaller retailers were more likely to sell to households. Sales to households accounted for less than 24% of the value of online sales by large firms. Small firms, those with fewer than 20 employees, reported that 41% of the value of their online sales was to households. Overall, e-business adoption by SMEs was found to grow only slowly.

Exhibit 2: Value of Internet Sales (Canada)

		2000	2001	2002	2003	2004
		Internet Sales With or Without Online Payment (in CAD / € million)				
Private Sector	CAD	5,549.8	6,336.6	10,815.3	18,164.4	26,438.0
	€	4,054.9	4,572.6	7,309.7	11,495.3	16,373.6
Public Sector	CAD	111.2	180.3	263.6	756.5	1,881.5
	€	81.2	130.1	178.2	478.8	1,165.3
TOTAL	CAD	5,661.0	6,516.9	11,078.9	18,920.9	28,319.5
	€	4,136.1	4,702.7	7,487.9	11,974.1	17,538.8

Source: The Daily, April 20, 2005 (based on Statistics Canada. SECT 2004).

From a sector perspective, four sectors (wholesale, transportation and warehousing, manufacturing and retail trade) accounted for about two-thirds of online sales by private companies in 2004, virtually unchanged from the year before. For the fourth consecutive year, the wholesale trade sector accounted for the largest value of e-commerce sales. Wholesalers sold over CAD 6 (•3.7) billion worth of goods online in 2004, nearly one-quarter of total private sector e-commerce. Firms in the transportation and warehousing sector were second with about CAD 4.6 (•2.8) billion in sales, or 17% of the total.

E-Business Monitoring in Japan

Institutional Background and Main Surveys

In Japan, a decentralised statistical system is adopted. Basic and common statistical surveys, for instance the Population Census are conducted by the Statistical Survey Department of the Statistics Bureau, Ministry of Public Management, Home Affairs, Posts and Tele-communications (MPHPT), while other statistical surveys necessary for the policy-making of the ministries and agencies are conducted within their respective jurisdiction.

Within this framework, the Japanese Statistics Bureau *(www.stat.co.jp/)* plays a key role. The Bureau is responsible for coordinating the statistical activities of different ministries. The Bureau is part of the Ministry of Internal Affairs and Communications (MIC). Several surveys are conducted by the Japanese Statistics Bureau that address issues related to electronic business development. Topics include the engagement of companies in e-commerce, the ratio of e-commerce by industry, by networks used, by partners for trade, and by size of enterprise.

One of the main surveys on ICT use by enterprises and organisations is CUTS (Communications Usage Trend Survey). CUTS consists of two sub-surveys:

- CUTS Offices-Establishments, which MPHPT carries out annually as a nation wide sample survey to 5.600 establishments with more than 5 regular employees;
- CUTS Enterprises, which MPHPT carries out annually as a nation wide sample survey of 3,000 enterprises with more than 100 regular employees.

An important other data source is ECOM (Electronic Commerce Promotion Council of Japan), which conducted a joint e-commerce survey with the Ministry of Economy, Trade and Industry (METI), and NTT Data Institute of Management Consulting in 2002.

Main Results

According to the CUTS 2003, nearly 80% of corporations surveyed had established a website in 2003. Positive responses were comparatively higher in the service industries, including financial and insurance services.

30% of corporations responded that they had implemented B2B (Business-To-Business) e-commerce, while 11.5% said they practised B2C (Business-To-Consumer) e-commerce. From a sectoral perspective, manufacturing firms were most likely to use B2B (34%), while financial and insurance firms were leaders in B2C use (26%). While the percentage of companies that used B2B e-commerce increased in most sectors from 2002 to 2003 (with the exception of financial services), the share of firms that engaged in B2C had stagnated or even slightly decreased. In financial services for example, the percentage had dropped from 31% to 26% (rounded), in 'services and other services' from 17% to 14%.

75% of corporations said they had invested in computers and other ICT equipment over the last year (i.e., in 2002). The most common purpose of IT investment given was "to improve business efficiency and speed" (85%). Out of the companies that had made investments, 71% observed a positive effect on their business.

B2B was projected to account for close to 90% of total e-commerce sales in 2005, down from 99% in 1998. B2C was estimated at roughly 10% (up from a 1% in 1998). In B2B trade, electronic commerce already accounts for about 14% of total revenues. In B2C markets, e-commerce is estimated to account for 4.5% of revenues

Broadband adoption: At the end of 2004, about 74% of companies (with 100 or more full-time employees) that used the internet had introduced Cable TV lines, DSL lines, optical lines or wireless access. The maximum bandwidth exceeded 1.5 Mbps in 61 % of companies.[3]

E-Business Monitoring in Korea

Institutional Background and Main Surveys

The Korean National Statistical Office (KNSO - *http://www.riso.ao.kr/enalish*) collects, monitors and disseminates data and information on ICT adoption. However, it is not the only relevant source for information on e-commerce and e-business. Various organisations are involved in promoting e-commerce through research and project implementations in co-operation with the Korean government.

KNSO has developed a set of indicators measuring changes of the knowledge and information society and is monitoring and measuring changes in e-business at a national scale. Its definition of e-commerce coincides with that of the broad

3 Ministry of Internal Affairs and Communications (2005). Information and Communications in Japan. Stirrings of u-Japan. White Paper 2005.

OECD definition. KNSO monitors the adoption of e-business in Korea mainly by means of two dedicated surveys:

- a monthly B2C survey, called 'Cyber Shopping Mall Survey', and
- the quarterly B2B and B2G survey, which is called the 'e-Commerce Survey.

Both surveys measure the type of e-commerce, the amount of e-commerce sales/purchases, and the number of business establishments involved. The monthly 'Cyber Shopping Mall Survey' (B2C) was first released in August 2000. The 'E-commerce Survey on Enterprise' (B2B) was first released in June 2001. and the 'E-Commerce Survey on Government' (B2G), being incorporated into the B2B survey, was first released in September 2001. The two surveys were approved as designated statistics in February 2004 by the Korean Statistics law.

Main Results

Korea has gained much ground in e-commerce According to KNSO's "Report on the E-Commerce Survey" (2004), the total e-commerce transaction volume was KRW 235.Q25 billion (• 176 billion) in 2003 (including B2B, B2G and B2C transactions). This is a growth of 32% from 2002. Data for the 1st quarter of 2004 indicated further growth of about a third compared to 2003.

B2B has emerged as the major type of e-commerce accounting for close to 90% of the transaction volume in 2003 (see Exhibit 3) B2B has also shown the highest growth rates over the past few years. In 2003 the e-commerce transaction volume in inter-firm trade increased by more than 30%.

B2C has also significantly increased by about 20% in 2003, according to KNSO. However, the total transaction volume accounts for only about 3% of total e-commerce. Nevertheless, further growth is expected for the years to come in line with a trend that can be observed for many countries these days. In the case of Korea the fast catching-up in household internet penetration (compared to the late 1990s, when other advanced economies were still ahead of Korea in that respect), coupled with the general rise of the internet may well lead to extraordinary growth rates in future B2C e-commerce. Back in 2002, approximately 20% of all internet users in Korea were identified as B2C

Exhibit 3: E-business Volume in Korea by Type of Customer (B2B, B2G, B2C)

	billion KRW	ratio	billion KRW	ratio	billion KRW	Changeover previous year +/- rate
Total E-Commerce	177,810 (€ 151 b)	100.0	235,025 (€ 176 b)	100.0 (€ 25 b)	57,215	32.2
Business-to-Business (B2B)	155.707	87.5	206.854 (a)	88.0	51,147	32.8
Business-to-Government (B2G)	16.632	9.4	21,634	9.2	5,002	30.1
Business-to-Consumer (B2C1)	5.043	2.8	6,095 (b)	2.6	1,052	20.9
Other	427	0.2	442	0.2	15	3.5

Notes:

(a) KRW 206,654 billion for B2B is the sum of KRW 206,336 billion estimated by the E-commerce survey on Enterprise and KRW 518 billion by the Cyber Shopping Mall Survey.

(b) KRW 6.095 billion for B2C and 21.634 billion KRW for B2G were estimated from the results of the Cyber Shopping Mall Survey & E-commerce Survey and Government respectively.

Source. KNSO, 2004.

e-commerce users. It can be speculated that this percentage has significantly increased since.

"Closed transactions" (i.e., transactions between large corporations and their long-term suppliers) accounted for about two thirds of the total e-commerce transaction volume in 2003. "Open transactions" (i.e., transactions via bidding or open markets) accounted for about one third.

E-Business Monitoring in the USA

Institutional Background and Main Surveys

The most important authority for measuring e-business in the United States of America is the US Census Bureau of the Department of Commerce (*DoC. www. census, ciov/eos*). Pre-eminent collector and disseminator of timely, relevant, and quality data about the people and the economy of the United States. The Census Bureau conducts a population and housing census every 10 years, an economic census every five years, and more than 100 demographic and economic surveys every year, all of them evolving from the first census in 1790.

E-Stats *(www.census.doWestats)* is the US Census Bureau's internet project site devoted exclusively to Measuring the Electronic Economy. It features recent and upcoming releases, information on methods, classification systems, and background papers.

ICT and e-business-related data are collected mainly through the following Census Bureau surveys:

- The Annual Survey of Manufacturers (ASM),
- The Annual Trade Survey (ATS),
- The Service Annual Survey (SAS),
- The Annual Retail Trade Survey (ARTS) and
- The Economic Census."[4]

Another relevant source is the US Economics and Statistics Administration (ESA -httcs:*/Vwww.esa.doc.aov'i*) which publishes the "Digital Economy" reports. The latest one was the Digital Economy 2003 report, the Department's fifth annual report on conditions in US information technology industries and the effects of ICT on national economic performance.

Main Results

The latest edition of E-Stats, the official news bulletin of the US Bureau of Census (May 11, 2005) reported the following e-commerce highlights for the USA:

- E-commerce, on a percent change basis, outperformed total economic activity in all four major economic sectors (i.e., manufacturing, merchant wholesale, retail trade, service industries) measured between 2002 and 2003. For example, in manufacturing the percentage change in shipments was 1.5% in total, but 12.1% for e-commerce. E-commerce as percent of total shipment increased from 19% in 2002 to 21% in 2003[5].

---

4 In 1999, the Census Bureau conducted the Computer Network Use Survey (CNUS). Results of CNUS have been frequently used in ICT related research in combination with evidence from the annual industry surveys mentioned.

5 Source: *http://www.census.gov/eos/www/papers/2003/tu- hichnis*

- Business-to-Business (B2B) activity, which depends critically on Electronic Data Interchange (EDI) dominated e-commerce. For example. EDI as percent of total sales in merchant wholesale trade increased from 10.5 to 11.3% from 2002 to 2003.
- Most e-commerce occurred in a handful of industry groups within each sector. Among 21 manufacturing industries, for example, transportation equipment manufacturing accounted for almost 40% of the e-commerce shipment value, followed by chemical manufacturing which accounted for 10%.

While more comprehensive synthesis results for all industries, as reported by E-Stats, are only available for the year 2003, data for US retail e-commerce sales are collected and reported on a quarterly basis. Historically, the US Bureau of Census has begun collecting e-commerce sales from retailers included in the monthly retail survey (sample of about 12,000 retailers) in October 1999. Since then, data has been collected quarterly, which allows precisely tracking the growth of e-commerce.

Exhibit 4 shows data for US retail e-commerce sales as percent of total quarterly retail sales for the time period of 1999 to 2004. It shows that e-commerce retail sales represent a slowly, but steadily increasing share of total retail sales, in terms of both value and volume. The total e-commerce retail sales volume (in millions of dollars) has been estimated at USD 13.4 billion (•14.3 billion) for the fourth quarter of 2004, an increase of 47% from the third quarter of 2004 (left axis). Total e-commerce retail sales amounted to only 2.0% of total retail sales in the fourth quarter of 2004 (right axis). However, this e-commerce volume is nearly twice as large as that of 2001 (1.1%) and almost four times as large as 1999 (0.6%).

The steady growth of e-commerce is also supported by the fact that the growth rate of total retail e-commerce for the first quarter of 2004 was 28% (compared to 2003), while the rate of growth of total retail in the same period was only 9%. A report by UNCTAD[6] projects this positive trend to continue:

---

6 UNCTAD (United Nations Conference in Trade and Development) (2004). E-Commerce and Development Report 2004, Geneva

Notes:

(a) Estimates are adjusted for seasonal variation and holiday and trading-day differences, but not for price changes.

(b) E-commerce sales are sales of goods and services where an order is placed by the buyer or price and terms of sale are negotiated over an internet, extranet, Electronic Data Interchange [EDI] network, electronic mail, or other-online system. Payment may or may not be made online.

Source: US Bureau of the Census (2004).

"On current trends, retail e-commerce in the United States could amount to USD 100 billion by mid-2006, at which moment it could represent between 25 and 30% of total retail sales in that country" (p. 12).

Synopsis of Findings and Comparison to the EU

Exhibit 5 provides a comparative overview of the main instruments used for collecting e-business data in the five countries, and highlights some of the main results of these monitoring activities. As outlined in the sections above, e-business monitoring activities in Australia, Canada, Japan, Korea and the USA differ in their structure and focus. Therefore, the international comparability of results from different sources is limited and problematic. A truly international benchmarking of e-business developments requires special studies that have the resources to conduct primary research on their own. This also applies to the comparability of data with results for European enterprises. Some general conclusions, however, can be drawn regarding the state-of-play of e-business in Europe.

Exhibit 5: Overview of International E-business Monitoring Initiatives and Snapshots of Key Results

	Australia	Canada	Japan	Korea	USA
Main Survey(s)	Business Use of Information Technology Survey (BUIT)	Survey of Electronic Commerce and Technology (SECT)	At least 41 official statistical surveys with questions related to ICT use. Most relevant for E-Business: CUTS (Communications Usage Trend Survey), EEC (Establishment and Enterprise Census), and Surveys by ECOM (Electronic Commerce Promotion Council of Japan)	Cyber Shopping Mall Survey E-commerce Survey on Enterprise (B2B)	Data are collected in five separate Census Bureau surveys, focusing on different segments of the economy: for manufactures (ASM), wholesale trade (ATS), services (SAS), retail trade (ARTS), and the Economic Census.
Sampling Frame	ANZSIC	NAICS	JICS	KSC	NAICS
Snapshots - Main Findings	85% of firms use a computer, 74% use the internet and 25% have a web presence. 31% of firms place orders on the internet (+3%-points compared to 2002/03). 12% have received orders via internet or web. Out of those, 44% generated 5% or more of their total income in this way.	The volume of e-B2B transaction is CAD 19.8 (-12.3) billion, representing 75% of total e-commerce by private firms. The volume of e-B2C transactions is CAD 6.6 (-4.1) billion (25% of total e-commerce). 7% of firms, representing 27% of gross business income, engage in e-commerce.	In 2003, 80% of corporations had a website, 30% engages in B2B e-commerce, 12% in B2C e-commerce. While B2B increased, B2C was stagnating. Projections for 2005 estimate that e-commerce will account for 14% of total B2B and 4.5% of total B2C trade volume.	B2B transactions account for about 88% of total e-commerce. In 2003, the B2B transactions volume increased by more than 30% compared to 2002. B2C transactions account for about 3%, B2G (Business-to-Government) for about 9% of electronic transactions. B2C increased by 20% in 2003.	E-commerce accounts for 16.3% of total B2B and 2.0% of total retail sales. 92.7% of total e-commerce is B2B, 7.3% B2C. In manufacturing, e-commerce accounts for more than 20% of the total value of shipments. E-commerce outperforms total economic activity in all sectors studied.
Main Trends Identified	Dynamic overall development, but stagnation in the percentage of firms that sell on the internet	B2B sales drive e-commerce growth. E-commerce has high growth rates, but still accounts for less than 1 % of total e-commerce sales. B2C has recently stagnated	The major e-commerce adopter in the Asia-Pacific region. B2B drives the development, accounting for close to 90% of total e-commerce sales. B2C has recently stagnated.	Enormous growth rates in e-commerce; e-transaction volume grew by 32% from 2002 to 2003, and by 31% from 2003 to 2004 (1st quarter comparison). 2003	B2B is dominating, but B2C retail e-commerce is growing fast, particularly in specific sectors (e.g. books, textiles).
Reference Year	2003/4	2004	2005 (projected)	2003	2004

Source: Developed by E-Business W@tch (2005) from various international sources.

Similar State-of-Play in E-Business in Advanced Economies

Most e-business data indicate that the maturity of ICT adoption and e-commerce activity among enterprises is at a similar stage in all major economies. The percentage of enterprises' total turnover from e-commerce, for example, appears to have reached similar levels in Europe (EU-25), the USA and Australia with about 7-10% in each of these economies.[7] This indicates that the significance of e-business activity for sales transactions is comparable, at least on the aggregate level.

However, as argued in the summary box below, gaps are more pronounced when comparing individual ELJ Member States. Eurostat reports that enterprises from the EU-25 make 8.6% of their total turnover from e-commerce.[8] Figures vary considerably between Member States. For Greece, for example, Eurostat reports a share of 1.6% of turnover, for Poland 2.8%. In contrast, shares are highest for Ireland (20%), the UK (13.7%), Denmark, Finland, Sweden and Germany.

Exhibit 6: Main Conclusions on the Performance of EU Enterprises in E-business

- **Head-to-Head:** On average, EU enterprises are head-to-head with their counterparts in other advanced economies in terms of electronic business activity.
- **Gaps within the EU:** However, gaps in E-Business adoption within the European Union (between Member States) are clearly more pronounced than on aggregate level in international benchmarks, that is between firms from the EU-25 and the USA, Australia or Japan (and others). Of course, the same observation could be made for other large economies, notably for the USA, where digital divides between states or regions also exist.
  - EU countries as international benchmark: Firms from those EU Member States which are most advanced in their information society development (the Nordic countries in particular) are not only 'e-leaders' within the EU, but constitute international benchmarks of ICT infrastructure adoption and E-Business activity.

Contd...

[7] Sources: Eurostat (EU); ABS-BUIT 2003/4 (ALPS). US Census Bureau 2005 (USA).

[8] Eurostat survey on ICT use by enterprises (2004). Data for this indicator are available on the Eurostat website *http.//epp.eurostat.cec.eu.int/portal/page?* paciekl=0.1136195.0 45572097& dad=portal& schema=PORTAL (downloaded in July 2005) Percentages relate to the base of enterprises with at least 10 employees and using computers.

Contd...

- Major EU economies aligned with international development: Many EU countries are well aligned with the international state-of-play in E-Business. This holds true for some of the major economies in the EU, for example the UK Germany, the Netherlands and Spain. For France and Italy, results are mixed; some indicators point at a lower adoption of E-Business activity.
- Digital divide concerns mostly the 'third tier1: ICT and E-Business adoption is comparatively low among firms from EU Member States which constitute the least advanced group in information society development. This group includes some of the newEU Member States, Greece and Portugal.

• Cultural similarities reflected in E-Business activity? International findings on E-Business activity are strikingly comparable in particular for Europe (EU-25). the USA. Canada and Australia. Results for Japan and South Korea suggest some differences in specific areas, 48 notwithstanding that the overall dynamic is still similar. The same observation could be made for countries within the EU, where Member States with a similar culture show comparable patterns in E-Business adoption.

Recommendations for Policy

Considering the importance of ICT as a driver and enabler of globalisation processes, further initiatives to facilitate the international comparison of e-business developments and their impacts should be encouraged. There are several possibilities how this goal can be addressed. Three approaches are suggested as feasible options. They are discussed in more detail, in terms of their requirements, strengths and weaknesses, in the full special report.[9] These options are not necessarily substituting or excluding one other. The proposed measures can also be conducted in parallel. In particular, approach 1 should be viewed as a complementary and preparatory activity in relation to either approach 2 or 3.

An improved international cooperation in e-business monitoring would certainly make sense, both in terms of effectiveness and efficiency. International cooperation can be expected to be effective, as it creates an added value when (national) monitoring results can be put into an international perspective. Cooperation will normally also be efficient, as the total cost of the individual efforts involved should not be significantly higher than if carried out without coordination. There are more arguments for an increasingly international

9 See *www.ebusiness-watch.org* ('resources')

Possible Policy Approaches for Improving the Availability of Internationally Comparative E-business Data

Approach	Focus	Potential initiator(s)
1. Coordination of methodology development	• Focus on development of common definitions, guidelines and instruments • Encourage adoption of these instruments in as many surveys as possible	• OECD • UN • Statistical Working Groups • Official Statistical Offices in EU. USA Japan etc • Government (Ministries or departments responsible for E-Business) • European Commission • EU Research Programmes (FP 7) • World Bank
2. International cooperation of official statistical institutes	• The (European) Community Survey on ICT Use in Enterprises as a model for an international survey • Central coordination of methodology development • Local data collection in participating countries • Implementation of an international observatory	
3. The International E-Business W@tch	• Observatory put in charge of collecting data and preparing reports • Possibly in international cooperation (e.g., EU - USA)	

orientation in monitoring activities. These include demand for a better understanding of causal links between e-business developments and international (cross-border) trade developments, implications for SMEs, and impacts on growth, productivity and employment in different parts of the world.

(This article is based on the "European e-business Report 2005", the 4th Annual Synthesis Report by the e-business w@tch of the European Commission, Enterprise and Industry Directorate General. E-Business w@tch was launched by the European Commission in late 2001 to monitor the growing maturity of electronic business across different sectors of the economy in the European Union. The observatory has analysed ebusiness developments and impacts in about 20 manufacturing, financial and service sectors since. All publications are available on the internet at www.ebusiness-watch.org. E-Business w@tch is implemented by an international research team which is coordinated by empirica GmbH, Germany (www.empirica.com). Editor of the "European e-business Report 2005": Hannes Selhofer, empirica GmbH., Germany (www.empirica.com).)

Section III

Applications and Cases

12

E-Tourism: An Innovative Approach for the Small and Medium-Sized Tourism Enterprises (SMTEs) in Korea

Chulwon Kim

This paper deals with e-tourism, innovation and growth. The Internet is revolutionising the distribution of tourism information and sales. The Korean Small and Medium-sized Tourism Enterprises (SMTEs) with well-developed and innovative Websites can now have "equal Internet access" to international tourism markets. This paper examines problems and solutions related to electronic commerce in the tourism industry and suggests recommendations for successful e-commerce strategies in tourism to be applied by the industry and the government of Korea.

Introduction

The definitions of tourism innovation (e.g., product, service and technological innovations) remains unclear, with the exception maybe of the Internet. New technologies can produce an essential contribution to tourism development.

For tourism businesses, the Internet offers the potential to make information and booking facilities available to large numbers of tourists at relatively low costs. It also provides a tool for communication between tourism suppliers, intermediaries, as well as end-consumers. OECD (2000) revealed that the advent of Internet-based electronic commerce offers considerable opportunities for firms to expand their customer base, enter new product markets and rationalise their business. WTO (2001) also indicated that electronic business offers SMEs the opportunity to undertake their business in new and more cost-effective ways.

According to WTO, the Internet is revolutionising the distribution of tourism information and sales. An increasing proportion of Internet users are buying on–line and tourism will gain a larger and larger share of the online commerce market. Obviously, the Internet is having a major impact as a source of information for tourism. However, the SMTEs are facing more stringent impediments to the adoption of new information technology, in particular, e-business. Part of the problem relates to the scale and affordability of information technology, as well as the facility of implementation within rapidly growing and changing organisations. In addition, new solutions configured for large, stable, and internationally-oriented firms do not fit well for small, dynamic, and locally-based tourism firms.

Despite these challenges, SMTEs with well-developed and innovative Websites can now have "equal Internet access" to international tourism markets. This implies equal access to telecom infrastructure, as well as to marketing management and education. According to a UN report (2001), "it is not the cost of being there, on the online market place, which must be reckoned with, but the cost of not being there." It is certain that embracing digital communication and information technology is no longer an option, but a necessity. Thus, one of the most important characteristics of electronic commerce is the opportunity and promise it holds for SMTEs to extend their capabilities and grow.

Recent Research on E-Commerce in Tourism Industry

The study of e-commerce in the tourism industry has emerged as a 'frontier area' for information technology. The literature on e-commerce in the tourism industry was critically reviewed with a view to developing a framework suitable for this study. E-commerce is defined as the process of buying and selling or exchanging products, services and information via computer networks including the Internet (Turban, Lee, King & Chung, 2000). However, adoption of Information and Communication Technologies (ICT) is only part of the story. In particular, network access costs, dissemination of information on electronic commerce, training, skill development and human resources provide big challenges for smaller companies.

The difficulty in addressing issues of trust and confidence also makes SMTEs more vulnerable than large firms to problems linked to authentication/certification, data security and confidentiality and the settling of commercial disputes (Buhalis, D. & Schertler, W. 1999, OECD, 1999).

However, a SME Electronic Commerce Study done by APEC reported that "Small and medium enterprises are significant players in business-to-business electronic commerce, which constitutes more than 80 percent of the entire e-commerce activities. SMEs that can demonstrate their capabilities to use e-commerce will have a competitive advantage in the e-commerce marketplace."

Many researchers suggested that government plays an important role in facilitating the use of electronic commerce for the tourism industry and in increasing their ability to reap the benefits, (e.g., via awareness building and training programmes). Governments in partnership with the private sector should establish a more comprehensive and consistent policy approach towards the tourism industry and electronic commerce, and apply evaluation mechanisms to assess what works and does not work (UN 2001, OECD, 2000, Korea Information Society Development Institute 2000, APEC-TEL 1999).

Key Factors for Successful E-Commerce for SMTEs

Research was performed to collect the secondary data regarding e-commerce for the tourism industry. Based on those data, a questionnaire was developed to get information on the challenges and opportunities faced by the tourism industry. The survey covered e-commerce activities, benefits, barriers and key success factors. It covered essentially the Korean SMTEs. SMTEs are defined as businesses that have 300 or fewer employees or sales from $2 million to 20 million, depending on the characteristics of business.

Benefits of E-Commerce for SMTEs

Respondents considered that the main benefits of e-commerce for tourism enterprises are 'providing easy access to information on tourism services,' 'providing better information on tourism services,' and 'providing convenience for customers'. This result implies that respondents are less aware of many other benefits of e-commerce, such as 'creating new markets,' 'improving customer services,' 'establishing interactive relationships with customers', 'reducing operating cost', 'interacting with other business partners', and 'finding new business partners' (Figure 1).

Figure 1: Benefits of E-Commerce

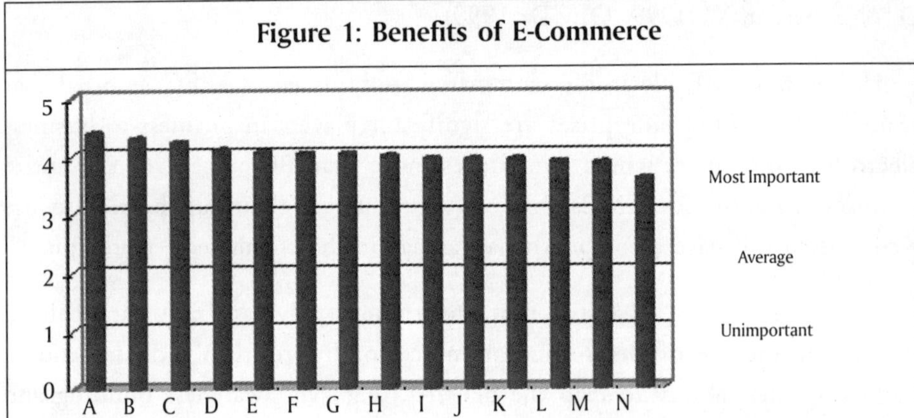

A: Providing easy access to information on tourism products and services B: Providing better information on tourism products and services C: Providing convenience for customers D: Expanding choices by customers E: Creating new markets F: Establishing interactive relationship with customers G : Improving customer services H : Improving image and public recognition of the small & medium sized tourism enterprises I: Saving time for providing tourism services J: Providing customized & specialized tourism products & services K: Reducing operating cost L: Simplifying the process business M: Interacting with business partners N: Finding new business partners

Barriers of E-Commerce for SMTEs

There are a number of barriers for SMTEs in adopting e-commerce in Korea. These barriers include 'limited knowledge of available technology,' 'lack of awareness,' 'cost of initial investment,' 'lack of confidence in the benefits of e-commerce,' and 'cost of system maintenance.' These barriers also include 'shortage of skilled human resources,' and 'resistance to adoption of e-commerce.'

In terms of market situation, one might also mention 'insufficient e-commerce infrastructure,' and 'small e-commerce market size' (Figure 2.).

Figure 2: Barriers to Adopting E-Commerce

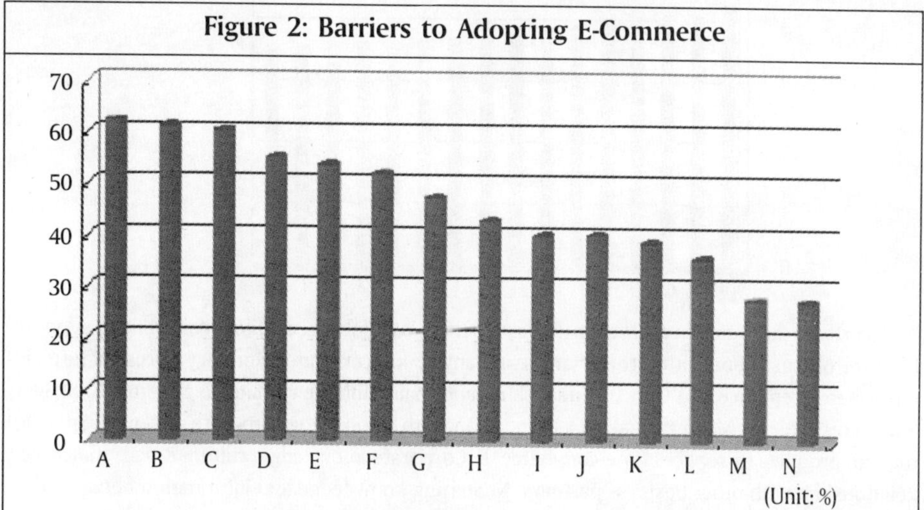

A : Limited knowledge of available technology B: Lack of awareness of e-commerce C : Cost of initial investment D : Lack of confidence in the benefits of e-commerce E: Cost of system maintenance F: Cost of securing skilled human resources for e-commerce G : Shortage of skilled human resources H: Difficulty with integrating e-commerce & existing system I: Cost of training human resources for e-commerce J: Insufficient e-commerce infrastructure K: Lack of government support L: Relatively small e-commerce market size M : Fear of changes incorporate culture N: Resistance to adoption of e-commerce

Factors for Successful SMTEs E-Commerce Practices

The two main factors for conducting successful e-commerce are 'security of the e-commerce system' and 'user-friendly Web interface', thus recognising that building customer trust and convenience for customers are essential to succeed. 'Top management support,' 'IT infrastructure,' and 'customer acceptance' were also considered as important factors. On the other hand, most SMTEs do not recognise the importance of 'sharing knowledge and information between SMTEs' and 'business partnerships' as (Figure 3) as e-commerce successful strategies.

Importance and Performance of SMTEs' E-Commerce

The study used Importance and Performance (IP) analysis to examine e-commerce strategies. For 'Importance' respondents indicated the importance of each of the

Figure 3: Important Factors for Successful E-Commerce

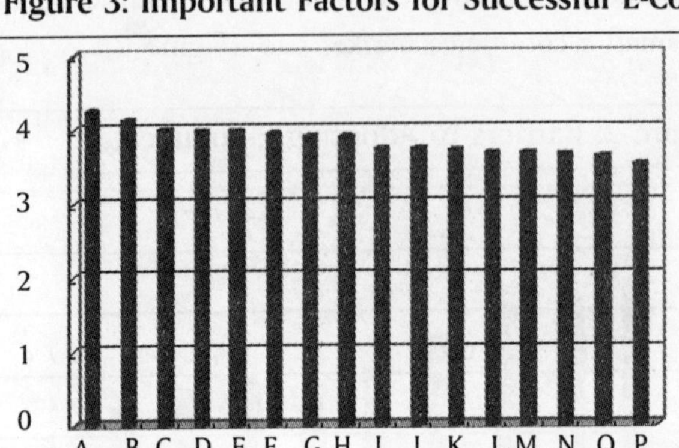

A : Security of the e-commerce system B: User-friendly Web interface C: Top management support D: Level of trust between customer and company E: Information technology infrastructure F: Customer acceptance G : Cost of establishing and maintaining e-commerce system H : Skilled human resources I: Market situation J: Integration w ith the existing corporate system K: Specific tourism products or services for e-commerce L: Corporate know ledge, culture & acceptance M: Relationship w ith other business partners N: Sharing know ledge and information between the small & medium-sized tourism enterprises O : Internal communication P : Government support.

16 proposed factors for a successful implementation of e-commerce by SMTEs. For 'Performance,' respondents indicated how well their member economy performs regarding e-commerce, in relation to their response to 'Importance.'

Four IP categories emerge from this analysis. The 'Keep up the good work' category means that both 'Importance' and 'Performance' are high. The category 'concentrated efforts' refers to 'high importance' and 'low performance' responses. The 'low priority' category refers to 'low importance' and 'low performance' responses. The 'Possible overkill' includes 'high performance' with low importance".

Keep up the Good Work

Respondents considered the following factors as important; 'Security of e-commerce,' 'User-friendly Web interface,' 'IT (Information Technology) infrastructure,' 'Level of trust between customer and company,' 'Customer acceptance.' All factors are strongly related to consumer issues such as security and user convenience. These factors were also considered as relatively well-performed.

Concentrated Efforts

The factors in this category include 'Top management support' and 'Skilled human resources'. These factors are considered as very important for implementing e-commerce, but are considered as performed insufficiently. Thus, more efforts need to focus on these factors.

Low Priority

'Government support,' 'Sharing knowledge and information between SMTEs,' 'Integration with the existing corporation,' and 'Relationship with other business partners.' received low marks in importance and performance. These factors, however, are actually critical to successful e-commerce of SMTEs. This implies that managers have limited information and knowledge on e-commerce. More information should be delivered to entrepreneurs about the importance of those factors.

Possible Overkill

'Market situation' falls in the 'Possible overkill' category. According to the survey results, managers of SMTEs utilise the Internet for market analysis (may include competitor analysis), but do not consider this factor as important. Researchers believe that this result has some discrepancy with previous reports that SMEs (Small and Medium-Sized Enterprises) usually do not use the Internet for market research.

Remainder

Three factors including 'Specific tourism products or services for e-commerce,' 'Corporation knowledge, culture, and acceptance,' and 'Internal communication' fall somewhere between 'Low Priority' and 'Possible overkill.' One factor, 'Cost of establishing and maintaining e-commerce system' is between the 'Concentrated efforts' and 'Keep up the good work' categories. These factors were assessed relatively similarly as 'low importance' and 'middle performance.'

Figure 4: Importance-Performance (I-P) Analysis

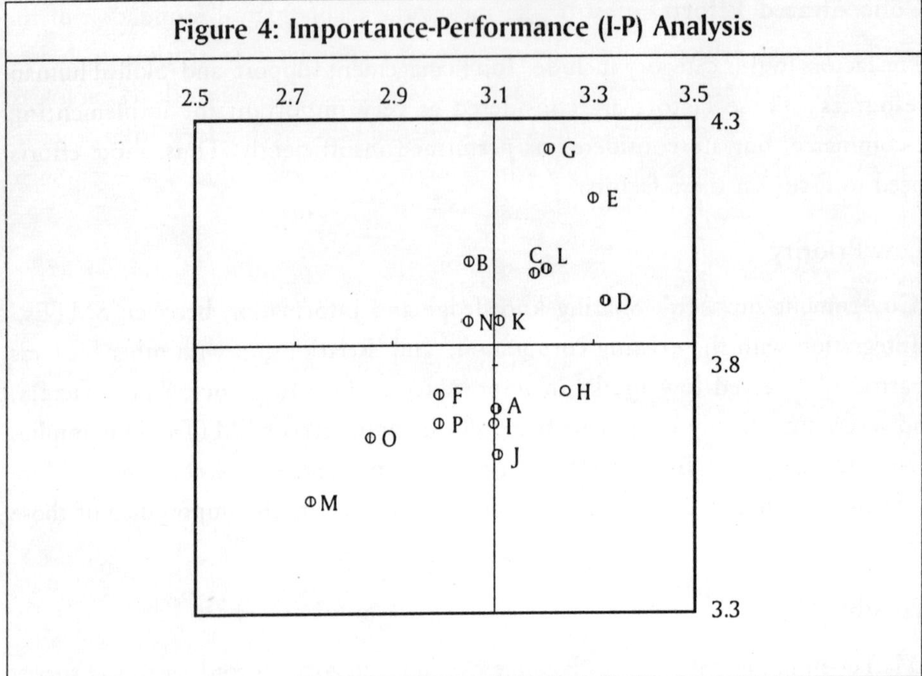

A: Specific tourism products or services for e-commerce B: Top management support

C: Information technology infrastructure D: Customer acceptance

E: User-friendly Web interface

F: Integration with the existing corporate system G: Security of the e-commerce system H: Market situation

I: Corporate knowledge, culture and acceptance J: Internal communication

K: Cost of establishing and maintaining e-commerce system L: Level of trust between customer and company M: Government support

N: Skilled human resources

O: Sharing knowledge and information between the small & medium sized tourism enterprises.

E-Commerce Strategies for Innovation of the SMTEs

For Rayport and Jaworski (2002), e-commerce strategy should be implemented with the four critical forces – technology, capital, media, and public policy infrastructures. An infrastructure is defined as the foundation of a system. E-commerce strategies refer to these four infrastructures:

- The technology infrastructure means the technological foundation of the Internet, which enables the running of e-commerce enterprises, including the hardware of computers, servers, routers, cables, network technologies, software, and communications. Understanding technology infrastructure – and thus understanding what is and is not achievable – is essential to formulating travel and tourism's vision and strategy.
- The capital infrastructure relates to how to secure funding for an e-business and subsequently value that business.
- The media infrastructure is an important issue for all e-commerce managers because the Internet is a mass communication platform. Managers who run online enterprises must learn to manage a staff responsible for design interface, stylistic choices, and editorial policies, and content choices associated with the new communication venue. Therefore, the e-commerce manager is now a publisher of digital content on the Web. He/she should make choices about the types of media employed (e.g., print, audio, video), the nature of the media, and editorial policy, including style, content, and look-and-feel.
- Finally, all of the decisions related to technology, capital, media, and strategy are influenced by laws and regulation, that is, public policy decisions. The public policy infrastructure affects not only the specific business, but also direct and indirect competitors. E-commerce managers should understand both the current laws and how the laws may affect their businesses and those around them.

This paper suggests different strategies according to the e-commerce infrastructure of the business and stage of e-business development:

- Internet start-up SMTEs should adopt a business model appropriate for their own e-business objectives and environments. External service providers have great potential for them. Marketing should be done selectively. Earning a good reputation in the local market should be the top-priority. Internet start-up SMTEs can develop a strategy to access international markets directly to sell their tourism products and services.

- Established SMTEs should focus on two key strategies: 1) expanding the range of services and products and 2) upgrading their quality. They should re-design their Websites to focus more on 'customer retention' than 'customer acquisition' to ensure quality of service. The Internet is a useful tool to reach international markets. E-partnerships between SMTEs or large firms are important. They should utilise their resource to build an e-community.

Their e-business strategies should be formulated according to their business environments. Linkage to a site of Destination Management Organization (DMO) is critical to success. Development of an online booking system is the most important technological aspect. Various measures to overcome lack of trust and confidence of consumers should be taken, such as utilization of 'about us,' 'Frequently Asked Questions (FAQs),' and 'call center' services. Established SMTEs should consider e-strategy issues, including: 1) target market segments, 2) building trust and confidence of e-consumers, and 3) expanding e-commerce activities.

Implications for Tourism Policy

The role of government is very important. The key principle is that the private sector leads the market. The government should avoid creating undue obstacles to e-commerce and its aims should be to support and enforce a predictable, minimal, consistent and simple legal environment if governmental involvement is needed. Active government support to foster an entrepreneurial culture is important. Key policy agendas include; 1) improving the legal and regulatory framework, 2) moving government procurement on line, and 3) facilitating e-transformation in industry sectors.

Legal and regulatory issues should consider consumer protection, legal resource mechanisms in disputes (e.g., e-commerce mediation committee), intellectual property protection, and validity and enforcement of contracts. The policies covers the issues such as what taxes should apply to Internet transactions, the identification and residence of users, and the problem of tax avoidance. The guidelines of international organisations such as APEC and OECD can be a basis for e-commerce laws and regulations. To support consumer trust and confidence, a programme of e-trust certification could be effective. Online government procurement and government participation in e-transformation of industry sectors should be planned and implemented in the medium- and long-term. Government support can be provided in tax reductions, monetary support, and sharing of knowledge and information between industries and research organisations.

In Korea, a pilot project aims to construct a B2B network in all key industries. The government has also implemented a 'System to Certify Venture Tourism Business,' which indirectly supports the industry. In 2001, 11 companies were selected as venture tourism businesses and can receive support and benefits. Applications for the status of venture tourism are evaluated twice a year. Most domestic software companies in Korea do not have distribution channels of their own. Therefore, they pay a commission of almost 40% to distributors of their products. This is a major disadvantage in the competitive market. To solve this problem the government established a software cybermall. The Internet shopping mall, which opened in 1998, provides product demonstrations and the ability to purchase products electronically. The mall is linked to the sites of many vendors.

Finally, government could help the growth of e-commerce in various ways through, planning, creating the legal and regulatory framework, building capacity in information technology infrastructure, skill formation and manpower planning, and also undertaking promotional and incentive measures. The government should function as a facilitator, promoter, educator, and 'anchor tenant' for testing and pilot deployment of new applications. It is expected that OECD member countries facilitate international strategic alliances at Government-To-Government (G2G) and Industry-To-Industry (I2I) levels and help local firms to grow, regionalise and also globalise. Government can also help create markets in emerging areas at the initial stage and help remove regulatory obstacles that may impede the growth of markets and businesses. Again, the ultimate objective of the government remains the promotion of private sector initiatives in e-commerce development (Kahn, 2002).

Conclusions: Recommendations for E-Tourism Innovations

In conclusion, this paper suggests some recommendations for decision-makers, entrepreneurs and practitioners in the tourism industry field, particularly for

SMTEs. These recommendations are made to the Korean e-tourism market, however, they can probably apply to the tourism industries in other countries.

The government should develop a national vision, a strategic plan and policy guidelines for SMTEs e-commerce activities. The development of e-commerce strategies should involve all tourism stakeholders. The policy-makers are also responsible for establishing the appropriate laws, regulations and service standards that will enable to build trust and consumer confidence.

Entrepreneurs need to adopt business models which are tailor-made for their own e-business objectives and the SMTEs environment. SMTEs can combine various e-business models. External service providers have great potential to assist SMTEs.

Stakeholders should also find ways to integrate SMTEs into industry-wide associations. This will encourage SMTEs to stop competing at the destination level, and to develop networks for mutual benefit. In line with this co-operation, they need to formulate and implement networking or strategic alliances through partnerships with other SMTEs or large firms, especially in the area of brand management, customer relationship management, and human resources management.

As regards marketing, association with e-shopping will allow SMTEs to conduct Internet-based e-commerce without bearing all the start-up costs, improvements cost, advertising and technical difficulties, which could be shared by all the merchants in the mall instead. Associations of e-shopping will provide SMTEs with the opportunity to take advantage of e-commerce systems e.g., interactivity, mass customisation, real time and a database of customers.

In the established stage, SMTEs may need to re-design their website to focus more on 'customer retention' than 'customer acquisition'. They should also try to develop and manage their own digital brand. Brand power is more important on line than off line because the main stage of e-business is the virtual world where consumers are more dependent on recognised brands.

Finally, both the policy-makers and the entrepreneurs should work together to raise awareness of e-commerce through training and education for stakeholders, employees and consumers. E-commerce cannot be implemented without empowering and enabling tourism stakeholders to take advantage of new Internet and e-commerce technologies.

(Chulwon Kim, Professor, College of Hotel and Tourism Management, Kyunghee University, Korea.)

References

"Asia-Pacific Economic Cooperation (APEC)" (1999). SME Electronic Commerce Study, TEL50/97T

Briggs, S (2001). "Successful Web Marketing for the Tourism and Leisure Sectors", Kogan Page.

Buhalis, D & Schertler, W. (1999). "Information Communication Technologies in Tourism" 1999, SpringerWien. NewYork.

Dayal, S, Landesberg, H & Zeisser, M (2000). "Building Digital Brand", The McKinsey Quarterly, Number 2.

Khan, H (2002). "Best Practices on E-Commerce Strategies for SMTEs in Singapore, APEC" International Tourism Symposium, Seoul.

Korea Information Society Development Institute (2000). "The Activation of E-commerce for SMEs in APEC Region".

Organization for Economic Co-operation and Development (OECD) (2000). "Realizing the Potential of Electronic Commerce for SMEs in the Global Economy", Conference for Ministers responsible for SMEs and Industry Ministers. Bologna, Italy.

Plant, R (2000). "E-Commerce: Formulation of Strategy", Prentice Hall.

Rayport, JF & Jaworski, BJ (2002). "Introduction to E-commerce", McGraw Hill.

Trepper, C (2000). "E-Commerce Strategies", Microsoft.

Turban, E, Lee, J, King, D, & Chung, H M (2000). "Electronic Commerce: A Managerial Perspective". p 451.

"United Nations Conference on Trade And Development (UNCTAD)" (2001). E-commerce and Development Report 2001.

World Tourism Organization (WTO) (2001). "E-business For Tourism, Practical Guideline For Tourism Destination and Business".

Why Should Countries Embed ICTs into SME Policy

– Carol Chyau

Summary

Most governments have policies to encourage the growth of local Small- and Medium-Enterprises (SMEs), because they can help to alleviate poverty by increasing income levels and creating jobs. As the global economy becomes increasingly reliant on Information Communication Technologies (ICTs) to receive, process, and send out information, SMEs in developing countries should not be left behind. Otherwise, they will lose out on opportunities to integrate into the global supply chain, bid for outsourcing businesses, and increase productivity.

This APDIP e-Note highlights three main ways ICTs can benefit SMEs: (1) increase productivity in the production process; (2) increase efficiency of internal business operations; and (3) connect SMEs more easily and cheaply to external contacts, whether locally or globally.

Despite the obvious and concrete benefits that ICTs can bring to SMEs, SMEs in most developing countries have been slow to adopt it. At the same time, most governments have not embedded ICTs into SME policy. This APDIP e-Note introduces examples of how Asian governments have launched initiatives to encourage and enable SMEs to use ICTs.

Hong Kong targets training at different sectors; Japan provides tax rebates for SMEs using ICTs; Republic of Korea provides a web forum for SMEs to showcase their products to an international market; Philippines is working to reduce the cost of international phone calls by deregulating Voice-over-Internet Protocol; and Singapore subsidizes computer training for SMEs employees and provides the foundation for developing secure e-payment services.

Introduction: Why are SMEs Important to Poverty Reduction?

"The only way to reduce poverty in a sustainable way is to promote economic growth, through wealth and employment creation. In developing countries, SMEs are the major source of income, a breeding ground for entrepreneurs and a provider of employment." ~ United Nations Industrial Development Organization

The idea that SMEs can promote economic growth is not a novel one. While the definition of SMEs, which is usually based on employment, assets, or a combination of the two, varies from country to country,[1] SMEs usually make up a very significant part of the economy. In fact, SMEs in Hong Kong comprise 98 percent of total manufacturing establishments.[2] SMEs can fuel economic growth because it creates new jobs, expands the tax base, and is a driver of innovation.

How can Governments Support the Growth of SMEs?

Since SMEs have great potential to drive economic growth, the best response for governments is to support SMEs by removing constraints and creating an enabling environment. Some policies to encourage the growth of SMEs include:

- Simplify registration and other legal processes
- Create incubators and science parks
- Provide business skills education

1 In Thailand for example, SMEs are firms with less than 200 employees for labour intensive sectors and less than THB100 million (USD2.43 million) for capital intensive sectors. In Indonesia, SMEs are firms with less than 100 employees.

2 APEC Centre for Technology Exchange and Training for SMEs *<http://www.actetsme.org/hong/hong98.htm>*

Contd...

Contd...

- Provide business consulting services
- Provide SME financing
- Help create SME linkages with larger companies
- Implement favourable tax and trade policies

What Benefits do ICTs Bring to SMEs?

The information revolution has transformed the way modern businesses are conducted. ICTs have enabled people to exchange large amounts of information quickly and cheaply. Those who can best receive, process, and innovate now become the winners.

We are in the era of the knowledge economy where those who have access to ICTs are closely connected to a virtual network regardless of geographic location, race, and gender.

Given this context, ICTs can benefit SMEs in three main ways: (1) increase productivity in the production process; (2) increase efficiency of internal business operations; and (3) connect SMEs more easily and cheaply to external contacts, whether locally or globally. This all falls under the term, e-business.[3]

Concrete examples of how ICTs can benefit SMEs include the following:

- Improve inventory management systems
- Decrease wastage in production processes
- Improve communication between different departments within the firm
- Improve accounting and budgeting practices
- Reduce communication costs and geographic barriers with global suppliers and clients
- Expand client base through e-marketing (e.g., websites, portals and mailing lists)
- Link to local and global supply chains and outsourcing opportunities
- Share and learn new business practices
- Facilitate capacity building of owners and employees through e-learning platforms
- Simplify government services such as business registration and filing taxes
- Introduce new methods of payment through e-commerce

Why Should Governments Embed ICTs into SME Policy?

Despite the obvious and concrete benefits that ICTs can bring to SMEs, SMEs in most developing countries have been slow to adopt it. Even in a technology savvy country such as the Republic of Korea, the industrial information index for its three million SMEs is still below 50 percent.[4] SMEs are faced with constraints such as:

- Limited ICT literacy
- High fixed cost (purchasing hardware and software, disrupting existing business practices, and IT maintenance)
- Poor communication infrastructure leading to high costs of accessing ICTs

[3] UNDP-APDIP's e-primer on e-commerce and e-business defines e-business as, "the transformation of an organization's processes to deliver additional customer value through the application of technologies, philosophies, and computing paradigm of the new economy." (p.6)

[4] Survey by Korea Information Management Institute for SMEs.

Contd...

Contd...

- Inexperience in integrating ICTs into the business process
- Undeveloped legal policy for electronic payment and security issues

Several countries have launched initiatives to overcome these obstacles:

Limited ICT Literacy

Singapore launched an Infocomm Competency Programme from November 2003 to March 2005 to increase the computer literacy of its workforce. The programme subsidized SGD5.00 (USD3.00) per trainee per hour for SMEs on broad-based ICT courses such as Office applications, desktop publishing, workgroup applications, and webpage design.[5]

High Fixed Cost

To encourage SMEs to use ICT equipment to increase productivity, the Japanese government allows corporations to deduct up to 6 percent of total lease payment on brand new machines from annual income tax payments. The government also subsidizes up to 25 percent (with a cap at JPY2.5 million or USD22,000) lease payments for corporations in agribusiness management, lumber supply, and aquaculture.[6]

Poor Communications Infrastructure

The Philippines National Economic and Development Authority (NEDA) is pushing for the full deregulation of Voice-over-Internet Protocol (VoIP)[7]. In most parts of the world, governments are more inclined to ban VoIP, because it is in direct competition with state-owned telecom companies and will decrease government revenues from incoming international call tariffs. NEDA however, firmly believes that VoIP can help spur "growth, investment, and jobs" because it can reduce charges for international calls by 75 percent.[8] Skype, the leading programme for VoIP now has more than 27 million users worldwide, of which 30 percent, primarily SMEs, use it for business purposes.[9]

Inexperience in Integrating ICT into the Business Process

The Hong Kong Productivity Council[10] sponsors various sector-specific programmes that help businesses to increase its productivity through better utilization of ICT resources. Their Enterprise Resource Planning Centre[11] provides training, consulting, and a software platform for its subscribers. In addition, the Vocational Training Council of Hong Kong provides e-learning courses by sector.[12]

5 National Infocomm Competency Centre, Singapore *<http://www.nicc.org.sg/products/icp_introduction.aspx>*

6 Leasing Policies *<http://www.leasing.or.jp/english/industry/effect1.html>*

7 VoIP (also called Internet telephony) is essentially a phone network that uses the Internet. It is the method by which voice is digitized and transmitted over Internet Protocol in digital packets rather than in the traditional circuit-committed protocols of the public switched telephone network.

8 NEDA Press Release, 22 February 2005 *<http://www.neda.gov.ph/ads/press_releases/pr.asp?ID=559>*

9 IT for SMEs: Cost savings by making the switch, UK Financial Times, 23 March 2005.

10 Hong Kong Productivity Council *<http://www.hkpc.org>*

11 Hong Kong Enterprise Resource Planning Centre *<http://www.e-factory.org>*

12 Hong Kong Information Technology Training and Development Centre *<http://www.ittdc.org>*

Contd...

Contd...

The Korean government created the Korean Market Place Website[13] to showcase products of Korean SMEs to global buyers. Local SMEs can easily connect to the global network by posting offers to buy or sell products. It currently hosts over 20,000 homepages of SMEs and e-catalogues of over 120,000 products.

Undeveloped Legal Policy for Electronic Payment and Security Issues

Between 1998 and 1999, the Singapore government passed the Electronic Transaction Act[14] and Electronic Transactions Regulations[15] to legitimize electronic signatures in the legal framework. This provided a foundation for key public and private sector leaders, including the Monetary Authority of Singapore, Cisco Systems, and Visa International, to develop more secure e-payment services over a public key infrastructure.

Conclusion

Since ICTs have obvious benefits for the growth of SMEs, governments should embed ICT components into SME policy. However, while some countries have incorporated ICTs into their SME policies, most countries still lack a comprehensive and focused approach. In addition, governments need to recognize that SMEs in different sectors use ICTs differently and will adopt them at different rates.

The willingness of SMEs to integrate e-business practices depends on how much they can directly improve their core business and how much the potential benefits outweigh the definite costs. A tour operator may be more likely to purchase computers and Internet connectivity in order to service its clients than a grocery store owner is willing to convert his/her cash register system into point of sale technology to better manage inventory.

By recognizing these differences and focusing their efforts on removing the constraints for SMEs to adopt ICTs, governments can play an important role in encouraging SMEs to use ICTs to both improve business processes and link SMEs to the global economy.

Acknowledgements

UNDP-APDIP would like to thank Vadim Kotelnikov, Founder, Ten3 Business e-Coach for his comments and contributions to this APDIP e-Note.

[13] Korean Market Place <http://eng.bestsme.com>

[14] Legal Guide to the Electronic Transactions Act 1998.

[15] Salient Features of the Certification Authority Regulations.

13

Walk, Don't Run: E-Business Readiness in Canadian SMEs

*Michelle Saulnier and Philip Rosson**

The Internet is widely regarded as an encouraging entrepreneurship and facilitating international business expansion. If these views are real, then the Internet is of particular importance to Small and Medium-sized Enterprises (SMEs), which stand to gain or lose competitive position as a result of their own and others' actions. Several conceptual models have been proposed concerning the adoption of Internet technology and a growing number of empirical studies shed light on SME practices. This paper adds to our knowledge by reporting results from exploratory research on the readiness of Canadian SMEs to engage in e-business. The study is based on field interviews in 15 SMEs in Nova Scotia, and analysis of their websites. The paper first reports on general e-business implementations to date, supply and demand chain actions, and website features, with comparisons made to those from other jurisdictions. In overall terms, Nova Scotia SMEs appear to have embraced Internet technology similarly to those elsewhere, although

* Corresponding Author

somewhat less fully and more slowly. The paper then attempts to uncover factors related to Internet implementation and, hence e-business readiness. Implementation does not appear to be related to company size, age, market focus, or customer served. Not surprisingly perhaps, the degree to which owners and/or managers regard e-business as being critical to their business is most strongly correlated with Internet implementation.

Introduction

The importance of entrepreneurship to the health and vitality of the economy is by now well known and accepted (Schumpeter, 1934). Such entrepreneurship is often linked to the exploitation of new technologies either through new business formation or changes to existing enterprises. This paper focuses on entrepreneurship and technology adoption. Much has been written in recent years about Internet technology and its potential to change "everything." Although these claims have been exaggerated, the importance of Internet technology is clear. As Porter (2001: 64) writes "The key question is not whether to deploy Internet technology—companies have no choice if they want to stay competitive but how to deploy it." A growing number of studies attest to the importance of the Internet in firm growth and international expansion (Prasad *et al.*, 2001; Dulipovici, 2002; Mustaffa and Beaumont, 2004). This paper reports on the deployment of Internet technology by Canadian Small and Medium-sized Enterprises (SMEs). The study is exploratory in nature, (1) presenting data on the readiness of 15 Nova Scotia SMEs to engage in e-business, (2) making comparisons to the readiness of companies in other parts of Canada, and (3) examining factors that might explain the behaviour in question.

Before framing the study within the literature, clarification of several terms is in order. In this context "e-business" refers to business that is transacted over the Internet, including the buying and selling of goods and services, management of customer relationships, and collaboration with business partners. "E-commerce" is a subset of e-business, involving the processes whereby goods and services are exchanged online. "Internet marketing" is often used synonymously with e-commerce, but is increasingly used to connote those activities that support an enterprise's online marketing objectives, including driving traffic to the website, running online promotions, interacting with customers through e-mail, etc.

SMEs and the Internet

The literature on the adoption and impact of Internet technology on business is substantial, but as is the case with any new field, current knowledge is based more on speculation and anecdote than scientific evidence. This is changing as a more theoretical approach is brought to bear on the behaviour in question, and as findings from empirical studies are published. The latter typically involve small-scale research efforts employing either a case study or survey approach to understanding company practices.

Frameworks developed in the fields of innovation, information systems, marketing, and international business typically guide these theoretical and empirical approaches. In this section, a number of relevant contributions from the literature are discussed. The following headings are employed: (1) Internet benefits and barriers, (2) Internet adoption, stages and impacts, (3) the Internet and international expansion, and (4) Canadian SME practices.

Internet Benefits and Barriers for SMEs

Numerous lists have been developed of the benefits that Internet adoption can confer on companies. One identifies the following benefits: abolition of distance and time; better supply chain management; process acceleration and automation; marketing and promotion efficiencies; enhanced customer relations; and greater efficiency and bargaining power (Mustaffa and Beaumont, 2004). Other researchers (Piers and Aisbett, 2003) identify more than 50 benefits from their review of the literature (as well as 40 disadvantages). These are alluring possibilities for all companies but are particularly attractive for SMEs, which stand to gain much from efficiency improvements and ready access to new markets and customers.[1] The benefits of Internet technology are viewed as potentially "leveling the playing field" for SMEs located in peripheral regions of developed nations or,

1 For some companies, Internet technology is the basis for the business. Although it was ultimately closed down, Napster is perhaps the best example of a company for which the Internet was "everything" (Menn, 2003).

indeed, those located in developing countries. Research from Atlantic Canada (Industry Canada, 2000) provides some support for the former notion, and from Bangladesh (Prashantham and Young, 2004) and South Africa (Moodley, 2003) for the latter notion. The benefits of Internet technology are recognized by many SMEs, with surveys showing adoption by a large and increasing number of SMEs around the world (Canadian e-Business Initiative, 2003).

Where SMEs have not embraced Internet technology, this is usually for a good reason. Firms in The Netherlands, for example, reported not adopting Internet technology because they were unsure that it would deliver the supposed cost reductions and business efficiencies, or there was a belief that it was not appropriate for a given industry (Walczuch *et al.*, 2000). Another study shows that adoption often occurs as a result of an external "push" rather than as a deliberate strategy. Many Australian SMEs did not invest in Internet technology until they were pressured to do so either by suppliers or, more frequently, by customers (Poon, 2000). Even among those companies that have adopted Internet technology, the benefits are not enjoyed automatically; rather they have to be realized through an investment of time and money—resources that are in short supply in most SMEs. Mostafa *et al.* (2004), argued that the entrepreneurial behaviour exhibited in a company is key to Internet technology adoption and successful use, while other factors (e.g., relationships with distributors, type of product, and level of resources) will either facilitate commitment to the Internet, or act as a barrier to its adoption.[2] In the next section, the steps that often follow initial adoption are outlined.

SME Internet Adoption, Stages and Impacts

Innovative behaviour, such as adopting Internet technology, should not be seen as a single and discrete event. Rather, the adoption decision marks a first step in a continuing commitment to develop new ways of conducting business. Various models have been presented of stages of Internet technology development. Rao *et al.* (2003) identify the factors that facilitate or obstruct the transition from one stage to the next. The stages are: (1) presence—a website that acts as an electronic

---

2 Although the model presented in this research has an international business emphasis, it appears relevant to business operations more generally.

brochure; (2) portals—a website that encourages two-way communication with customers or suppliers; (3) transactions integration—financial exchanges are possible for the first time; (4) enterprises integration—the full integration of business processes means that the old-line business cannot be distinguished from the online business. Cost, technology demands and complexity increase from stage 1 to stage 4. Consequently, none of the SMEs examined had reached the "enterprises integration" stage. Other researchers also offer stage models (Houghton *et al.*, 2001; Buttriss and Wilkinson, 2001), although these incorporate contrasting factors and depict somewhat different processes.

Four of the many factors identified in the literature—on innovation adoption generally and information systems specifically are examined in this study: firm size, age, market focus, and customer served. A firm's resources will determine its ability to invest in new technology, as well as to manage its implementation and development (Thong, 1999; Lal, 2003; Patterson *et al.*, 2003). Company size is frequently used as a measure of the resource base. Organizational readiness has been shown as influencing the adoption of information systems (Mehrtens *et al.*, 2001; Chang and Cheung, 2001).

Company's age is used here as a measure of readiness. New firms and young firms are less fettered by established ways of doing business and thus more open to new technology. In fact, new technology sometimes provides a company's raison d'être. The market focus of a company reflects both its owner/managers' vision and the company's operational base. SMEs that compete in local markets may be viewed as less open to opportunities and/or less pressurized by competitors than others and, thus, less likely to innovate through technology adoption (Lal, 2003; Grandon and Pearson, 2004). A final factor of interest concerns the type of customer served. The initial uptake of Internet technology was seen most strongly in the Business-To-Consumer (B2C) domain (UCLA, 2003), whereas its application in a B2B environment was often seen as less appropriate (Oppel *et al.*, 2001). Accordingly, operating in a B2C setting is a fourth factor examined below.

Two other studies should be mentioned at this point. Feindt *et al.*,'s (2002) report on Internet start-up companies that have achieved high rates of growth. These small companies (5–49 employees) have progressed from start-up, through a growth and maturity stage, to become higher volume, more mature businesses in a short period of time. Critical success factors of various types were identified, including four (content, convenience, control, and interaction) that are relevant from the outset for all companies involved in e-commerce. In terms of impact, Mustaffa and Beaumont (2004) find that implementing Internet technology does indeed produce intermediate benefits. This research also reveals some strong relationships between Internet adoption and final benefits such as cost reduction, revenue growth, and sustained competitive advantage.

The Internet and SME International Expansion

One of the most frequently cited benefits of Internet adoption is that it opens up world markets to SMEs.[3] It therefore follows that theoretical and empirical attention has focused on the link between e-commerce and international business behaviour. An example of the former is provided by Samiee (1998), who distinguishes between the ability of the Internet to improve business processes and generate revenue, and makes the point that these advantages will appeal differently to a "sporadic" as opposed to "experienced" exporter. Chrysostome & Rosson (2004) discussed the role that the Internet can play in SME internationalization, concluding that there are both beneficial and problematic aspects. Thus, while foreign markets may be entered more quickly and effectively, cost savings may be hard to achieve, legal issues persist, and competition is likely to become more intense. Theories of internationalization and agency/transaction costs are used by Petersen *et al.* (2002) to examine the potential effect of the Internet on foreign market expansion. Three possible outcomes are envisaged: modest expansion, faster expansion, and rash foreign market expansion. Loane *et al.* (2004) describe the influence of Internet technology on the international development activities and paths of SMEs in Europe and North America. This work supports the idea that "marketspace"[4] (Brock and Berry 2004) is relevant in firm internationalization.[5]

---

3 The corollary is that open markets lead to more competition.

4 The term marketspace is used to connote the virtual world of digitized information, which has the potential of significantly reducing information and resource-related barriers to company expansion, particularly for SMEs.

5 "Internationalization" is the "process of increasing involvement in international operations" (Welch and Luostarinen, 1988).

A number of conceptual models have resulted from case study research. Tiessen *et al.* (2001), for example, developed a model of SME international e-commerce from an examination of 12 Canadian companies in two sectors that serve the Japanese market. In this model, a company's international web use (resource commitment, functional sophistication and cultural adaptation) is influenced by external factors (market changes and industry norms) and firm factors (capabilities and business relationships[6]). Another example is provided by Chulikavit and Rose (2003), whose work in Thailand lead them to identify factors (e.g., the creativity, markets, products, experience and information access of the firm) that are likely to influence the use of e-commerce to increase export performance.

Canadian SME Practices

Numerous studies reveal that Canadian companies have made steady progress in adopting Internet technology. Some 78% of firms reported using the Internet and online sales reached $19.1 billion in 2003, representing a 40% increase over 2002 (Industry Canada, 2004). The increased influence of the Internet is explained to a degree by leading practices in the US and that nation's ownership of key sectors of the Canadian economy. Another factor is the commitment made by the federal government to position Canada as a leader in e-business, which has led to various policy changes and support programs. Organizations such as the Canadian e-Business Initiative (2002, 2003) and Industry Canada (2004) report in detail on levels and trends in Internet technology adoption, and provide comparisons with other countries. Venkat (2001) provides an Atlantic Canada perspective on the Internet as an enabler of export expansion.

Recent research reveals that Canadian SMEs tend to lag larger companies in the adoption of Internet technologies, but usage levels are greater among "innovative" SMEs when compared to their non-innovator counterparts. The main reasons reported for non-adoption are that Internet-based transactions are

---

6 The Internet was earlier expected to cause widespread "disintermediation" (or make it possible to circumvent traditional business networks and trading relationships). In most settings this has not happened; SMEs and others are therefore forced to integrate Internet technology within existing channels to market, making the best of Internet efficiencies and the face-to-face contact provided by intermediaries. See Prashantham and Berry (2004) on the Internet and business networks.

inappropriate for the products or services in question, and that face-to-face interaction is preferred. Security concerns and website costs are less frequent barriers to adoption (Gault & Earl 2004). Most Canadian companies have yet to progress much beyond the promotional or basic transactional level with their websites (Computing Canada 2003). Further, buying online (37% of companies) is much more prevalent than selling online (7%) (Industry Canada, 2004). However, use of the Internet is shown to impact on the growth of Canadian SMEs, their performance expectations, and export behaviour (Dulipovici, 2002). Case studies illustrate that Internet-based methods have been successfully employed by SMEs in entering international markets or expanding foreign business operations (Rosson, 2004). The picture that emerges from these studies is that at the macro level the e-business readiness of Canadian companies is on a par with those in other developed nations, but that some ground is being lost as SMEs elsewhere accelerate their use of Internet technology. At the micro level, however, individual Canadian SMEs are successfully exploiting the technology.

The Present Study

Scope

The primary objective of the study was to examine the e-business readiness among SMEs in Nova Scotia, Canada. Data was collected in the summer of 2003. The first phase of the research was carried out through on-site interviews in 15 companies that had recently received assistance from consultants under an e-business mentoring program funded by the Atlantic Canada Opportunities Agency (ACOA), a regional development agency. The objective of the mentoring program was to provide advice that would enhance business efficiency and international trade prospects. In order to build on existing knowledge and to facilitate comparisons, the questionnaire employed was modeled on one used in a similar study carried out in Ontario (Ontario, 2001). The respondents were either business owners (60%) or senior managers (40%), and the interviews took an average of one hour to complete. Both quantitative and qualitative questions were posed, focusing on matters of strategy, technology infrastructure, and e-business applications. In the second phase of the study, a detailed review was conducted of each of the SME's websites. The objective here was to assess design and content features of the websites. The work of Nielsen (2003) guided the examination of website usability, while Boisvert's (2002) approach was used in studying website functionality. Since one company no longer had a website at the time of the study, and another had pages on a third party's site, the analysis on websites is based on data compiled for the remaining 13 SMEs.

The Study Sample

The SMEs studied are profiled in Table 1. Whether measured in terms of sales revenues or employees, most of the companies are small; 60% of the companies have less than $2 million in annual revenues and two-thirds have 20 employees or less.[7] Although the majority of companies (40%) were established from five to ten years ago, new and longer established entities were also included. The sample is dominated by manufacturing enterprises (87%), which operates in a variety of industrial sectors. Companies providing services to consumer and business markets make up the balance. Regarding the market focus of companies, most were firmly rooted at home, where they generate a median of 80% of revenues in the regional market, and 12% in markets in the rest of Canada. The US was also a significant market for many companies, as shown by the number serving that market and the revenue data (median = 20%). Only one SME was active outside of North America, generating 60% of its revenues in Europe, Asia and Latin America.

Descriptive Findings

General e-Business Readiness

The overall e-business readiness of companies is indicated by their Internet strategies and technical capabilities. For the most part, SME owner/managers saw e-business to be important to their business, particularly in terms of reaching customers and partners in new markets, and in effecting efficiencies through streamlining internal operations. The extent to which these general statements about e-business have been turned into concrete action is reflected in data shown in Table 2.

---

7 One company with a much larger workforce and higher sales is an outlier in the present sample. Revenues and employee numbers were highly correlated ($r = 0.636$, $p \leq 0.01$, one-tailed). Neither revenues nor employee numbers were associated with company age.

Almost one-half of SMEs have implemented one or more e-business initiatives, 33% are in the process of making such an implementation, and the remaining 20% plan to do so. Two-thirds of respondents agreed that e-business was a top priority of the SME's senior management, but fewer (40%) reported that this objective had been turned into a robust vision or strategy. Even fewer (27%) agreed that e-business priorities had been translated into successful training programs for professional staff. The lack of a concrete strategy and trained staff perhaps explains why just 38% of SMEs agreed that they had the necessary infrastructure in place to execute e-business initiatives. Fewer still (19%) felt the company was equipped with e-business applications that would permit significant growth in operations. Although not shown in Table 2, this situation is not the result of the negligence. Fully 87% of SMEs reported having spent "substantially" or "somewhat more" money on e-business initiatives in the previous two years, with 100% of companies expecting to invest more in the next two years. Further, 40% of companies indicated that major suppliers had integrated some of their business processes into the SME's e-business systems. This most frequently took the form of transfer payments through online banking and ordering supplies online.

The SMEs surveyed had recently received e-business and export advice offered through an ACOA support program. Whether SMEs will be able to use such advice to their advantage is not clear. Although most of the companies valued the advice received about marketing from their websites and how technologies affect internal efficiency, many reported implementation challenges and/or barriers. Time (69%), people (63%) and financing (56%) were most frequently stated to be problem areas. Other challenges/barriers mentioned were skills (38%), market information (19%), and legal/regulatory issues (6%).

Supply and Demand Chain Actions

Companies were asked questions about e-business initiatives in their supply and demand chains. Slightly more than one-half of the companies reported making purchases through online marketplaces. Table 3, presents responses to other supply chain questions. Responses are relatively uniform across the three areas of initiative. Whether it is placing orders, tracking order status, or online information, the number of SMEs providing positive and negative responses are split almost equally.

One-third or more companies have an e-business implementation in process or already done, with another 20% at the planning stage. Others do not intend to make supply chain changes. In 13% to 33% of the companies, this is explained by the non-critical nature of e-business to overall operations.

The data on demand chain initiatives are more encouraging. SMEs have already achieved more implementations, have more in process and planned than was the case for supply chain initiatives. Completed implementations (40%) were greatest in the areas of order placement and customer care. The record for order tracking and online billing initiatives was less stellar, with respectively 7% and 13% of the SMEs having made implementations to date. However, considerably more initiatives are in the pipeline. As was the case for supply chain developments, because e-business is not seen as critical to operations, between 13% and 27% of SMEs will not make demand chain changes. A final indicator of demand chain e-business implementations is that 60% of SMEs drive traffic to their websites through portals, affiliated sites, banner ads, and online marketplaces. The majority (47%) employed one to five methods to encourage website visitors, with six to 10 methods, and more than 10 methods each used by 7% of companies.

Website Usability and Functionality

The SME websites were inspected with respect to the ten most violated design guidelines, as identified by Nielsen (2003). Table 4, shows the percentage of Nova Scotia SMEs that do not violate these principles (i.e., are in compliance). The mixed nature of the results is striking. On the first five items, companies score quite strongly, whereas the reverse is true for items six to nine. It is not obvious why Nova Scotia SMEs would score very well on some design guidelines but poorly on others (see below). The two final items merit separate mention. First, Nielsen does not deal with foreign language content. However, given the interest in internationalization among Nova Scotia SMEs, the use of languages other than English on the website was recorded. In fact, none of the sites provided foreign language content. This is not surprising, given the SMEs' present emphasis on domestic and US markets. However, it indicates an area for attention when non-English speaking markets are targeted and might well discourage unsolicited enquiries currently. Second, item 10 in Nielsen's list of guidelines concerns stock quotes. The SME emphasis meant that this item was not relevant in this study.

In addition to meeting customer (and other) needs regarding usability, websites should satisfy certain functionality requirements. Boisvert's (2002) approach was employed in assessing the websites of Nova Scotia SMEs. The scores shown in Table 5, indicate the extent to which 18 website's functions were represented on the websites examined. As was the case with usability, the results varied substantially from one functional feature to another. Companies scored well on the following features: "identification" (94%); "FAQS/discussion forum" (66%); and "services/ locations" (57%). However, many functionality features were absent; 13 of the 18 features are represented on less than one in 20% of the sites. Notable among the low scores are "security" (0%) and "privacy" (9%) features.

Comparative Analysis

E-Business Readiness

In order achieve greater perspective; some of the Nova Scotia findings on e-business readiness are now compared with those from a study conducted in Ontario (Ontario, 2001). Any comparison of the data must recognize some inherent limitations. First, the two studies were undertaken at different points in time, with two years separating the fieldwork in Ontario (2001) and Nova Scotia (2003). Second, the size of the two samples differs. The Ontario data is based on responses from 180 SMEs, whereas that in Nova Scotia is much smaller (15 SMEs). Third, the composition of the two samples varies. On average, Ontario companies are less often manufacturers (55% versus 87%), more often in services (26% versus 13%), and are larger entities (e.g., 8% have less than $2 million in revenues versus 60%). Despite differences in the two samples, it is instructive to compare the results from Nova Scotia with those from Ontario.

Ontario SMEs have a stronger record of e-business implementation (59% versus 47%), whereas Nova Scotia companies have more implementations in process (33% versus 13%). It appears that Ontario companies show a greater and earlier degree of general e-business readiness. This is also suggested by data showing that Ontario companies score higher on evaluating competitor' websites (60% versus 53%), providing professional staff training in e-business (34% versus 27%), and having the infrastructure necessary to executive their e-business initiatives (50% versus 33%).

The results for supply chain initiatives yield no clear pattern of differences between the two provinces. The degree to which orders are placed and tracked online differs, but not greatly. In contrast, Ontario SME use of the Internet for online and billing information is twice the level in Nova Scotia (80% versus 40%). Other findings include: 40% of SMEs in both provinces report having integrated some business processes with major suppliers, and Nova Scotia companies purchase supplies online more often (47% versus 37%) than those in Ontario. However, it is difficult to take too much from these findings.

Demand chain initiatives were more evident in both provinces than those in the supply chain. There is also a reasonably consistent pattern of implementation – customer care functions have been most frequently provided (Ontario 66% versus Nova Scotia 87%), followed by ordering online (O 61% versus NS 80%), and order status tracking (O 57% versus NS 60%). Access to billing functions has received less attention (O 40% versus NS 60%). Nova Scotia SMEs score higher on all four areas of activity. They also report greater use of methods to drive traffic to their websites (50% versus 44%).

Comparisons of Nova Scotia and Ontario SMEs reveal that the latter exhibit a greater degree of e-business readiness in general. Regarding supply chain initiatives the record of companies in both locations is somewhat similar. Demand chain initiatives have occurred at a somewhat higher level and with a similar emphasis in both provinces with Nova Scotia SMEs appearing to lead those in Ontario. These comparisons should again be viewed in the context of the study timing and sample composition differences mentioned earlier.

Website Usability and Functionality

With regard to website usability, the Nova Scotia results are compared to those reported by Nielsen (200?). No concrete information is presented about the number or composition of the companies assessed by Nielsen. However, a sense is given that these might be in the hundreds and that large companies are included as well as SMEs. No other data are reported regarding these usability measures and so, despite likely sample differences, these are the only comparisons that can be made at this time. On four of Nielsen's guidelines, Nova Scotia SMEs score higher than the comparison group: "graphics" (95% versus 35%); "breadcrumbs" (66% versus 39%); "active link" (53% versus 41%); and "offer" (46% versus 27%). The low compliance rate of Nova Scotia companies on other usability guidelines was noted above. Not surprisingly, the comparison group score higher on these items: "access" (6% versus 37%); "liquid layout" (0% versus 28%); "search" (0% versus 40%); and "colour links" (0% versus 33%). Thus, Nova Scotia companies are strong on some guidelines and weak on others, in comparison to data presented by Nielsen.

In terms of functionality, comparisons are made between the websites of Nova Scotia SMEs and those of their counterparts in Ontario and Quebec. The latter data are provided by Boisvert (2002) in his study of 5,935 SMEs in a wide variety of industry sectors. For 13 of the features, Nova Scotia SMEs exhibit lower levels of functionality, while for three features similar levels are evident. In only two instances ("FAQs/discussion forum" and "accreditation") did Nova Scotia SMEs score higher than those in Ontario and Quebec. In making these comparisons, it should be recognized that that the Ontario/Quebec research was conducted at least a year earlier that that in Nova Scotia. Thus, lower website functionality scores for Nova Scotia companies gives some cause for concern.

Further Analysis

Having examined the absolute and relative e-business readiness of Nova Scotia SMEs, attention now turns towards the factors which might explain the behaviour. A number of factors identified in the literature as influencing e-business readiness were correlated with variables already discussed, as well as summary variables constructed with this analysis in mind. The variables are listed and defined in Appendix A.

Association with Company Characteristics

Four company characteristics were correlated with 10 e-business readiness variables. Table 6 shows the resulting Pearson product-moment correlation coefficients. Because it is demanding of resources, some view company size to influence e-business readiness. In this study, size was represented by "revenues" and, with the exception of "supply chain actions" ($r = .461$, $p \leq 10$), is not significantly related to e-business readiness behaviour. The age of a company is used here as a measure of organizational readiness to adopt Internet technology. "Company age" is not related to behaviour in this study. Another explanation for e-business readiness behaviour is that, as is the case with other business innovation, this is more likely among companies that are more open to opportunities and pressured by competition.

"Regional sales" was used as a proxy measure: companies with sales concentrated in the Atlantic Canada region were regarded as less open and pressurized. Two of the coefficients show significant result, but these were in the reverse direction to that anticipated. "Process integration" ($r = .453$, $p \leq .10$) and "demand chain actions" ($r = .570$, $p \leq 05$) were greater among SMEs with higher concentrations of regional sales. Finally, the literature suggests that company uptake of Internet technology has been more pronounced among those serving consumer markets (as opposed to B2B). This was not supported in the present study. Two significant coefficients emerged from the analysis: B2C companies exhibited less "readiness for growth" ($r = -.473$, $p \leq .10$) but more "supply chain actions" ($r = .481$, $p \leq 10$) than B2B companies. Clearly, the analysis did not support views expressed in the literature as being linked to ebusiness readiness. Therefore, it appears difficult to profile companies' e-business readiness in terms of general characteristics and/or simple ideas about what drives the adoption of Internet technology.

The Criticality of e-Business and Readiness Responses

It was earlier reported that e-business was considered important in a general way by the SMEs surveyed and, of course, mention was made about their participation in a mentoring program that had an emphasis on the employment of Internet technology. However, in answering questions about supply and demand chain actions, a number of companies indicated that e-business was not critical to their operations. This seemed to be a significant response and one that was worth exploring further. A new variable labeled "e-business non-critical" was therefore developed from responses on seven specific supply and demand chain questions (see Appendix A). When correlated with e-business readiness behaviour, the right-hand column in Table 6 reveals that six of 10 coefficients are statistically significant. Only "readiness for growth," "use of e-markets," "website usability" and "website functionality" are not related to e-business readiness behaviour. Thus, as one might expect, companies have not readied themselves so much if e-business is not seen as critical to the survival and prosperity of their business. The coefficients in the bottom row of Table 6 show that "e-business non-critical" is unrelated to company size, age, or outward focus. It is related, however, to the type of customer served. B2C companies are less likely to view e-business as being non-critical ($r = -.518$, $p \leq .05$) than B2B SMEs.

In order to examine the criticality question further, the sample was divided into groups labeled e-business is "more critical" and "less critical." The resulting mean scores for e-business readiness were compared using the student-t test. The results are shown in Table 7. As expected, SMEs for which e-business is more critical score higher on every readiness variable, with the exception of "website functionality." The difference in the mean scores is significant at the $p \leq .05$ level in the cases of "spending," "process integration," "use of portals" and "demand chain actions."

Concluding Comments

In this section, the research findings are summarized, a number of limitations identified, and suggestions made for future study.

Summary of Results

An examination of the e-business readiness of 15 Nova Scotia SMEs revealed that they had implemented Internet technology to different degrees. In general terms, expressions made about the importance of e-business have not been fully matched by actions taken, particularly in the areas of staff training, technology infrastructure, and applications to deal with growth. Companies have taken more concrete steps within their demand as opposed to supply chains. With regard to their websites, Nova Scotia companies displayed both high and low scores on usability factors and functionality features. These results are more meaningful when compared with others. On the question of general e-business readiness and supply and demand chain actions, Nova Scotia SMEs have embraced Internet technology less fully and somewhat more slowly than their equivalents in Ontario. However, this is a summary statement and on some individual measures, Nova Scotia companies score better. As far as website usability is concerned, Nova Scotia

SMEs score better and worse than those in Nielsen's (2003) data set. Finally, the websites of the companies studied exhibited fewer functionality features than SMEs in Ontario and Quebec. These results suggest that while the importance of e-business is understood, Nova Scotia SMEs appear to lag those in other parts of Canada. A third element in the analysis focused on factors that might explain e-business behaviour. No support was found for an association between behaviour and company size, age, market focus, or customer served. A strong relationship was found between behaviour and the criticality of e-business to the company. A related notion to criticality is "perception of strategic value" (Grandon *et al.*, 2004).

Limitations and Future Research

The present study has a number of limitations. The most obvious of these are sample size, industry sector coverage, measures employed, and cross-sectional methods. The sample size (15 companies) restricts the ability to generalize from this study about Nova Scotia SMEs, let alone SMEs more generally. Small samples also limit the statistical analysis that can be carried out, particularly of sub-groups within the sample. They can also limit the range of response on a given questionnaire item (as was the case with company size and market focus here). Clearly, a larger sample would be preferable in future research (unless deep analysis of a few cases was intended). The sample of Nova Scotia SMEs was drawn from several manufacturing industries and this potentially impacted on the findings since each provides a different operating context for companies. Even sub-sectors of a given industry might provoke different types of e-business responses. For example, a company that runs a catering service for weddings might view e-business quite differently from a food processing company that supplies grocery chains.

Subsequent studies would do well to think carefully about the sample frame from which companies are selected. Research in new fields is hampered by the lack of agreement about what should be measured and how. E-business is no exception: there is little agreement about the constructs or their measurement. In order to make comparisons with other researchers' findings, this study used a questionnaire and website approaches that have been employed elsewhere. In retrospect, however, other approaches may have yielded results that were more illuminating about SME behaviour. This point leads to the next one concerning methods. Cross-sectional approaches such as those employed here often provide a good snap shot of a situation. But pictures at one point in time do not reveal the changes that are taking place, or of the drivers and consequences of change. Few longitudinal studies are undertaken but when they are, they invariably deepen our understanding of change processes.

Like all exploratory research, this paper raises as many (or more) questions as it has answered. However, by providing more empirical data on e-business readiness, making comparisons to SMEs in other locations, and examining factors that might explain behaviour, it is hoped that some contribution is made in this emerging and important area of business activity.

(Michelle Saulnier, Faculty of Computer Science and Philip Rosson, Corresponding Author, School of Business Administration, Dalhousie University).

References

Boisvert, H (2002). "Smart web development". CMA Management, 76 (8), November. Retrieved July 3, 2004 from: *www.managementmag.com/index.cfm/ci_id/583/la_id/1.htm.*

Brock, J & Berry, M. (2004). "Marketspace and the internationalisation process of the firm". Working paper, Strathclyde International Business Unit, University of Strathclyde.

Buttriss G, & Wilkinson I (2002). "Towards a process model of internetalisation: Becoming an e-business". Retrieved July 24, 2004, from: *www.marketing.unsw.edu.au/HTML/mktresearch/workingpapers/Buttriss_Wilkinson03_6.pdf*

Canadian e-Business Initiative. (2003). "Net impact study Canada: The SME experience". A preliminary report, November. Retrieved August 5, 2004, from *www.cebi.ca.*

Canadian e-Business Initiative. (2003). "Net impact study Canada: The international experience". Interim report, May. Retrieved July 15, 2004, from *www.cebi.ca.*

Chang, M & Cheung. W (2001). "Determinants of the intention to use Internet"/ *WWW at work: A confirmatory study. Information & Management, 39, 1–14.*

Chrysostome, E & Rosson, P. (2004). "The Internet and SME internationalization": Promises and illusions. Proceedings, International Business Division, Administrative Sciences Association of Canada Conference, Quebec City, June, CD-ROM.

Chulikavit, K & Rose, J (2003). "E-commerce and the internationalization of SMEs". In H. Etemad & R. Wright (eds.), Globalization and Entrepreneurship: Policy and Strategy Perspectives, Cheltenham, Edward Elgar, 205–222.

Dulipovici, A (2002). "The impact of Internet use in small and medium-sized Canadian businesses during a recession". The 6th. International Francophone Congress on SME, October. Retrieved August 3, 2004, from *www.cfib.ca/research/report/default_e.asp.*

Feindt, S, Jeffcoate, J & Chappell, C. (2002). "Identifying success factors for rapid growth in SME e-commerce". Small Business Economics, 19 (1), 51–62.

Gault, F & Earl, L (2004). "Innovative firms: A look at small firms". Ottawa, Statistics Canada. Catalogue no. 88F0006XIE–No. 010.

Grandon, E & Pearson, M (2004). "Electronic commerce adoption: An empirical study of small and medium US businesses". Information & Management, 41, in press.

Houghton, K, Winklhofer, H & Ennew, C (2001). "Factors affecting the adoption of the Internet for global marketing in UK exporting SMEs: Development of a conceptual model". Proceedings, European Marketing Academy Conference, May, Bergen.

Industry Canada (2000). "E-business in Atlantic Canada: The knowledge economy in action", Ottawa.

Industry Canada (2004). "Highlights from the 2003 Survey of Electronic Commerce and Technology". Retrieved July 3, 2004, from *http://e-com.ic.gc.ca/epic/internet/inecic-ceac.nsf/en/gv00237e.html*

Lal, K (2002). "E-Business and manufacturing sector: A study of small and medium-sized enterprises in India". Research Policy, 31, 1199–1211.

Loane, S, McNaughton, R & Bell, J (2004). "The internationalization of Internet-enabled entrepreneurial firms: Evidence from Europe and North America". *Canadian Journal of Administrative Sciences*, 21 (1), 79–96.

Menn, J (2003). "All the Rave: The Rise and Fall of Shawn Fanning's Napster". New York, Crown Business.

Mehrtens, J, Cragg, P & Mills, A (2001). "A model of Internet adoption by SMEs". Information & Management, 39, 165–176.

Moodley, S (2003). "E-commerce and export market: Small furniture producers in South Africa". *Journal of Small Business Management*, 41 (3), 317–324.

Mostafa, R, Wheeler, C & Dimitratos, P (2004). "Internet-enabled international entrepreneurship: A conceptual model". In M Jones & P. Dimtratos (eds.), Emerging Paradigms in International Entrepreneurship, Cheltenham, Edward Elgar, 155–172.

Mustaffa, S & Beaumont, N (2004). "The effect of electronic commerce on small Australian enterprises". Technovation, 24, 8595.

Nielsen, J (2003). "The ten most violated homepage design guidelines". November 10. Retrieved January 20, 2004, from: *www.useit.com/alertbox/20031110.html*

Ontario (2001). "The wisdom exchange e-business readiness assessment". Report No, 4. Ministry of Economic Development and Trade, Queen's Printer for Ontario, Toronto.

Oppel, K, Hartmann, E, Lingenfelder & Gemunden, H (2001). "Electronic marketplaces—Impact on B2B transactions and relationships?" Proceedings, 17th International Marketing and Purchasing Conference, Oslo, CD-ROM.

Patterson, K, Grimm, C & Corsi, T (2003). "Adopting new technologies for supply chain management". Transportation Research Part E, 39, 95–121.

Petersen, B, Welch, L & Liesch, P (2002). "The Internet and foreign market expansion by firms". *Management International Review*, 42 (2), 207–221.

Pires, G & Aisbett, J (2003). "The relationship between technology adoption and business strategy in business-to-business markets: The case of e-commerce". Industrial Marketing Management, 32, 291–300.

Poon, S. (2000). "Business environment and Internet commerce benefit—A small business perspective". *European Journal of Information Systems*, 9, 72–81.

Porter, M (2001). "Strategy and the Internet". *Harvard Business Review*, 79 (3) 62–78.

Prasad, K, Ramamurhty, K & Naidu, G (2001). "The influence of Internet-marketing integration on marketing competencies and export performance". *Journal of International Marketing*, 9 (4), 82–110.

Prashantham, S & Berry, M (2004). "The Internet and the internationalisation of small knowledge-intensive firms: A conceptual approach". In M Jones & P Dimtratos (eds.), Emerging Paradigms in International Entrepreneurship, Cheltenham, Edward Elgar, 192–213.

Prashantham, S & Young, S (2004). "The Internet and the internationalisation of small knowledge-intensive firms: Promises, problems and prospects". *International Journal of Entrepreneurship and Small Business*, in press.

Rao, S, Metts, G & Mora Monge, C. (2003). "Electronic commerce development in small and medium sized enterprises: A stage model and its implications". *Business Process Management Journal*, 9 (1), 11–32.

Rosson, P (2004). "The Internet and SME exporting: Canadian success stories. In: H, Etemad (ed.) International Entrepreneurship: The Globalization of SMEs' Orientation", Environment and Strategy. Cheltenham, Edward Elgar, 2004, in press.

Samiee, S (1998). "Exporting and the Internet: A conceptual perspective". *International Marketing Review*, 15 (5), 413–427.

Schumpeter, J (1934). "The theory of economic development: An inquiry into profits, capital, credit, interest and the business cycle". Cambridge, MA, Harvard University Press.

Thong, J (1999). "An integrated model of information systems adoption in small businesses". *Journal of Management Information Systems*, 15 (4), 187–214.

Tiessen, J, Wright, R. & Turner, I. (2001). "A model of e-commerce use by internationalizing SMEs". *Journal of International Management*, 7, 211–233.

UCLA (2003). "The UCLA Internet report: surveying the digital future". UCLA Center for Communications Policy, November. Retrieved August 8, 42004 from: *www.ccp.ucla.edu.*

Venkat, R (2001). "Global e-commerce: An Atlantic Canadian perspective". In D Chaundy (ed.), Atlantic Canada's International Trade in the Post-FTA Era, Atlantic Provinces Economic Council, 93–116.

Walczuch, R, van Braven, G & Lundgren, H (2000). "Internet adoption barriers for small firms in The Netherlands". *European Management Journal*, 18 (5), 561–572.

Welch, L & Luosatrinen, R (1988). "Internationalization: Evolution of a concept". *Journal of General Management*, 7 (3), 36–64.

APPENDIX A

Variables Used in Further Analysis

Variable Label	Description and Scoring
Company Characteristics:	
Revenue	Gross revenue for most recent year. Scored from (1) under C$100,000, to (5) C$10 m–$50 m.
Age	Years the company has been in business. Scored from (1) 1–3 years, to (5) More than 20 years.
Regional sales	Dependence of company on regional market. The percentage of company gross revenues generated in Atlantic Canada.
B2C	Whether the company serves consumer (B2C) markets. Scored (0) no, or (1) yes.
E-Business Related:	
(i) General	
Implementations	Current status regarding e-business implementation. Scored from (1) e-business initiatives are not in our plans over the next 12 months, to (4) we have implement one or more e-business initiatives.
Specific Actions	A summary measure of concrete e-business actions. Includes response on four items; Our company: has developed a robust vision or strategy for e-business; has senior management that have made creating a competitive advantage through e-business a top priority; routinely evaluates our competitor's websites and capabilities; and has successfully provided e-business training for our professional staff. Items scored from (1) disagree, to (5) agree.
Spending	A summary measure of spending on e-business initiatives. Includes response on two items—spending over the past two years, and over the next two years. Items scored from (1) decreased substantially, to (5) increased substantially.
Readiness for Growth	A summary measure of a company's readiness to capitalize on growth. Includes response to two items; Our company: currently has the technology infrastructure necessary to execute our e-business initiatives; and currently has e-business applications that are capable of handling significant growth in number of transactions, customers, or employees. Items scored from (1) disagree, to (5) agree.

Contd...

Process Integration	Extent to which major suppliers have integrated some business processes into the company e-business systems. Scored from (0) no integration, to (4) greater than 30%.
(ii) Supply Chain	
Use of E-Markets	Degree to which company makes major purchases through third-party online marketplaces. Score from (0) no purchases, to (4) greater than 30%.
Supply Chain Actions	A summary measure of the supply chain actions taken by a company. Includes response on three items; Which statement best classifies your company with respect to: procurement by utilizing the Internet to place orders with your major suppliers; utilizing the Internet to track the status of orders from your major suppliers; and utilizing the Internet to access online and billing information, including making payments to your major suppliers? Scored from (1) these e-business applications are not in our plans over the next 12 months, to (4) we have implemented one or more of these e-business applications.
(iii) Demand Chain	
Use of Portals	Number of portals (MSN, Yahoo, AOL, etc.), affiliated sites, banner ads, or online marketplaces used to drive traffic to company website. Scored from (0) not used, to (3) more than 10.
Demand Chain Actions	A summary measure of the demand chain actions taken by a company. Includes response on three items; Which statement best classifies your company with respect to: allowing customers to place their orders online; allowing customers to track the status of orders online; allowing customers to access billing functions, including payment online; and allowing customers to access customer care applications (customer service, product inquiries, etc.) on line? Scored from (1) these e-business applications are not in our plans over the next 12 months, to (4) we have implemented one or more of these e-business applications.
(iv) Website	
Usability	Extent to which a company's website complies with nine usability guidelines developed by Nielsen (2003) Scored from (0) zero compliance, to (9) full compliance.
Functionality	Number of functions (as defined by Boisvert 2002) that are represented in company website. Scored from (0) zero functionality, to (18) full functionality.

Table 1: Profile of Companies (n = 15)

Company Characteristic			**%**
Revenues (C$)			
<$100,000			13.3
$100,000–$500,000			26.7
$500,000–$2 million			20.0
$2 million–$10 million			33.0
$10 million–$50 million			7.0
Employees			
1–20 employees			67.7
21–50			26.7
101–300			6.7
Age			
1–3 years			19.0
5–10			40.0
10–20			26.7
>20			13.3
	No. of Companies	Revenue Range %	Median Revenue %
Markets Served and Revenues			
Atlantic Canada	13	3–100	80
Rest of Canada	11	5–55	12
United States	9	1–95	20
Other Markets	1	60	NA

Table 2: General E-Business Readiness (n = 15)

Variable/Items		Yes %
Implementations		
As of today, our company:		
Has implemented one or more e-business initiatives		47.0
Is in process of implementing one or more e-business initiatives		33.0
Is in planning stages of implementing one or more e-business initiatives		20.0
e-business initiatives not in plans over next 12 months		0.0
	Agree %	Somewhat Agree %
Specific Actions		
Our Company:		
Senior management has made creating a competitive advantage through e-business a top priority	66.7	6.7
Has developed a robust vision or strategy for e-business	40.0	33.0
Routinely evaluates our competitors' websites and capabilities	53.0	33.0
Has successfully provided e-business training for our professional staff (not applicable 20.0%)	27.0	20.0
Readiness for Growth		
Our company currently has:		
The technology infrastructures (hardware, software, people) necessary to execute our e-business initiatives	38.0	13.0
e-business applications that are capable of handling significant growth in number of transactions, customers or employees (not applicable 13.0%)	19.0	19.0

Table 3: E-Business Actions in Supply and Demand Chains (n=15)

Variable/Items	Done	In Process	Planning to %	Not Planned	E-Business not Critical to Business
Supply Chain					
Utlilize the Internet to place orders with major suppliers	27.0	7.0	20.0	13.0	33.0
Utilize the Internet to track the status of orders from major suppliers	26.7	6.7	20.0	20.0	26.7
Utilize the Internet to access online and billing information, including making payments to major suppliers	47.0	13.0	20.0	7.0	13.0
Demand Chain					
Customers are able to place their orders online	40.0	20.0	20.0	0	20.0
Customers are able to track the status of their orders online	7.0	20.0	33.0	13.0	27.0
Customers are able to access billing functions, including payment online	13.3	13.3	33.3	13.3	26.7
Customers are able to access customer care applications (service, product enquiries, etc.) online	40.0	13.3	33.3	0	13.3

Table 4: Website Usability (n=13)

Usability Guideline		Compliant %
Use graphics to show real content, not just to decorate		95
Include breadcrumb or short site description in window title		66
Don't include an active link to the homepage on the homepage		53
Emphasize what the site offers, and how it differs		46
Group all corporate information together under "About us"		38
Make it easy to access anything recently featured		6
Use a liquid layout that lets users adjust homepage size		0
Provide site search capability		0
Use colour to distinguish visited and unvisited links		0
Show percentage of change for stock quotes		NA
Language:	English	100
	Other language	0

Table 5: Website Functionality (n=13)

Functionality Feature	Represented %
Identification	94
Faqs/Discussion Forum	66
Services/Locations	57
E-catalogue	39
Navigation	22
Image	19
Product Ads	18
Partners	15
Contracts/Shipping	15
Customer Services	14
Accreditation	14
Expertise	12
E-Commerce	12
Privacy	9
Customer Loyalty	6
Employment	3
Investor Information	0
Security	0

Table 6: Relationship Between Company and E-Business Readiness Variables

E-Business Variable	Revenues	Age	Regional Sales	B2C	E-Business non-critical
E-Business Actions	-.158	-.082	.300	-.336	-.485*
Spending	-.072	.241	-.128	-.082	-.580*
Readiness for Growth	-.123	.350	.286	-.475*	.032
Process Integration	.158	-.011	.453*	.131	-.454*
Use of E-markets	.039	-.223	.087	.051	-.198
Supply Chain Actions	.461*	-.086	.332	.481*	-.525*
Use of Portals	-.009	-.048	-.143	.203	-.512*
Demand Chain Actions	.106	.136	.570*	.311	-.844**
Website Usability	-.295	.090	.047	-.269	-.124
Website Functionality	-.124	.076	-.126	.246	-.242
E-business Non-critical	.051	.132	-.299	-.518*	–

** $p \le .01$. * $p \le .05$, one-tailed; n = 13-15.

Table 7: Readiness in Companies where E-Business is More or Less Critical

E-Business Variable	Mean: More Critical (n=7)	Mean: Less Critical (n=8)	T-Statistic	df	Significance
E-business Actions	4.19	3.55	1.034	13	.320
Spending	9.29	8.25	2.183	13	.048
Readiness for Growth	6.29	5.17	.695	11	.502
Process Integration	2.00	.14	2.517	12	.027
Use of E-Markets	1.00	.50	.871	13	.400
Supply Chain Actions	7.57	6.14	1.058	12	.311
Use of Portals	1.43	.38	3.105	13	.008
Demand Chain Actions	11.43	7.14	5.023	12	.000
Website Usability	4.00	3.57	.525	11	.610
Website Functionality	8.00	8.00	.000	11	1.000

14

E-Business Developments in the Irish Agribusiness Industry

Paul Brandon, John O' Connell**, Dermot Ruane and Padraig Wims*

A study of Irish Agribusiness companies was conducted in 2002 to determine the extent of and to assess the likely future developments for e-business. Fifty five percent had a website. Large multi-position businesses were the most likely to have developed a website (66%) while 54% had one. Respondents indicated that their main reasons for developing a website were to improve their promotion strategy (78%) and for external communications (69%) with customers. The use of e-business on the supply side was beneficial to 20% of respondents but was seen as having future prospects. Customers not yet ready for e-business was the main obstacle in the way of continued e-business growth as reported by 71% of respondents while the costs of developing a website and the lack of technological skills in many businesses were also identified as inhibiting factors (69% each). Eighty five percent of businesses which did not have a website intended to develop one in the future while 72% of respondents agreed that e-business would change the way business is done in their industry in the next 5 to 7 years.

Source: Journal of Farm Management, 2004, Vol. 12. This was presented at EFITA Conference in 2003.

1. Introduction and Background

The agribusiness industry has traditionally been one of the cornerstones of the Irish economy. Though there are number of definitions used to describe agribusiness, both narrow and wide, in this paper the definition used comprises businesses involved in the manufacture and distribution of food products as well as businesses supplying inputs to the agricultural industry such as chemicals/ pharmaceuticals, machinery and consultancy. Mueller (2000) defined e-business as business transactions conducted over electronic networks. This paper reports on an exploratory study carried out to examine the levels of e-business development and website adoption amongst Irish agribusinesses in 2002. The study concentrated on business-to-business transactions over the Internet but includes the wider uses of e-business such as Internet, intranet, extranet and e-mail. Under this definition payment may be made either online or offline. Three main objectives specified for this study were: (1) To determine the extent and type of e-business developments in the Irish agribusiness industry as defined above (2) To assess future prospects for e-business in the industry and (3) To compare e-business developments in the Irish Agribusiness Industry with those in other countries.

2. Methodology

Two research methodologies were utilized: (1) A comprehensive and detailed postal questionnaire was mailed to a random sample of 404 registered agribusinesses in the Republic of Ireland; (2) Case studies were carried out with senior managers in 5 agribusiness companies identified from the survey and chosen because of their commitment to e-business. The data from the postal questionnaire were analysed using SPSS. Of the 404 surveyed, 155 returned completed questionnaires: this was a response rate of 38.4%.

3. Results and Discussion

3.1 Web Characteristics of Irish Agribusinesses

Fifty five percent of respondent agribusinesses had a website, and 48% of these were developed between 1996 and 1999, a period when the attendant publicity concerning usage of internet and e-business was high. Figure 1 indicates the progress of website development. It indicates that Irish agribusinesses have continued with website development despite the adverse publicity associated with e-business during the "dot-com" collapse in 2000. These Irish results are broadly similar with results from Irish and international studies (Ehmke *et al.* 2001, Clark *et al.* 2001, Chambers of Commerce of Ireland 2001, Information Society Commission 2000).

The results also showed that in businesses without a website, 28% of respondents had plans to develop a website in 2002. A further 15% indicated their positive intentions in 2003, while a further 43% of respondents indicated an intention to develop a website at a future time. Fourteen percent of responding businesses had no plans for such a development. Table 1 shows an e-profile of the

Figure 1: Period when Irish Agribusiness Websites were Developed (Prior to 1996 -2002)

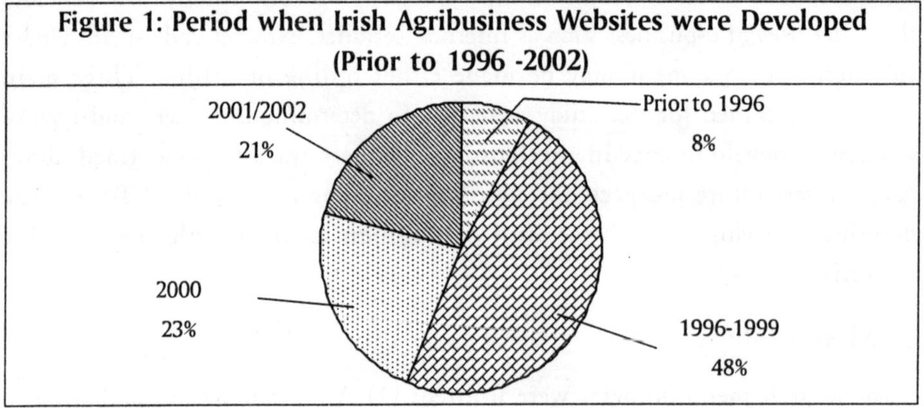

Irish Agribusiness Industry in Ireland in 2002 by position in the supply chain, sector, size and scope of the business.

The results show that larger, more internationally focussed, multi-position and multi-sector businesses were the most likely Irish agribusinesses to be involved in e-business. The food component of the industry had the highest sectoral involvement in e-business.

3.2 Features Found on Websites

Sparkes and Thomas (2001) suggested that a good agribusiness website will contain information needed to facilitate a buying decision and will also have entertainment value. All Irish agribusiness websites contained basic information on the businesses themselves, the products they sold and services provided.

"Advanced" features listed were: online ordering, business intranets, extranets and interactive facilities and some or all of these were found on 31% of websites. This was higher than recorded by Henderson *et al.* (2001) who reported that 19% of US agribusinesses had advanced features on their websites.

Table 1: E-Business Profile of the Irish Agribusiness Industry by Position, Sector, Size and Scope of the Business

Characteristics of the business	Percentage of businesses which had a website	Characteristics of the business	Percentage of businesses which had a website
Position in the supply chain		**Size**	
Manufacturer	47%	Small	39%
Manufacturer / distributor	59%	Medium	61%
Multi-position	66%	Large	94%
Sector		**Scope**	
Food industry	54%	Local / regional	44%
Animal feed	27%	National only	49%
Chemical / pharmaceutical	37%	National and international	66%

The association between first development of websites and the level of complexity of these websites was found to be significant at the 95% level (chi square significance). Businesses with longer established websites were much more likely to have an advanced website than recently developed websites. Seventy percent of websites developed prior to 1996 were advanced websites as were 38% of those developed between 1996 and 1999. Only 21% and 11% of websites developed in 2000 and 2001/2002 respectively were advanced websites. Three possible explanations for this finding are suggested:

1. Businesses initially develop a relatively simple website and continue to invest in their website until it becomes a more complex site. These businesses may have been satisfied with their websites and then decided it was strategically important to further develop their web presence. The case study data support this proposition.

2. Businesses that developed their websites since the "dot-com" collapse of 2000 were reluctant to invest significantly in creating a more advanced site.

3. Businesses which developed their websites prior to 2000 were likely to be the innovators and early adopters of the industry (Rogers 1995). These businesses may have been more adventurous.

3.3 Reasons for Investing in E-Business

When Agribusiness companies with websites were asked to identify their reasons for investing in e-business, the following were the three most important reasons for developing a website (with the complete results shown in Figure 2). These were:

1. **More effective promotion of the business:** Seventy eight percent of respondents with websites said that this was their key reason for investing in e-business.
2. **Keep up with/ahead of competitors:** Sixty nine percent stated that was a significant reason for website development.
3. **Communication links to customers:** Sixty nine percent of respondents felt that this was a key factor in their decision to invest in e-business.

"Procurement of supplies", "increased internal cost efficiencies" and "communication links to suppliers" were listed as the least important factors for investment in e-business. While "communication links to customers" was one of the most important reasons for investing in e-business, improving communications on the supply side of their businesses was seen as less important. Irish agribusiness companies were mostly concerned with improving sales and after-sales service using e-business and were not concerned about the possibilities for using e-business on their supply side at the time of the survey.

3.4 Factors Inhibiting the Development of E-Business

The key obstacle to e-business development for both businesses which had a website and those which did not have a website was "customers not yet ready for e-business". Table 2 shows the factors inhibiting the development of e-business and outlines the differences in responses between website and non-website businesses and the level of significance. The results showed that the respondents in non-website businesses believed that there were a smaller number of factors inhibiting the development of e-business in their industry, each of whose relative importance depends on how well-prepared or otherwise each individual business was for e- business. The results showed further that the businesses that developed websites found a majority of the factors listed in Table 2 as significant inhibitors for the development of e-businesses compared to those identified by non-website businesses. It is likely that the experience of establishing the website brought these factors into more focus among the website developers.

Figure 2: Distribution of Reasons for Investment in E-Business (Legend Shown Below)

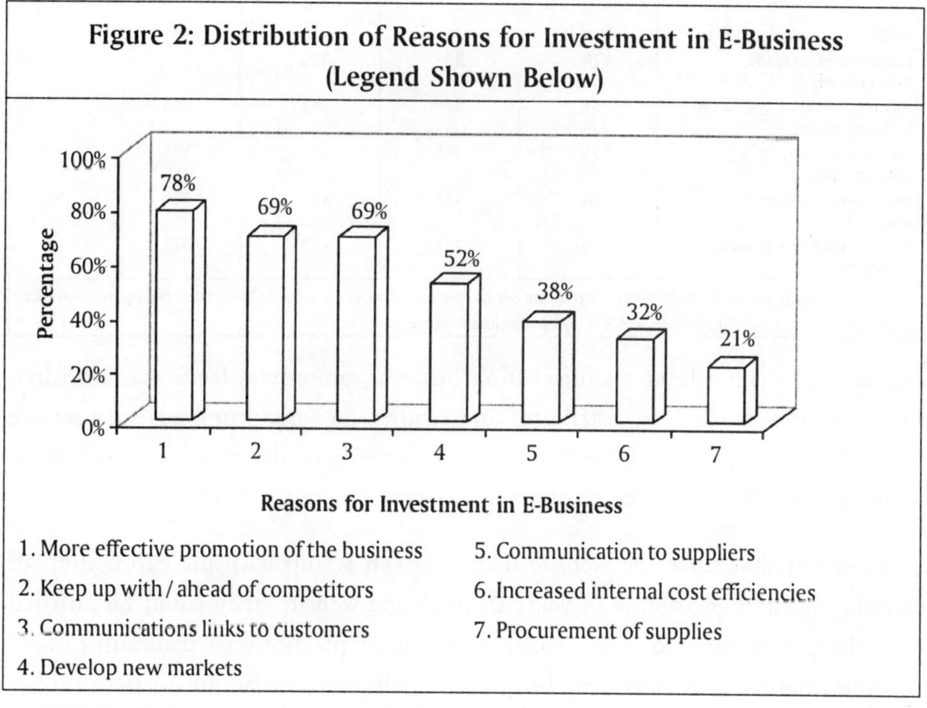

Irish businesses were concerned about the opportunities to develop e-business links with their customers. Clark *et al.* (2000) reported in a study on New Zealand Small and Medium Enterprises (SME's) that respondents observed "low customer use of e-business" as a key barrier to e-business growth. High cost of computing and network technology and a limited knowledge of how to use these technologies were also major factors to the respondents in that survey.

3.5 Satisfaction with E-business

The case studies focused on the respondents' satisfaction with their websites and their plans for further investment in e-business. The businesses involved in the

Table 2: Key Obstacles to E-Business Development for Irish Agribusinesses (Non Responses Excluded)

Factors inhibiting the development of e-business	Type of Business				Significance
	Website Businesses		Non Website Businesses		
	Was a Factor (%)	Not a Factor (%)	Was a Factor (%)	Not a Factor (%)	
Customers not yet ready for e-business	72%	28%	60%	40%	NS
Lack of in-house technological expertise	69%	31%	34%	66%	*
High initial development costs	69%	31%	19%	81%	*
Suppliers not yet ready for e-business	67%	33%	23%	77%	*
No online ordering system for Irish agribusiness	56%	44%	25%	75%	*
Lack of required trust to transact online	55%	45%	13%	87%	*
Insufficient return on investment	53%	47%	39%	61%	NS
Lack of advice on e-business strategies	54%	46%	13%	87%	*

* = significantly different at the 95% level. Significance is calculated between the website businesses and the non-website businesses for each individual obstacle. NS = no significant difference

case studies were: a food manufacturing business, an animal feeds manufacturer, an agricultural machinery distributor and retailer, an agricultural advisory service provider and a large multi-sector agribusiness. All of the five businesses were satisfied with the performance of their websites but not extremely satisfied.

They felt that since the website had not been set up with the expectation of carrying out a large volume of trade through the website, they could be satisfied with the performance of the website in terms of promotions, communications and information provision. The businesses attributed satisfaction to the number of "hits" on their website as well as from favourable comments from trading partners. None of them however was prepared to make an estimate of level of business conducted that could be attributed to the website. None of the case study businesses described their website as being central to their strategic plans. The businesses agreed that their investment in e-business in the coming years was likely to increase as the website begins to record more trade.

3.6 E-business Strategies for the Future

Table 3 shows the responses from the questionnaire survey of both website and non-website agribusinesses to six statements on the future of e-business in their industry. Agribusiness companies felt that e-business would have an impact on their industry in 5to7 years. Respondents were confident that e-procurement would become much more important in that time period. This is in agreement with other reports that showed that e-business would offer great opportunities to streamline inventory management (Friochol (2001), Lucking-Reiley and Spulber (2001) and Enterprise Ireland (2002)).

It would not be surprising if developments on the supply side commenced after the sales side has been set up, and is operational. Therefore, it is reasonable to suggest that e-procurement is likely to become a more important issue for Irish agribusinesses in the future. The results are also supported by the case study findings in this research. Case study respondents indicated that as with all aspects of business, development of e-business on the supply side would continue as more companies come online. In addition, the case study respondents felt that extranet-type features on websites would become more important in the future while one of the case study businesses had already commenced making a significant investment in mobile e-business (m-business) at the time of the survey.

Respondents in US studies showed that US agribusinesses had similar points of view on the future of e-business in their industry when they were asked to respond to a list of similar questions (Henderson *et al.* 2001, Ehmke *et al.* 2001). E-business is still new in the Irish agribus iness industry. While 55% of agribusinesses had a website, almost one quarter of these have only been online for the past year and 14% of respondents expressed no interest in e-business and indicated no intention of ever developing a website. Forfas (2002) suggested that Irish businesses are now adopting a "wait and see" approach to the adoption of e-business and many may be in this mode at present, given Irish national and wider international economic uncertainty.

Though businesses have been concentrating on getting their websites established and functioning in recent years little progress has been made on the further development of these sites, mainly the sales and procurement side of the business over the web. The website is being used in most businesses as a support and key promotion-communications tool. It can afford a business a greater level of after-sales service and allows them to be able to support customers in a much

Table 3: Future Direction of E-business in the Irish Agribusiness Industry

Statement on future direction of E-Business in the agribusiness industry	Type of Business				Significance
	Website Businesses (N = 86)		Non-Website Businesses (N = 69)		
	Agree with with statement	Disagree with statement	Agree with statement	Disagree with statement	
E-business will change the way business is done in the agricultural industry in the next 5–7 years	73%	27%	71%	29%	NS
E-business will reduce the role for local agricultural retailers in the next 5–7 years	27%	73%	25%	75%	NS
E-business will improve ability to manage inventory levels in the next 5–7 years	48%	52%	60%	40%	*
Information on complex products is difficult to provide over the internet	37%	63%	42%	58%	NS
E-procurement will become commonplace in the agricultural industry in the next 5–7 years	56%	44%	58%	42%	NS
Distribution issues will limit sales of agricultural products over the internet	48%	52%	51%	49%	NS

* = significantly different at the 95% level (chi-square). Significance is calculated between the website businesses and the non-website businesses for each individual statement. NS = no significant difference

more pro-active way. It may be assumed that if more agribusinesses were to develop effective websites, it would have an impact on reluctant competitors to use these new technologies. If an agribusiness company's customers were online and were using their website for both communication and other purposes, then these businesses would need little direct re-assurance that it would be in their interests to build their own website. However, given that most businesses stated that they were not interested in using their websites on the purchases side at present, it is difficult to envisage major development of e-procurement activity over the web in the short term.

4. Conclusion

Irish agribusinesses are in the process of embracing the e-business culture. Those which have developed websites are strategically well positioned in the e-business world to gain the full benefits in terms of cost savings, information and communications. Many are still in the process of developing e-business and while e-procurement is likely to be the next important phase, this process may yet take some time. A minority of Irish agribusinesses however are in a less competitive position for e-business and appear to be hoping that their business will remain unaffected by e-business.

(Paul Brandon, John O'Connell, Dermot Ruane and Padraig Wims are associated with Department of Agribusiness and Rural Development, University College Dublin, Ireland).

References

Chambers of Commerce of Ireland (2002): SME E-business survey, *www.chambersireland.ie* (4/ 10/ 2002)

Clark, D, Bowden, S, Corner, P, Gibb, J, Kearins, K, Pavlovich, K, (2001): "Adoption and Implementation of E-business in New Zealand: Empirical Results 2001." University of Waikato Management School, NZ

Ehmke, C, Ernst, S, Hopkins, J, Tweeten, L, (2001): "The market for E-commerce services in Agriculture." Select paper for the AAEA Annual meetings, Chicago, Illinois, Aug. 5-8.

Enterprise Ireland E-business Basics Guide (2002) *www.enterprise-ireland.com/ebusiness/print_basics.htm June17th*

Forfas (2002): E-business: Where are we and where do we go from here? Dublin, Forfas

Friochol, M, (2001): "There's no business like E-business." IIE Solutions, Vol. 33, Issue 3, p.38.

Henderson, J R, Dooley, F, Akridge, J, Boehlje, M, (2001): "E-business and Distribution Channel strategies in Agribusiness Industries." American Agricultural Economics Association Meetings.

Information Society Commission (2000): "How the Business Community is adapting to the Information Society in Ireland". Information Society Commission findings, September 2000.

Lucking-Reiley, D, Spulber, D F, (2001): "Business to Business Electronic Commerce." *Journal of Economic Perspectives*. Vol. 15, No. 1, Winter, pp. 55-68.

Mueller, R A E, (2000): "Emergent E-commerce in Agriculture." AIC Issues Brief, No. 14, December.

Rogers, E M, (1995): Diffusion of Innovations, 4th Ed. New York; London: Free Press 1995.

Sparkes, A and Thomas, B, (2001): "The use of the internet as a critical success factor for the marketing of Welsh agri-food SMEs in the twenty-first century". *British Food Journal*, Vol. 103, No. 5, pp.331-347.

ITC's E-Choupal: The Next Frontier in E-Business Innovation

Launched in June 2000, the 'e-Choupal' initiative has been fruitful in exploiting the benefits of Information and Communication Technologies (ICTs) in over 600,000 agricultural villages of rural India, thereby connecting nine states (Madhya Pradesh, Haryana, Uttaranchal, Karnataka, Andhra Pradesh, Uttar Pradesh, Maharashtra, Rajasthan and Kerala) and bridging the rural-urban 'digital-divide'. This market-led innovative business model has been enhancing the competitiveness of Indian agriculture by generating higher productivity and incomes, enabling farmer risk management and encouraging further investments. The 'e-Choupal' model has been exclusively designed to address the challenges faced by Indian agriculture, like fragmented farms, weak infrastructure, involvement of multiple intermediaries, etc. By leveraging Information Technology, the initiative virtually clusters the value chain participants, viz; farm input companies, farmers, traders, procurers, processors, retailers, exporters, consumers both institutional and retail, etc to the same effect as that of vertical integration in mature agricultural economies like the USA. Besides, serving as an e-commerce hub, it is a place of social gathering for exchanging information.

'e-Choupal' utilizes the physical transmission capabilities of the existing intermediaries like aggregation, logistics, counter party risks, etc., and eliminates the middleman from the chain of information flow and market signals, thereby, reducing wasteful intermediation.

A combination of the click and mortar capabilities, the village Internet kiosks help the Indian farmers to access real-time crop information (on weather and market prices) and customized knowledge (like farm practices and risk management) in their native languages. These kiosks are managed by the farmers called the 'sanchalaks' who guide the agricultural community with the relevant agri information. This benefits the farmer's decision-making capacity, thereby assisting him to better align his farm output to the projected demand in both Indian and global markets. Moreover, by creating a direct marketing channel that virtually links to the 'mandi' system for price discovery and related information, it eliminates wasteful intermediation and multiple handling, thereby minimizing transaction costs.

However, setting up and managing the 'e-Choupal' have been a challenging task, especially when the infrastructural requirements like power supply, telecom connectivity and bandwidth, have not been fully met. There exists the additional challenge of training the farmers in remote and inaccessible parts of rural India to the required Internet skills. However, a lot of innovative solutions like mobile choupals, 24x7 helpdesk, power back-up through batteries charged by solar panels, etc, are being deployed to overcome these challenges.

Considering the good response from the farmers, ITC has planned to extend these choupals from the present nine to a total of fifteen states in India. This e-business innovation is also expected to deliver other services like micro-credit, health and education, through the same 'e-Choupal' infrastructure. Besides India, where it has originated, this model is also becoming popular in all the developing countries.

It is noteworthy to mention that ITC's 'e-Choupal' has won numerous awards like the Stockholm Challenge 2006 and Innovation for India Award 2006 in the Social Innovations Category.

Ref: http://www.itcportal.com/agri-exports/e-choupal_new.htm.

15

Improving Citizen-Government Interface Through Innovative E-Governance: A Study of India

Y Pardhasaradhi

The search for smaller government through efficiency, re-engineering of service systems, performance management, transparency of government operations, and emphasis on citizen service with citizen satisfaction as a strategy are the buzzing words for administrators. Quick decision-making, data based-planning, effective implementation through quantitative techniques seemed to clinch the issue in its favour. The Information revolution promises to change the world like never before. The objective of this paper is to examine and analyzing the improving citizens interface with the government through electronic means in India. For this purpose we selected the Andhra Pradesh (herein after referred as AP) state in India. In the state of AP, IT is an important tool for governance. AP is the first state in India to design a state-wide computerization programme covering all levels of the administrative spectrum from the smallest – the village level revenue offices to the top

---

Source: unpan/un.org/intradoc/groups. © Y Pardhasaradhi. This article was presented at AIT Bangkok Conference 2003 with the title Improving Citizen-Government Interface through E-Governance: A study of India. Reprinted with permission.

most, largest and most powerful. The successful implementation of e-Governance in the administration in AP has indicated positive response by various communities. The analysis indicates that almost 100 percent respondents are appreciating the electronic means of operation of citizen services and use of computers in administration. It is saving their valuable time and money. The e-governance is helpful in establishing a two-way information communication network vertically and horizontally across the public and administrative system and helps in re-installing and re-inforcing people's faith in government.

Introduction

The last two decades have witnessed many changes in managing the public sector and public services and they had an effect on the social, economic and political aspect of the state. These changes not only affected the size and composition of public sector, but also the ways in which public organizations were structured and managed. Citizens are demanding smaller, effective and efficient governments. The challenges forced the governments everywhere to launch major innovations.

The classical administrative model with its major emphasis on structure, hierarchy, rules, differentiation and several functional features were itself under serious threat for administrators. The search for smaller government through efficiency, re-engineering of service systems, performance management, transparency of government operations, down sizing or rightsizing the government workforce, strong emphasis on citizen service with citizen satisfaction as a strategy have become the buzzing words for administrators. Quick decision-making, data based planning, effective implementation through quantitative techniques seemed to clinch the issue. These changes forced the governments in search of new techniques and technologies. The impact of managerialism has been greatest within the public services and it has changed the orientation of the public services. The traditional principles of public administration were changed towards the principles of 'public business' and 'customer awareness', focusing on the instrumental objectives of economy, efficiency, effectiveness and quality through the agency more professionalised management. The governments experimented to achieve efficiency and citizen satisfaction through various measures, and recognized the importance of Information and Communications Technologies (ICTs) and started exploiting the capabilities ICTs. The 'new' public services with the use of IT created a new 'informational logic' for public administration. 'A new public administration is being forged, and new information flows, and the computer networks which facilitate and mediate them, are fundamental to the innovation process'. The purpose of this study is to discuss the significance and impact of Information and communication technologies for managing and delivering the public services.

The Impact of Mangerialism on Public Services

Public sector consists of many organizations and it is very difficult to generalize their goals, structures and styles of management. These public organizations have have a common feature that is they are created by governments to achieve political goals and to support political objectives and policies. The present trend is on the principles of 'public business' and customer awareness, focusing on the instrumental objectives of economy, efficiency, effectiveness and quality through the agency of more professionalized management. These changes gave a way to private sector and using the techniques of private sector to public organizations. Private sector management is largely market driven. This means that the ways in which private organization are managed reflects the market environment in which they operate. Success, growth or even survival for private organization depends on the ability of their managerial cadres to manage effectively the dynamic economic environment facing their business. Private organization must be both profitable and economically efficient to survive in the market place. Private organizations have less complex, more easily stated and less disputed goals than those of public organizations. This is because they are market centred enterprises. All organization whether it is private or public are ultimately responsible though their governing bodies, for the actions they take, to achieve their goals and objectives. Public service organizations are managed with private sector management ideas, techniques and practices penetrating the public services.

Information technology will facilitate an open government and access to information and knowledge by providing transparent and open dealing in government services through simultaneous use of infinite, expandable, diffusive and instant transmission of information. It becomes feasible through re-engineering of the system and procedures to reap the benefits of new media and new technologies. New means of involving citizens through wide access, procedures to gain access, knowledge about the available systems, services, communication channels and the degree of involvement built in, is going to be the greatest challenge faced by the administration, technology providers and the citizenry. Information technology has been found to be very useful technology to reinvigorate government by enhancing the administrative capacity and organizational efficiency of the public and development administrative system. The current experience with the application of IT world in government business and transactions is that, it leads to:

- Increased transparency in administrative processes, there by re-installing people's faith in the government.
- Opportunities for promoting participation of the people and their organizations in government processes.
- Openness in the functioning of the government.
- Encourages innovations and introduction of new ideas and concepts in government transactions, and
- The evolution of intuitive solutions to development issues and problems facing community.

E-Governance

Given the extraordinary pace of changes in the IT industry, the term e-governance, itself is some what new and essentially implies upgrading of their efficiency and effectiveness of the administrative machinery through the combination of Information Technology and sophisticated multimedia to deliver better, cost – effective and speedy services to the citizens. The present generations are in the rapidly changing periods in the history. There has been a shift in importance from the traditional inputs of a production process to the processes involved in the creation, storage and use of information. The new technology has already had impact in the manner in which large organizations functions. Many of these organizations have had to restructure themselves to create a flatter – less hierarchical- structure. At the same time one of the principal efforts of all organizations have been devoted to the creation and sustenance of an environment of learning in view of quantum increases in knowledge and changes in technology. In government the transition to electronic delivery of services will not only involve to changes to the systems, procedures and processes of the relevant services, but will also the effect the way in which the public and business community deals with the government. Customer will no longer need to interface directly with government officials in order to secure a particular service. They also do not need to know which agency is a service provider, as the service can be obtained through a kiosk or a personal computer. The important benefit to the customer is to secure the required service speedily and easily. These new trends will influence the nature of government administration and management, there by reinventing the government to make it experience seamless to the citizens.

The Present Study

The above discussion raises specific aspects of the use of Information Technology in general covering number of areas of administration. We are in the age of 'Digitalization process'. Use of IT in administration was initiated particularly in developed world, but not in the developing world. The availability of the literature is purely from the developing world, may not be compared to ours. The literature and studies in this area is very scanty in our country. The yawning gap in the body of the knowledge on this imperative and innovative development must be supported by new studies and research. The present study therefore is an attempt on the working of Information technology in Andhra Pradesh.

Objectives of the Study

The study aims at examining and analyzing e-seva (Electronic Citizen Services) with special reference to Andhra Pradesh. In particular, the study examines:

- Analyzing the role of e-governance in improving citizen services;
- The methods of restructuring the government for change;

- To identify the citizen awareness activities on e-seva; and
- To study the people's satisfaction on e-seva.

Methodology

The present study is basically an analysis of e-seva in Andhra Pradesh. The data was collected through net, official documents, discussions, questionnaires and interview schedules. The areas of study are: (i) Citizen Services through Technology; (ii) Restructuring of Administration; (iii) Public-Private Partnerships. We selected the state of Andhra Pradesh for this research as it has moved faster on the road to e-governance than any other state in India. The state has undertaken various e-government initiatives to provide better, most efficient, transparent and responsive services to the citizens and promote greater efficiency within the government. The first department of IT in the country was formally established in Andhra Pradesh in 1998, to focus upon IT and give the sector the impetus that it deserves. Andhra Pradesh provide better services to citizens by establishing Simple, Moral, Accountable, Responsive and Transparent (SMART) government. The state has initiated a number of e-government projects under the concept of SMART government, which have been successful and appreciated. Significant among these are CARD (Computer Aided Administration in Registration Department), e-Seva (Electronic Citizen Services), FAST (Fully Automated System for Transport), APSWAN (Andhra Pradesh State Wide Area Network) etc. The primary reason for selection was because of the states IT initiative in various sectors. The researcher's familiarity with the environment is another important, but a secondary factor, in the selection. The study is basically concerned with the citizen satisfaction on the use of IT in services and the restructuring of administration with public –private partnerships.

E-Seva (Electronic Citizen Services)

As citizens had to run around various departments for payment of utility bills and had to spend long hours to pay the utility bills, Government of Andhra Pradesh has taken a vital leap in providing citizens with convenience and comfort in all transactions with the government. E-seva is one of the major IT project undertaken by the government of Andhra Pradesh as a part of e-governance. E-seva is the first kind of service in the country, providing a wide spectrum of citizen-friendly services that will save citizens running around various departments. E-seva is built on the success of TWINS (Twin Cities Network Services) pilot project, which was launched in December 1999 in Hyderabad, the state capital. It is designed to provide citizens of Hyderabad and Secunderabad to handle integrated 19 services pertaining to six departments for delivery on a one-stop mode. Services range from utility bill/tax payments, issue of certificates, provision of information and facilitation. TWINS has been renamed e-seva as the state government plans to extend it to major towns and municipalities in the state. E-seva is a citizen service with a difference, which provide a clean, transparent, efficient and effective administrative system through state-of-the-art electronic technology. Citizens are benefited by the direct interface between government, which saves time, energy and money and gives hassle free dealings with the administration. All the administrative departments come to the customer under one roof offering the citizen a wide range of citizen friendly services.

Structure of the Department

The main department is headed by the Director, who is an IAS Officer, and the head office is situated at Banjara Hills (Address: MCH Building, Road No. 7, Hyderabad). Down the hierarchy is Deputy Director 1 & Deputy Director 2, followed by additional director (Technical) and Additional director (Public Relation Officer), followed by Manager, Assistant Manager, Accountant and below than computer operator. This hierarchical structure is found in Head Quarters. At present 18 e-seva centres (with over 200 services counters) spread over the twin cities. Manager followed by Assistant Manager, Accountant and computer operator, heads each centre.

Public-Private Partnership

E-seva is a government organization build on public-private partnership model. Infrastructure and building are provided by the government. Staff is provided by government as well as by the private. Government recruits the staff through deputation and the respective departments pay salaries. Private hire the staff through tenders and they are protected by minimum wage act. Private organizations provided the network and the software. The technological partnership is provided by the M/s CMS computers Ltd and M/s Ram Informatics

Ltd. Apart from technological aspect, maintenance, telephone bills, connection charges, electricity charge, day-to-day charge, security and office boys are taken care by the private organizations.

Salient Features of E-Seva

- All services can be availed at any center.
- All services can be availed at any counter within the centre, i.e., a consumer need not visit one counter for one service and another for another service.
- There are no jurisdictional limits. A resident of Secunderabad can pay his bills at the old city of Hyderabad and vice-versa.
- Services can be availed on holidays as well.
- Bill payment can be made over the Internet.
- Online service: e-forms, e-filing, and e-payments.

Mode of Payment

At all the e-seva counters payment can be made through cash, cheque, demand draft & credit card. E-seva receipt is treated as a conclusive proof of payment. As the payment particulars get updated on the departmental servers from time to time.

Direct Debit System

For using direct debit system, one has to register with *www.esevaonline.com*. This process is similar to an e-mail registration and secondly one need to have an Internet banking account with any of the following banks with whom e-seva has an agreement. They are UTI/GTB/HDFC/IDBI/ICICI and planning to extend with other banks.

- Once registered you can add services like payment of electricity bills, telephone bills & property tax etc., on line.
- After selecting the bank where the customer has an account, the control is transferred to the bank site. Here the customer log in with the user name and password given by the bank and the amount is debited from the account and credited to e-seva account. The transaction is updated online on the departmental server.

- Citizen gets a receipt, which can be printed. The transaction reference number can be quoted for any future correspondence.

Public Opinion on e-Seva

E-seva is the first kind of service in the country, which provide a wide spectrum of citizen-friendly services that saves citizens from running around various departments for the payment of utility bills. To find out the impact study of e-seva, around 11 questions are covered in the questionnaire and the data was collected from different localities of Twin Cities. Total 21 localities are covered from 6 centres 27 centers. The next section presents the details of the public opinion on e-seva.

Tables 1 to 4 explains the respondents gender, education qualification, localities, and occupation respectively. Tables 5 to 12 explains the time taken for the payment of utility bills before e-seva and after the implementation of e-seva. Table 13 explains the citizen benefits due to e-seva service.

Respondents

Gender: 100 people 90% are male and 10% are female.

Educational Qualification: Of 100 people out of which 10% are SSC, 12% Inter, 45% are graduates, 20% are postgraduates, 4% LLB graduates, 6% are Engineer Graduates and 3% Ph.D.

Occupation

5% are accountants, 23% are business people, 2% are engineers, 40% are working in government service, 5% are housewife, 2% are lecturers, 19% are working in private service and 4% are students.

Time Taken (Before and After e-seva)

38% says less than an hour and 62% say half an hour to 2 hours before e-seva.

Under e-seva we see that 77% says 1 to 5 minutes and 23% says 10 to 15 minutes.

Electricity Bill: We see that 18% says less than half an hour and 82% says half an hour to 2 hours before e-seva, but after e-seva we see that 77% says 1 to 5 minutes and 23% says 10 minutes to 15 minutes.

Payment of Water Bill: The time taken for the payment of water bill before and after e-seva. When 19% says less than half an hour and 81% says half an hour to 2 hours before e-seva and after e-seva 76% says 1 to 5 minutes and 24% says 10 to 15 minutes.

Property Tax: Before e-seva the time taken for the payment of property tax after e-seva.

We see that 19% takes less than half an hour and 81% takes more than half an hour to 2 hours before e-seva and under e-seva 76% takes 1 minute to 5 minutes and 24% take 10 minutes to 15 minutes.

Citizen benefits by e-seva service: 100% approves for e-seva. Above given data show the opinion of the people from different localities regarding department payment of bills and newly introduced e-seva service by the Government of Andhra Pradesh.

Difficulties Faced by Citizens While Visiting Various Departments for the Payment of Utility Bills

Citizens used to face lot of difficulties while paying utility bills in different departments; some of the difficulties faced are as follows: Manual operation used to take lot of time; Large queue; No cooperation from the staff; Always citizen argue with each other and time is wasted; Illiterate uses to face lot of problems as there are no concern person to direct these people. The above difficulties are expressed by the people while paying the bill in the respective departments.

Benefits Due to E-Seva

Though people face some difficulties due to e-seva service, there are many benefits provided by e-seva. They are as follows: Due to computerization lot of time is saved for citizens; Quick service, calm atmosphere providing mental relief to the citizen compared with their previous experiences; Friendly behavior of the staff;

Timing of e-seva suits all types of citizens, due to their long working hours and even on Sundays & holidays; Bills can be paid at any location; All the bills can be paid under one roof; E-Seva centres are located at walk able distances in various localities; There is no queue as everything is at fingertips.

Suggestions for Improvement of E-Seva Service

Though people are satisfied with the services provided by the e-seva at present, there are some areas where there is a need for improvement. The important suggestions given by the citizens are as follows:

1. To open more centres at each and every corner of the locality.
2. To undertake other services of central government and state government.
3. There should be no charge for any service offered by e-seva.
4. Particular about the month and other particulars of the bill should be mentioned in the receipt. E-seva centres should accept the bill after the due date along with the fine also.
5. There is lack of communication among the e-seva and concerned departments, sometimes creating hurdles for citizens.
6. E-seva must work 18 hours.
7. E-seva centres accept credit card bills are beneficial for the community.
8. Punctuality should be maintained. In some centres the employees are coming late.
9. There is no need for token system as there is not much rush. Due to token system it takes longer times and in the centers where there is no token system payment of bills takes only seconds and the lastly, citizen hopes that e-seva maintains the same tempo with the helpful attitude. Citizens hope that the maintenance of the premises as good as new and do not let it turn into another government buildings.

Conclusion

The launching of e-seva in Andhra Pradesh represents three important dimensions i.e., New Mangerialism, Public-Private Partnerships and the use of Technology for the benefit of the citizens. By all appearances, e-seva dramatically improved the interaction between citizens and government departments through quick and convenient access to automated services. The study clearly indicates that citizens are satisfied with the e-seva and they want to continue the same tempo of functioning in future. The maladies of bureaucracy and the performance of public office were totally restructured in the e-seva. 85% of the respondents were felt that their time of two hours and more to pay the utility bills were reduced to five to ten minutes and they can visit the center whenever they like, including holidays. It has witnessed not only growth in revenue collection, but also timely payment by the citizens is a positive indication of good citizenship. Public organizations should keep abreast of the changing needs and aspirations of the citizens. In other words, they should become, what Warren Bennis calls 'organic-adaptive' organizations to prevent them from becoming inefficient. Public organizations can continue to act as change agents when they become adaptive organizations.

(Dr. Y Pardhasaradhi, Associate Professor of Public Administration, Osmania University).

References

David Farnham and Sylvia Horton, Ed., 1996, "Managing the New Public Services", London, Macmillan Press.

Dunsire A 1995, "Administrative Theory in the 1980s", Public Administration, 73:1-15.

Garson GD 2000. Hand Book of Public Information Systems, New York, Marcel Dekker, Inc.

Garson GD 1999. "Information Technology and Computer Applications for Public Administration, Issues and Trends", London, Idea Group Publications.

Massey, A 1993. "Managing the Public Sector", Aldershot: Edward Elgar.

Hughes, O 1994. "Public Management and Administration". New York: St. Martin's Press.

Rogers W'O Okot-uma, "Electronic Governance: Reinventing Good Governance", London, Commonwealth Secretariat.

Taylor, J and Williams, H 1991 "Public Administration and the Information Polity", Public Administration, 69:2-21.

E-Procurement – Just Click Away

Samar Srivastava

India is now getting used to e-tendering. The Andhra Pradesh government's initiative is now a model for other states.

When was the last time you read those ugly tender advertisements in the newspaper? Maybe never, unless, of course, your business has something to do with responding to tenders. So far, the government's procurement process, too, has been a bit like those ads – dull and tedious.

But now, things are beginning to change. Indeed, a few years from now you may be hard pressed to spot a single tender in a newspaper. Various arms of the government are increasingly using the Internet to speed up and simplify procurement transactions. Call it tender e-procurement.

It began in the year 2002 in Andhra Pradesh. The State government projects had been stalled by delays in awarding tenders. Cartels regularly cornered the bulk of government contracts and bids were tampered with after closure. For N Chandrababu Naidu the tech-savvy chief minister in a hurry, this was unacceptable. He needed a way around the mess – and predictably by use of technology. There was, of course, the formality of appointing a cabinet committee to study all this, but the end result was unequivocal: implement e-procurement.

Ajay Prakash Sawhney, Andhra Pradesh's former IT secretary and the man responsible for implementing the project, recalls that it was "a most difficult project to implement". Preparing the new platform was a great challenge as employees had to be thoroughly trained, offices connected online, suppliers registered and taught how to use the system, and so on.

Project manager (e-procurement) K Bikshapathi says that initially, both departments and suppliers were unable to utilise the system due to lack of training. First year collections were way off the mark – only Rs. 14 crore worth goods were ordered online, though a Rs. 250-crore target had been set. The only good news: negligible resistance from government employees. They readily accepted the new procedure since its benefits were clear to them. They would no longer have to pander to the whims of their political masters and favour certain suppliers.

Now, 90 per cent of all the tenders in Andhra Pradesh are completed online. Last year, orders worth Rs. 15,000 crore were placed (See 'The Andhra Pradesh Numbers'). While it earlier took somewhere between 90 and 135 days to finalise a tender, today it takes only 35 days.

The suppliers are a happy lot as well. They no longer have to rely on resourceful touts to get tender documents. Both technical bids and cost bids are submitted online and the contract goes to the best bid on both counts.

G Kiran Kumar, account manager, HCL, who has seen both methods of tendering (manual and online), says: "The online system has removed a lot of tedious aspects, which has been the biggest boon for us. No longer do we have to fill out detailed forms and rush to offer clarifications." More importantly, all parties can view other bids once the tenders have been awarded. This level of transparency clearly eliminates any scope for bias.

This practice, which pays for itself, has been completely outsourced to a Delhi-based private company C1 India. C1 gets 0.024 per cent of the tender value as fees. That means the government doesn't have to pay to run this programme.

More significantly, greater competition (the average number of bids per tender has gone up from 3 to 4.5) has also reduced quotations. Prices quoted are down 16 per cent, which once again translates into savings for the government. "The project has paid for itself many times over if one looks at the cost savings for the Andhra Pradesh government," says Sawhney.

Contd...

Contd...

The Andhra Pradesh Numbers

No. of Departments/ Agencies	8 Departments	7 Departments, 9 PSUs, 17 Municipalities	8 Departments, 13 PSUs 17 Municipalities, 5 Universities
Value of Transactions Completed (Rs. Cr)	2,012	15,849	16,630
No. of Transactions Processed	564	3,746	7,931
Percentage of E-Procurement	20	80	90

Source: World Bank Report

Andhra Pradesh's experience has other states queuing up to set up their own e-procurement systems. In Karnataka, Antares Systems has set up e-procurement portals for state government undertakings such as the Karnataka State Road Transport Corporation (KSRTC), Bangalore Development Authority (BDA), and Bangalore Water Supply and Sewerage Board (BWSSB) to name a few. Kerala, Gujarat and Chhattisgarh have also recently followed suit.

Beyond cost benefits and the reduction of delays, e-procurement also benefits the small trader. In the past, they complained that they got to know of tenders only once the bids had closed, as the ads usually appeared in newspapers with low circulation. Submitting documents was also difficult, and their bigger competitors would often influence the final outcome.

Due to its various inherent advantages, e-procurement has made it a level playing field. Companies can now participate in tenders nationally. N.B.V. Satyanarayana, assistant general manager, IVRCL, a construction company, says that his company now participates in tenders across 14 states, something that would have been impossible in the past. They are also comfortable with the security mechanisms in place as all data is encrypted.

Today, though the Andhra Pradesh project is considered a model, similar initiatives in other countries show that there is still tremendous scope for improvement. Subhash Bhatnagar, a professor at the Indian Institute of Management, Ahmedabad, who has studied the project for the World Bank, argues that unlike the Korean model, the Indian model is not yet completely evolved. For instance, e-certificates are not yet issued by the government, and contractors still have to upload their certificates manually. (These are submitted by contractors as a record of their past work in the field.)

Such drawbacks notwithstanding, recently, the initiative received a further fillip when the central government, too, decided to adopt e-procurement. In April, the Directorate General of Civil Supplies and Disposal (DGS&D) launched its own programme. Though the DGS&D tenders for goods worth only Rs. 6,000 crore every year, all central government departments use its rates as a benchmark when deciding their requirements. This expands the scope to tens of thousands of crores. More than the amount transacted, several observers feel that this will send a strong message to states that have not yet come aboard.

Source: BusinessWorld, June 26, 2006.

16

Google in 2005: Innovating to Stay Ahead[1]

A V Vedpuriswar

In 2005, Google, well-known for its search engine was considering one of the most successful and innovative companies in the technological world. Having completed its initial public offering successfully in April 2004, Google finalised plans to widen its product range and minimise its dependence on search engines. Google also seems on course for a head to head clash with many bigger rivals in the industry including Microsoft. Google realises the only way to stay ahead will be to innovate. But as rivals come up with competing products, will Google be able to sustain its lead?

Introduction

In 2005, Google, well known for its search engine was considered one of the most successful and innovative companies in the tech world. Having completed its IPO successfully in April 2004, Google was finalizing plans to widen its product range and minimize its dependence on search engines. As it did so, Google seemed

1 This case is drawn heavily from the article "Managing Google's Idea Factory," by Elgin Ben from BusinessWeek (3rd October 2005, pp.72-74).

on course for a head to head clash with many bigger rivals in the industry including Microsoft. Google realized the only way to stay ahead would be to innovate. But as rivals came up with competing products, would Google be able to sustain its lead?

Background Note

Set up in 1996 by two Stanford students Larry Page (Page) and Sergey Brin (Brin), Google began as an academic search engine. By 1998, *Google.com* was answering 10,000 search queries a day. The number increased to over 5,00,000 queries a day in 1999. As 2000 ended, Google was already handling more than 100 million search queries a day. By the fourth quarter of 2001, Google announced that it had become profitable.

Google entered into a multi-year contract with America Online (AOL) in May 2002 for providing technology to enhance AOL's own search offering. Google took over AOL's traditional search function from Inktomi in early 2002. Google powered web search results for AOL sites in the United States, the United Kingdom, France, Germany, the Netherlands, Brazil, Mexico, Argentina, Japan, Australia and Canada. It provided paid listings to sites in the US, Japan and Canada. Google also provided search results to the AOL-owned sites of Netscape and CompuServe. When the contract was renewed in October 2003, Google's paid listings were integrated into AOL Yellow Pages listings.

In June 2005, Google's share of US searches hit 52% (up from 45% in June 2004). It was answering over 2 billion queries a day. Such was its rising popularity that Google, which had not been in the list of the 100 most powerful brands in the world till 2004, joined the list straight at the 38th position in 2005[2]. The survey valued the brand at $8.64 billion in 2005.

Google in 2005

Page and Brin had long declared their mission was to "organize the world's information." But for a long time, Google had primarily been a search engine that could locate intelligently and speedily content which was freely accessible on the web. Only in recent months had the staggering scope of Google's ambition

2 "Interbrand survey," *www.businessweek.com*, August 2004 and August 2005.

become visible. Google was moving to digitize the world's libraries, to offer all comers free voice calls, to provide satellite images of the world, and perhaps to give away wireless broadband service to millions of people. Google believed it could make every bit of information available to anyone anywhere, and direct all those bits – whether text, audio, or video – through its computers to users.

Google's meteoric rise had attracted various competitors, from giants like Microsoft and Yahoo! to upstarts like Technorati and Exalead. They were all attempting to grab market share from Google with comparable products.

An analyst mentioned[3]:

"People are used to typing in Google to search. But its competitors are doing a really good job of rolling out quality features and products."

Despite these moves by competitors, Google's search lead looked formidable. In June 2005, Google's share of US searches hit 52% (up from 45% in June 2004). The market share of its closest competitors, Yahoo and MSN had slipped to 25% and 10% respectively. Though many studies confirmed the near-parity of rival search technologies, changing searchers' habits was more difficult in 2005 than in the Web's early days. One major reason for this loyalty was Google's spartan home page, which included just 13 links or so – less than one tenth of the number at MSN and Yahoo.

An industry observer mentioned[4]:

"People are on a mission when they come to a search site. The last thing they want to know is what's happening with Tom Cruise."

Apart from internet search, Google was making successful inroads into other categories. A person could use Google software with any Internet browser to search the web and desktop, send and store up to two gigabytes of e-mail via Gmail (Hotmail, Microsoft's rival free e-mail service, offered 250 megabytes, a fraction of that). Customers could manage, edit, and send digital photographs

---

3 Chris Sherman, editor of the industry newsletter SearchDay.

4 Spool, Jared M founding principal at researcher User Interface Engineering.

using Google's Picasa software, which is considered as the best PC photo software available. Through Google's Blogger, customers could create, post online, and print formatted documents. Google was offering all these products for free.

For years, Microsoft had prided itself on attracting and retaining the best brains in the industry. Since 2004, every other month, Google had been hiring a top developer from Microsoft. Before Google's IPO in October 2004, Microsoft executives had dismissed this brain drain as a function of greed. But when the exodus continued after the IPO – especially when Marc Lucovsky, one of Microsoft's best engineers, left for Google – it was clear that Microsoft had a much bigger problem on its hands. As of March 2005, roughly 100 Microsoft employees had left for Google. Google and not Microsoft seemed to be the hot place for young techies. Apart from being attracted to the unsolved technical challenges that affected hundreds of millions of people daily, much of Google's magnetism was also a result of its zany culture perfectly suited to the geek lifestyle. Google pretty much seemed to have become what Microsoft was in the 1990s.

CEO Eric Schmidt pointed out,[5]

> *"One of the criticisms that the media makes is to compare Google to previous generation companies. Google is trying to solve the next problem, not the last problem."*

Privately, Google's executives understood exactly the impact they were having on Gates and his team. But in public, they projected a carefree image in part because it made business sense. They seemed to have history in mind. One blunder made by Netscape was that it had become aggressive to the point of telling the world how he intended to put Microsoft out of business. Google did not want to repeat that mistake. Moreover, many of the most influential people at Google understood Microsoft well. Schmidt had battled Gates as CTO of Sun Microsystems and CEO of Novell in the 1990s. Omid Kordestani, Google's head of advertising sales, had been a top executive at Netscape. Three of Google's directors, Ram Shriram, John Doerr, and Michael Moritz, had been on the front lines of Silicon Valley's war with Microsoft over the years.

---

5 ibid.

It was precisely this understanding of Microsoft that had encouraged Google to roll out so many new or improved products. Schmidt understood that innovation was the only way to stay ahead of powerful rivals. The moment Google allowed itself to slow, Microsoft could overwhelm it. To maintain the innovation momentum, Google paid extraordinary attention to exploiting the creativity of its talented employees.

Managing Innovation

Google's innovation initiatives were spearheaded by Marissa Mayer, Director of consumer web. It was in late 1998, when Mayer first heard about Google. When the Stanford University graduate was urged by her adviser to meet two people, who were developing ways to analyze the World Wide Web on the computer science building's fourth floor, she was initially skeptical.

Later, a headhunter persuaded Mayer to reconsider the search startup. Mayer, who ended up joining Google in early 1999, as a programmer, was only Google's 20th employee. Since then, Mayer had emerged as a powerful force inside Google. She championed innovation within Google, covering areas ranging from the look of its Web pages to new software for searching the hard drive. Mayer decided which new initiatives would get the attention of the company's founders and which would not.

Mayer's style of functioning was influenced by the philosophy of Google's founders who believed that good ideas could come from anywhere. So Page and Brin insisted that all engineers in the company had one day a week to work on their own pet projects. An ideas mailing list was open to anyone at Google who wanted to post a proposal. Mayer's job was to make sure good ideas bubbled to the surface and got the attention they needed. The task was becoming more complex as Google grew, into a large company with a workforce of 4,200 now and revenues expected to cross $3.7 billion in 2005. But Mayer persisted with her efforts, employing a variety of approaches to tap the creativity of employees.

During a casual chat in 2003, Mayer had come to know about the project of an Australian engineer, Steve Lawrence, who was developing a program to track and search the contents of his Linux based computer. Knowing Google had to figure out a way for people to locate files and documents on their own computers, Mayer tracked Lawrence down and asked him about developing a version of his software to search any PC. Seeing his enthusiasm, she put together a team to work with him. Google introduced its desktop search in October, 2004, two months before Microsoft.

Part of Mayer's challenge was realizing when to put an end to a project. For years she ran the company's Top 100 priorities list, which ranked projects by order of importance. But as Google's workforce grew, the list expanded to more than 270 projects. In 2005, Google decided it had run its course, and shut it down.

Meanwhile, Mayer took pains to make it known to employees that good ideas were always welcome. As Mayer put it,[6]

"I keep my ears open. I work at building a reputation for being receptive."

At 4 p.m., three-times-a-week, Mayer met Google engineers who had something new to discuss. It was a tradition Mayer had brought over from her days at Stanford, where she taught computer science to undergraduate students. Over the years, such meetings had spawned some big ideas, including Google's social-networking site Orkut. Mayer decided when the employees' pet projects were refined enough to be presented to the company's founders. Such decisions were often made through an established process. Mayer discussed these ideas during her open office hours or during brainstorming sessions. Yet she also met programmers informally in the cafeteria or hall-way.

In ones or twice, all the visitors got a brief hearing, typically five minutes. In one such meeting in mid-2005, she gently rejected a proposal to put a link to Hurricane Katrina information on Google's home page. The site for hurricane victims, did not seem useful enough yet. She brainstormed with a product manager on how to measure and compare the freshness of Google's search results with that of its rivals.

When one group marched in to discuss a personalized search product, Mayer paid all attention. Many experts described personalization as the Holy Grail in

[6] Elgin, Ben. "Managing Google's Idea Factory," BusinessWeek, 3rd October 2005, pp.72-74.

search. An engine that knew customer preferences and interests intimately could tailor the information delivered to improve results. Google had been offering rudimentary personalization for a year, but Mayer realized much more could be done. With two people in Mayer's office and another on speaker phone, she grilled the trio about the service's name. After a few minutes of discussion, Mayer emphasized the group on the product's features. Google's top management was having its next product-review session shortly, in which new ideas were either put on the fast-track or sent back for modification. So Mayer asked them whether they were ready to make a presentation to Larry Page the next day.

Meeting people was only one way in which Mayer kept in touch with the company's techies. Another was Google's ideas mailing list, the e-mail thread to which anyone could submit or comment on an idea. At times, the thread more resembled a form of 'techie Darwinism'. Google newcomers who offered an especially obvious suggestion ("Why don't we search blogs?"), or something mundane like how to arrange the cafeteria tables, often received rebukes. According to insiders, Google oozed with what one ex-employee called "geek machismo." Intellectual sparring can get heated. In the cafeteria, "food gets thrown," mentioned the former employee.

Mayer put in a different way,[7]

"It's about 50% new ideas, 50% indoctrination of new employees."

Google encouraged risk taking among employees. Mayer explained that for continued innovation it was essential for Google to keep its sense of fearlessness. She mentioned[8]:

"I like to launch [products] early and often. That has become my mantra," She mentioned Apple Computer and Madonna. "Nobody remembers the Sex Book or the Newton. Consumers remember your average over time. That philosophy frees you from fear."

---

[7] ibid.

[8] Elgin, ben. "Managing Google's Idea Factory," BusinessWeek, 3rd October 2005, pp.72-74.

Google had various ways to promote a collegial atmosphere among employers. An old Google technique was movie night, when perhaps 100 employees visited a local cinema. Over time, as the number of employees had grown, organizing such an event had become complicated. Yet Mayer handled several of these a year, from picking a movie to ordering thousands of tickets to writing the software that let her track who had received them.

An employee mentioned[9]:

"She still walks around with a laptop, handing out all the tickets beforehand."

The Road Ahead

Despite being hugely profitable and a favorite of the stock exchange, Google was a young company, largely controlled by its founders and dealing with the unavoidable pains of rapid growth. The search game was still in its infancy. Only a fraction of the content available online was actually searchable. For instance, even subscribers could not search current and archived issues of the Wall Street Journal or most other publications with a search engine. They had to go to the publication's site. This suggested that search engines that could get the world to list premium content on their platform might have a big advantage over competitiors. Microsoft had plenty of money to buy the rights to such content. It also owned powerful digital-rightsmanagement software, which helped copyright holders control who used their products and how often. Those might turn out to be major competitive advantages as many content companies worried about losing control of copyrighted text, music, and video on the Net.

Another advantage which Microsoft sensed was that search engines were still technologically primitive. They could not understand context, for example; if a person typed "chip," they could not tell whether customers were looking for snack food or high-tech equipment. As a result, the major search engines were scrambling to find ways to make search more personalized. The thinking was that the more a search engine knew about who was searching, the more accurate the results would be. Each company had the foundations of such a product in its

---

9 Ibid.

desktop-search software, which could tell what a person had on his or her computer's hard drive.

Perhaps Microsoft, because it understood Windows better than any other company, would be able to offer faster and more accurate searches. All the same, Microsoft was taking longer than expected to catch up with Google. Meanwhile, Google realized it could not afford to be complacent. In the past, Microsoft, with its formidable marketing and financial muscle had demonstrated that it could cut competitors down to size, ruthlessly. Would Google be able to maintain its so far brilliant track record in innovating?

(A V Vedpuriswar, Assistant Vice President, Satyam Computer Services, Hyderabad).

Bibliography

1. Mand, Adrienne. "Unlaunched Site Making Digerati Google-Eyed," *Brandweek*, 12th July 1999, Vol. 40, Issue 28, p-30.
2. Sreenivasan, Sreenath. "Google," *Columbia Journalism Review*, May/June 2000, p-9.
3. Mossberg, Walter S. "Google Is Smart, Fast, Honest and May Be Best Sleuth on the Web," *Wall Street Journal* - Eastern Edition, 1st March 2001, pp.B-1.
4. McCarthy, Jack. "Yahoo to port Google WAP technology," InfoWorld, 16th April 2001, p-16.
5. Wiggins, Richard W. "Google Seeks to Restore Deja Functionality," Information Today, June 2001, p-21.
6. Murphy, Kevin. "Teoma Hopes to Out-Google Google," Multimedia Futures, 20th July 2001, p-5.
7. Spangler, Todd. "Schmidt gets Google-Y eyed," *Interactive Week*, 13th August 2001, p-15.
8. Moody, Glyn and Doyle, Eric. "Google leads the search," *Computer Weekly*, 17th January 2002, p-25.
9. Fugazy, Danielle. "Will Google Search For More Through An IPO?" IPO Reporter, 11th February 2002, p-1.
10. Livingston, Brian. "Google's new news," InfoWorld, 8th April 2002, p-20.
11. Elgin, Ben. "Google's Offspring: Taking Baby Steps," *www.businessweek.com*, 9th March 2003.

12. Metz, Cade. "Google Watch," *PC Magazine,* 22nd April 2003, Vol. 22, Issue 7, p-28.
13. Fox, Steve. "Google and Amazon Put Books Online," *PC World,* April 2004, Vol. 22, Issue 4, p-51.
14. "Interbrand Survey," *www.businessweek.com,* August 2004.
15. Wildstrom, Stephen H. "Google's Magic Carpet Ride," *BusinessWeek,* 18th July 2005, p-22.
16. Wildstrom, Stephen H. "The Web Hits the Stacks," *BusinessWeek,* 25th July 2005, p-22.
17. "Interbrand Survey," *www.businessweek.com,* August 2005.
18. Elgin, Ben and Hesseldahl, Arik. "Google's Grand Ambitions," *BusinessWeek,* 5th September 2005, pp.36-37.
19. Beucke, Dan and Elgin, Ben. "Google's Crafty Star Search," *BusinessWeek,* 12th September 2005, p-16.
20. Elgin, Ben. "How Google Got Its Groove," *BusinessWeek,* 19th September 2005, p-144.
21. Elgin, Ben. "Managing Google's Idea Factory," *BusinessWeek,* 3rd October 2005, pp.72-74.
22. Fine, Jon. "Hard Questions from Google," *BusinessWeek,* 24th October 2005, p-28.
23. Wildstrom, Stephen H. "The Way to a Google Office," *BusinessWeek,* 31st October 2005, p-20.
24. Neilsen/NetRatings NetView
25. *www.searchengine.com*
26. *www.google.com*

Exhibit 1: Overall Share of Visits to Top 25 Search Engines and Portals, April 2004

Name	Share
Search-Specific Visits	42.4%
Portal Visits	46.8%
Visits to Rest of the Sites	10.8%
Total	100.0%

Source: searchenginewatch.com.

Exhibit 2: Some of the Major Online Services Offered by Google (December 2004)	
Service Offerings	**Brief Features**
Google Alerts	A user could receive automatic e-mail updates on the basis of registered search terms, information type and frequency.
Google Catalogs	This service offered users the convenience of searching online mail-order catalogs. It was a non-commercial offering as Google did not have any association with the vendors.
Google Directory	It was an integration of Google's sophisticated search technology with the Open Directory[10] pages.
Froogle	Froogle focused on product search through which users could search for products and locate stores in their neighborhood. One could also make product comparisons.
Google Groups	A group could open a homepage with Google and perform discussions online through announcement lists, mailing lists etc.
Google Image Search	One could search over 880 million images indexed for viewing.
Google Local	Provided search services for local stores and services through postal codes or names of towns or cities.
Google News Search	This service presented information from over 4500 news sources worldwide. The most relevant news was presented first.
Google Scholar	Enabled specific search for research papers, theses, books, abstracts, preprints, technical reports etc.
	Contd....

[10] The Open Directory Project was the largest, most comprehensive human-edited directory of the Web. It was constructed and maintained by a vast, global community of volunteer editors. *(http://dmoz.org/about.html).*

Contd....	
Google Wireless	Users could search the entire world wide web from their mobiles apart from 5 million pages of the "mobile web" created specifically for wireless devices.
Google Suggest	An advanced service from Google that automatically offered users a list of popularly used, related search terms by simply entering the first one or two keywords.
Google Toolbar	The web could be searched with Google from any site by typing keywords instead of URLs.
Google Translate Tools	One could search for web pages in a specific language or a country. Apart from it, the tool also offered translation services.

Source: www.google.co.in.

Exhibit 3: Top 5 US Destinations (January 2004)

Search Destinations	**Unique Audience (000)**	**Active Reach (%)**
1. Google	59,327	39.37
2. Yahoo! Search	45,774	39.38
3. MSN Search	44,651	29.63
4. AOD Search	23,394	15.53
5. Ask Jeeves	12,792	8.49

Source: Neilsen/NetRatings NetView, January 2004.

Exhibit 4: Search Engine Global Usage Share

Property	May 2004	Nov. 2003	May 2003	Jan. 2003
Google	56.4%	56.1%	55.2%	54.7%
Yahoo!	21.1%	21.5%	21.7%	22.1%
MSN Search	9.2%	9.4%	9.6%	9.5%
AOL Search	3.8%	3.7%	3.8%	3.7%
Terra Lycos	2.0%	2.3%	2.6%	2.8%
Altavista	1.7%	1.9%	2.2%	2.5%
Ask Jeeves	1.7%	1.6%	1.5%	1.5%

Source: Neilsen/NetRatings NetView.

Exhibit 5: US Search Engine User Demographics (for the 12 weeks ending May 15, 2004)

	Google	Yahoo! Search	MSN Search
Female	46.58%	50.76%	54.26%
Male	53.42%	49.24%	45.74%
18-34	43.57%	48.23%	39.53%
35-54	42.85%	39.83%	44.49%
55+	13.57%	11.94%	15.99%
Under $30k/year	20.00%	21.87%	21.01%
$30k-$100k	57.05%	57.69%	58.84%
Over $100k/year	22.95%	20.44%	20.16%

Source: Neilsen/NetRatings NetView.

Moon, Mars and Everything Else

– Mala Bhargava

"One can hardly keep count as Google introduces one new venture after another"

I still come across people who get startled out of their wits when they zoom in on their own houses on Google Earth. It's rather funny when you think of how the powers-that-be go to all the trouble to prohibit photography in various sensitive spots, only to have Google swoop in and give everyone an aerial view anytime, anywhere.

Well, governments may not be amused, but NASA doesn't take a dim view of it. Recently, it partnered with Google to map up Mars. Head to *mars.google.com* and you can zoom into the craters on Mars, or use three modes to view the planet's surface. No McDonald's yet, but Google has reportedly taken up all other planet domains for its future interplanetary plans. It's already mapped up the moon. I won't be surprised if the next astronaut sent into space turns out to be a Google executive.

But this isn't just about Google going galactic. Google has enough designs on the home planet. I've written about its global vision before. But I'm not to be blamed for the search king's coming up with one plan after another almost on a weekly basis.

One of Google's more talked-about ventures is its acquisition of Writely (*writely.com*), an online word processor. It is not the first, or the only one. But in Google's hands, its potential use could go up a few million times. Providing it 'by-invitation-only', G-mail style, has ensured that everyone wants a peek. (No use asking me for invites, please.) Writely has many Word-like features and is easy to use. You can create documents, download them to your PC and pop them back, or work with them online with other people in real time. Microsoft's format is supported. You can edit documents, track revisions, and use many of the features you're used to, like styles. Competition for Microsoft? Maybe, but Microsoft has no shortage of competition anyway. Besides, many businesses have already invested a lot in MS Office.

But could people use Google Writely more? And, being a collaboration tool, could it make a difference to content management systems? The most interesting thing about Writely is that one can create and publish web pages and blogs from right there. Future plans for revenue through subscription or advertising can easily be visualized. Writely may not be important by itself, but becomes much more powerful when combined with Google's online services – planned and existing. Rumour has it that Google will offer infinite storage space online on 'G-drive'. It is like any other drive, and can store user files, searches, bookmarks, etc. However, it remains to be seen whether users will entrust their data to anyone else.

If you're a Google Desktop user, you may know that it's been upgraded, and now has a handy tool that's already a favourite. Press the 'Ctrl' key twice and a search box pops up no matter what program you're in. Two more key presses, and it's out of sight. Combined with Google Suggest, that lets Google guess your search possibilities and offer suggested links, it can further speed up and narrow down searches. G-Mail and G-Talk will be developed further and used for many other services.

This month, Google acquired @Last Software and its 3D imaging program SketchUp. Used by limited segments like architects and gamers, it is supposed to bring '3D for everyone'. Google also launched its online video store, partnering with CBS and others. It plans to put the most popular content for users to download inexpensively on demand. And just this week, Google partnered with Nike to launch an invitation-only site for soccer fans worldwide, its first "social networking" site.

Keeping track of everything that Google launches is actually quite a challenge and I'll have missed dozens of ventures and entries into different areas. The Internet giant is currently grappling with a few court cases, including one with the US department of justice over giving information on search results, but that isn't stopping it from putting in one solid building block after another into Googledom.

Source: BusinessWorld, April 3, 2006.

17

Apple's New Operating System, "Tiger": Riding on the Success of iPod?

Shalini

On April 29, 2005, Apple launched Tiger, its latest operating system. With 200 features, Tiger is the most advanced powerful and user-friendly operating system for the Apple's Mac users to date. With innovative features like Spotlight and Dashboard, Tiger is poised to change the way people use computers across the world. While some opine that Apple has launched Tiger 'about time' when the company is basking in the success of iPod, others are skeptical whether the company can make Tiger as successful as iPod. Besides, Apple is also expected to face competition from Microsoft, which is expected to come out with 'Longhorn', an advanced version of its operating system Microsoft XP. The case study, while highlighting the product innovation strategy of Apple, provides the scope to discuss Apple's plans to promote Tiger by leveraging on the brand value of iPod.

Source: Icfai Business School Case Development Centre.

"Apple has been innovative and that has paid off with the iPod. Embedded in the stock price is the belief that it will continue to innovate."[1]

– *Zach Shafran,*
Manager of the Waddell & Reed Advisor[2], Science and Technology fund.

"Mac OS X Tiger is the most innovative and secure desktop operating system ever created. Tigers groundbreaking new features like Spotlight and Dashboard will change the way people use their computers, and drive our competitors nuts trying to copy them."[3]

– Steve Jobs,
CEO of Apple

"Analysts are predicting a halo effect for Tiger, with the system basking in the stunning popularity of the iPod and the slew of new products Apple has been releasing, like its $499 Mac mini."[4]

On April 29th 2005, Apple released its new version of operating system, Tiger, for its Mac computers. Tiger is reported to be the most advanced, powerful, user-friendly and attractive version of Apple's operating systems. In order to leverage on the success of iPod, it has been observed that Apple launched Tiger with 200 additional features that included an in-built powerful search tool named Spotlight. Spotlight is the major attractive feature in Tiger and is considered to be more powerful search tool than the search systems in its earlier Mac versions as well as the desktop search tool in windows. Apart from Spotlight, other key features include – Dashboard, Parental controls and inbuilt video conferencing systems. Apple stated that its new OS has many new features, which might not be made available by Microsoft for atleast the next one and a half years. Microsoft, which is working to improve its existing windows XP, is expected to come out with a new version code named "Longhorn" by the end of 2006.

However, Apple's Tiger has some limitations. Unlike some of its features like Spotlight and Safari Web browser, its other tools are quite slow, taking more than normal time, particularly Apple Mail. Apple has announced to tackle the limitations in the next few months. As against Apple's earlier innovations such as the graphical user interface, the mouse, the laser printer, the colour monitor, photos and videos in computers, windows for PC and on-screen icons that had benefited its rivals more than Apple itself; its latest innovations, especially the iPod helped soar company's revenues and profit considerably. By 2005, iPod has been contributing one-third of the total revenue of Apple. Although, the success of iPod is considered to have a halo effect on the company's Mac business, concerns have always remained on the durability of this effect on the company. According to David Yoffie, a professor of Harvard Business School – "Apple has some hot products, they outgrow the market for some time and those [periods] tend to be short-lived."[5] It was opined that after iPod and its software – iTune, Mac OS X Tiger would enable Apple to gain a sustainable competitive advantage in the PC market.

Apple's New Operating System, "Tiger"

On April 12th 2005, Apple announced to release its new operating system, Mac OS X 10.4 i.e. "Tiger". Steve Jobs said, For starters, "this is one of those rare occasions when a major software release is actually early."[6] With better speed, attractive graphics, utilities, security and simplicity, Tiger was considered better than its earlier versions and even Microsoft's XP. Tiger also offered no crashing of system, pop-up adds, spyware and viruses. Tiger was the continuation of Apple's attempts to improve the compatibility with Windows. Steve Jobs said, "It has turned out just wonderfully. It's our biggest leap forward since the original Macintosh in 1984."[7]

Tiger was priced at $129 in the US and €129 in Europe. The Mac OS X[8] Tiger Family pack was introduced for $199 per residence that would cover five users. Apple also sold a software bundle that consisted of Tiger, iLife[9] and iWork[10] for $249. Tiger was priced at $499 for a 10-client license and $999 for an unlimited-client edition.

Tiger's key offerings included its search tool, Spotlight [Annexure1] that allowed users to locate all the references related to a topic stored in their Mac systems by typing in keywords, the way it is done in Google. The idea of integrating Spotlight with Tiger struck Apple after observing the performance of iTunes instant search tool.[11] Spotlight, which is represented by a magnifying glass icon, is placed on the right of the menu bar that provides a drop down search field. When a user types in a key word, a new list appears with results sorted according to various types like, PDF documents and mail messages. Spotlight is adapted to run with most applications like Tiger's System Preferences, Mail and Address Book. Spotlight can also find data within spreadsheets and PDF documents. Spotlight also enables users to search a song from his iTune library by typing in the keyword in the iTunes search bar. For instance, if a user types 'April', it displays a list of searches that includes documents, calendar appointments and even e-mails that contain that term. Not just confined to file names, Spotlight searches include information not only about the files but any text contained in them. It can also search files on the basis of name of person who created and modified the file, file type, and also individual words in the document.

Further, Tiger also has the option of Smart Folders[12] that enables its users to store the search results.[13] With Smart Mail Folders in the 'Tiger', the organization of searches has been further simplified. Tim Deal, an analyst with Technology Business Research,[14] said, "The company is really underscoring the importance of Spotlight. I do think it will better enable users to manage the wealth of data they download or install on their computers."[15]

Apart from Spotlight, iChat is also updated on Tiger. iChat AV was first introduced in Apple's earlier version of operating systems, Jaguar and also in Panther.[16] But the conferencing was limited to one-to-one. The upgraded version in Tiger enables more Mac users to join in the conversation. Apart from increasing the number of users, Tiger's iChat is also considered to have high quality audio sessions.

Tiger employs next generation videos, H.264/AVC (also called MPEG-4 Part 10i) open-standard video codec (video compressor and decompressor).[17] With H.264, iChat allows users to do audio conferencing with 10 people and video conferencing with four at one time [Annexure 2]. The videoconferencing facility is overhauled in Tiger. The interface provides the user with a three dimensional view[18] of the video conferencing participants. H.264 codec benefits included high quality video and high quality image. It could also be used for iChat AV.

Tiger also has other important features like Dashboard and Automator. Dashboard helps users to access important information on weather reports and forecasts and stock quotations by employing a new kind of application called widgets. As many as 14 widgets (used by Apple for small programs) have been incorporated in Tiger, which include calculator, clock, currency translator, weather report tools, stock ticker and air-flight tracker [Annexure 3]. All widgets are enabled to access online information at the touch of a button providing live webcam updates to the users.

Tiger's new feature, Automator (a program for automating tasks on a computer) would save time for its users by managing repetitive tasks. Automator is considered similar to AppleScript,[19] but unlike apple script, users are not required to write programs. Instead, they can create a flowchart for actions to be performed. Apple itself has supplied over 100 actions on the left side of Automator's window. The users can drag these actions into the Workflow area in order of their sequence, thereby creating a complex task series.

Tiger's another tool, Safari 2.0, provides the users with the RSS XML links and is a new version of Web browser. SAFARI 2.0 is embedded with a purpose to streamline browsing. RSS[20] (Really Simple Syndication) technology enables Web publishers to create small text files that contain certain basic information about Web content. With RSS, users can view the summary of the latest news and information on RSS-friendly Websites. If users access any website with the help of Safari, a blue badge appears on the window indicating RSS feed. By clicking on the icon, users can view a better version of the website's content along with headlines. Apart from a RSS search box, Safari also includes Start Private Browsing command under its menu. Safari 2.0 would also enable its users to save old web pages on their computers and access them even if the Website removed the news item from its site.

Other features included Mac Sync, (which allows seamless synchronization of information among Apple computers), VoiceOver, (an enhanced universal interface that allows users to operate a Mac through speech and audible cues) and parental controls. Tiger also updated some features that included Mail 2, Apple's Mail application (sometimes referred to as Mail.app because of it NeXTStep heritage), Address Book 4.0 and iCal 2.0 [Annexure 4]. Phil Schiller, Senior Vice President at Apple, said, "Tiger delivers more features and capabilities to our customers and enables us to distance ourselves from any other computer platform."[21]

Tiger is expected to increase the share of PC business in Apple's overall business. The new Mac OS X is expected to be installed in more than ten million computers in the US, gaining a market share of over 4% in 2005. Merrill Lynch's Steven Milunovich said, "Unlike previous Mac OS X upgrades, Tiger should boost Apple hardware sales. Tiger represents the fourth version of Mac OS X. Apple saw its PC unit share decline on average by 3 basis points one quarter after the release of last three Mac OS updates. We believe the halo effect from the iPod craze will reverse this negative trend. We expect Apple to have about 2.5 percent of the worldwide market by the end of 2005, up from 2.1 percent in 1Q/05."[22]

The announcement of the launch of Tiger came at a time when the company was already tasting the success of iPod among other products like iTunes and MacMini. Tiger's customers outnumbered those of Panther, the earlier version of Tiger, which was released in October 2003. It was reported that Apple had never witnessed the 'launch of such epic propitiations.'[23] "The success of iPod and iTunes has made sure that anything that Apple does, makes big headlines and this latest one sure is important. Apple has just released the Mac OS X 10.4 Tiger in the retail market and it is already claimed to be a huge success."[24]

Leveraging on the Success of iPod?

"In what could only be labeled the 'It's about time' corporate move, Apple will finally begin to take on PC makers in 2005. Now that the iPod is firmly engrained on all digital music fans as the only device worthy of their digital music, Apple will spend its hard-earned PR capital on growing its Mac user base beyond the 2% worldwide user level."[25]

By the end of 2004, iPod audio player was dominating the digital portable audio player market with 65% market share. iPod had become successful after one and a half years of its release (in November 2001) when it garnered total sales of 1 million units. Since then, iPod recorded continuous increase in sales and by November 2004, Apple had sold 6 million units of iPod, which made it difficult for Apple's competitors – Dell, Rio and Creative Labs, to establish their hold in this market. Apple also continued to introduce new products based on iPod platform. In November 2004, two new models of iPod were introduced, the iPod Photo and iPod U2 Special Edition. On the release of new models of iPod, Steve Jobs said, "iPod has become a cultural phenomenon."[26]

Having witnessed the success of iPod, analysts were optimistic on Apple's new version of Mac OS X. Observing that the success of iPod was spilling on Apple's PC area, CSFB analyst Rob Semple, while commenting on Tiger, said, "We expect it to be Apple's most popular (operating system) iteration to date. Apple has broken records with each of its two previous updates (Jaguar and Panther), with Panther recording revenue of $US60-plus million (more than $A77 million) in its first quarter, which we expect Tiger to easily surpass. While iPod has been enormously successful and will continue to grow as a percentage of the total business, we believe the next leg of Apple's share price ascension will be driven by success in the PC market, where the Mac has just completed its second consecutive quarter of share gain."[27]

Lured by iPod success, new users are expected to get attracted to Tiger. Some view iPod as a product that has increased the demand for Apple's entire product line. By the end of 2005, iPod sales are estimated to increase to 30 million, which in turn would increase the sales of Apple's other product lines. It is estimated that the upgraded version of operating system, Tiger would be adopted by 14 million users of Mac OS X system. Steven Milunovich from Merrill Lynch expects that in the first quarter of its release, Tiger sales would range between $84 million and $100 million as compared to $60 million for the previous version of Mac OS X, Panther. The company expects Apple's share in the global PC market to increase from 2.1% in the first quarter of 2005 to 2.5% by the end of 2005. "Previous OS releases did not boost Apple's PC share. Based on the features of Tiger and the halo effect from the iPod, we think Apple's P.C share outlook is rosier this time."[28]

Initially, Apple was considered to cater only to the niche market pertaining to a particular group of "creative" users but it was opined that the success of iPod has broadened the reach of Apple by making it a desirable brand among consumers. Apple CEO Steve Jobs said, "Apple is firing on all cylinders, and we have some incredible new products in the pipeline for the coming year."[29] It has been opined that the success of iPod has changed Apple's image from a mere computer manufacturer to a strong player in consumer electronics and music. Steve Jobs said, "The great thing is that Apple's DNA hasn't changed. The place where Apple has been standing for the last two decades is exactly where computer technology and the consumer electronics markets are converging. So it's not like we're having to cross the river to go somewhere else; the other side of the river is coming to us."[30]

In the first quarter of fiscal year 2005 that ended on December 31st 2004 (Fiscal year is October-September), iPod and other music-related products constituted 40% of Apple's total revenues as compared to 15% in the same period, the previous year. Tiger is expected to become the next big thing for Apple after iPod, drawing more customers who are already witnessing the halo effect of iPod [Box 1].

However, some analysts are sceptical regarding iPod's ability to attract new users to Apple's Tiger. Although iPod's halo effect is considered effective on many other products of Apple that included iBook, PowerBooks, iMacs and Mac mini, some feel that it has not translated to Apple's PowerMacs. Mac systems have witnessed a decrease in the global market share to 1.8% in the quarter ending

Box 1

Miss Farker had started thinking about buying an Apple a few months earlier, after she got one of the company's iPod digital music players.

Her graphic artist boyfriend, a longtime Apple enthusiast who works part time at the company's Tysons Corner Center store, helped her choose an iBook laptop with a 12-inch screen. Apple sells the IBook for between $1,000 and $1,500. "I love it," Miss Farker said. Its best feature is that it is more compatible with her beloved iPod, she said. "You can sync your iPod with a PC, but it's a lot harder to do. It's not set up to be friendly." Apple executives and industry analysts call this the iPod "halo" effect.

They say it works like this: A consumer such as Miss Farker, who had primarily used computers that operate on a Windows-based operating system, gets an iPod.

They fall in love with it, so much so that they begin buying other Apple products, eventually replacing their PC with a Macintosh, an IBook or another kind of Apple computer. For now, the halo effect exists primarily as a theory in the minds of executives and some analysts, but evidence is emerging that it is becoming a real phenomenon.

Source: "IPod's halo; Music machine turns users into Apple lovers.(BUSINESS)", www.highbeam.com (The Washington Times), May 5th 2005.

October 2004 from 2.1% in the corresponding period last year. Unlike Apple's Mac computers, it was opined that iPod has been successful due to its reasonable pricing. Eugene Munster, an analyst with Piper Jaffrey issued a research note that stated, "Apple's domination in digital music is a critical piece to the story. But we don't believe that iPod is the only potential growth avenue for the company."[31]

However, Rob Enderle, an analyst, considered the so-called iPod's halo effect "a myth." He opined, "From what I'm seeing, the iPod simply drives people into the stores, and the foot traffic helps move product. The iPod benefits the entire Apple product line, but Apple could have done the same thing by having Paris Hilton, or some other celebrity, visit the Apple stores."[32]

Still, according to some, if not a halo effect, iPod is having a fertilizing effect on Apple's computer sales. "This in itself isn't enough to sell more computers. However, the combination of this desirability with the technical superiority of the new Tiger operating system makes the Apple computer a much stronger alternative to Windows PCs."[33]

Merrill Lynch, an investment firm, is also optimistic on the launch of Apple's Mac OS X 10.4 "Tiger". The company stated, "There is now solid evidence of the halo effect, so the company wants to strike while the iron is hot."[34] Shaw Wu, an analyst with American Technology Research, said, "Tiger could drive a new hardware cycle and that's pretty significant."[35] With Tiger, Apple aims to gain a bigger slice of the market dominated by Microsoft. According to some analysts, Tiger has enabled Apple to move ahead of Microsoft in terms of technological advances.

It is opined that Apple's Tiger is a stronger offer than Microsoft's XP. With Microsoft having no comparable offer to make till the end of 2006, Tiger is expected to attract more first time buyers of Apple computers.

Challenges Ahead

While Apple released Tiger, Microsoft was also working on a better version of its operating system codenamed Longhorn. Longhorn is the major upgrade after Microsoft launched Windows XP in 2001. With improvements over XP, Microsoft is expecting Longhorn to boost sales. Among major improvements, Microsoft's Longhorn would make data sharing much easier and faster, reduce power consumption by laptops, improve navigation system and has an appealing desktop. The first preview of Longhorn is expected in June 2005.

Longhorn would also feature a similar powerful search engine as that of Tiger's Spotlight that would be based on its Windows File System (WinFS) technology. Apart from Spotlight, Microsoft's Longhorn has promised to offer other similar features as those in Apple's Tiger [Annexure 5]. Although Microsoft also has a desktop search tool, Apple claims its Spotlight to be better as it is a built-in feature in the operating system rather than an add-on feature as in Microsoft's operating systems.

As Longhorn would enter the market already dominated by Windows, some analysts opine that Apple should be concerned about the halo effect of Windows media rather than that of iPod. They feel that the emotional attachment of people with Windows Media and MTV.com is quite strong, so much so that they expect customers to dump their Macs and buy new PCs. According to Jim Allchin, Microsoft's group vice president for platforms, the number of Windows sold in 2005 would be greater than the total Mac computers used across the world, and by the end of 2005, 730 million people would be using Windows. Further, Microsoft is also expected to launch a big ad campaign by June 2005 that would grow by 2006, the year of Longhorn's launch.

Tiger has enabled Apple to move ahead of Microsoft in terms of technological advances. Steve Jobs boasted, "Tiger will give customers one more reason to buy a Mac, because it's so far ahead of Windows. The people developing Longhorn are trying to copy everything they can from it."[36]

Although executives at Tiger were optimistic on the college market for Tiger sales, estimations remain low on the expected sales from market, comprising kindergarten through high school as state budget shortfalls have limited expenditures on public schools. However, it is expected that Apple would be able to garner more customers in the absence of Longhorn. Already delayed a number of times, Longhorn is expected to arrive by the end of 2006. Joe Wilcox, an analyst with Jupiter Research,[37] said, "Microsoft is months away from issuing a next-generation Windows beta, which will put Tiger well in front of most, early Longhorn hype."[38]

Wilcox added – "Apple also is in a position to exploit Microsoft missteps."[39] He further added that Spotlight was the main selling point for Tiger helping the users to do away with the "archaic file folder metaphor"[40]. "Do people think about where to file their memories in their brains? Robust search is much closer than file folders to how most people think. Apple can claim leadership, while Microsoft appears to fall behind."[41]

Further, the users of Microsoft Windows also face problems of viruses and spywares while the launch of Tiger is considered as right time for Apple to regain the market share in the PC area. It is opined that Tiger's retail success is more important to Apple than Longhorn's retail success to Windows as the sales of the Mac OS X is less than that of Windows.

Corresponding with the release of Tiger, Apple is planning commercials to demonstrate the power and ease of use of the operating system. A total of 25 commercials are planned to be launched by December 2005. "With Microsoft's Longhorn still 2 years away, the time to strike is now, and Jobs knows it. 2005 will be the year of the Mac, and millions of people who have fallen in love with their iPods are finally ready to consider other Apple products."[42]

(Shalini is associated with Icfai Business School, Case Development Centre.)

Endnotes

1 La Monica, Paul R. "Apple earns its stripes", *http://money.cnn.com/*, April 12th 2005

2 Waddell & Reed Financial is one of the US's oldest mutual fund managers. Its subsidiaries administer and distribute nearly 70 mutual funds (representing $38 billion in assets under management) under the names Ivy Funds, Target Funds, and W&R Advisors Funds. They also manage accounts for institutional investors and private clients.

3 "Apple to ship Mac OS X "Tiger" on April 29; More than 200 new features & innovations.", M2 Presswire, April 12th 2005

4 Wendland, Mike "Apple, Microsoft prepare for war with new systems", *http://www.freep.com/* March 31st 2005

5 "Will Innovation Translate Into Bigger Slice of Market For Personal Computers?" *The Asian Wall Street Journal*, April 29th – May 1st 2005, Pg A5

6 Burrows, Peter "Apple's Tiger, Burning How Bright?", *www.businessweek.com*, April 13th 2005

7 Ibid.

8 The character X is a Roman numeral and is officially pronounced "ten", continuing the numbering of previous Macintosh operating systems such as Mac OS 8 and Mac OS 9. Some people read it as the letter X and pronounce it "ex". One reason for this interpretation is the tradition of giving Unix-like operating system names ending with the letter x (e.g. AIX, IRIX, Linux, Minix, Ultrix, Xenix). Another reason is Apple's tendency to refer to specific versions in print as (for example) "Mac OS X version 10.4".

9 iLife '05 is the suite of tightly integrated applications that continues to lead the digital media revolution by offering new versions of iPhoto, iMovie, iDVD, and GarageBand and iTunes.

10 iWork '05 is the perfect companion to iLife. It consists of two applications: Pages and Keynote 2. Pages is a streamlined, yet powerful word processing application that makes it easy for anyone to create great looking documents, from a simple letter or invitation to a monthly newsletter or three-panel brochure. Keynote 2 makes it easy to create compelling presentations and interactive slideshows. Customers can enhance their presentations with animated text, new themes, and advanced build animations.

11 In iTunes search capability, the user simply selects the search box, starts typing, and iTunes dynamically limits the song list in the player to match the user's search text.

12 Smart Folders contain documents grouped together based on search criteria that you define instead of their physical location. Computer file systems are rigid: a file can only be in one folder inside a hierarchy of other folders on your disk. Smart Folders fundamentally change the way of organizing the stuff because now a file can literally be in two folders (or many) at once without duplicating or moving the underlying file.

13 To create a Smart Folder, users are required to navigate to the Finder and choose File, then New Smart Folder. This displays the New Smart Folder window, which provides a visual query builder similar to the playlist query builder in Windows Media Player. After this, by simply clicking on the Save button, users can save their new Smart Folder where they want it. Double-clicking on the folder instantly displays the results.

14 Technology Business Research, Inc. (TBR), headquartered in Hampton, N.H., is recognized as one of the leading market research and consulting firms specializing in the analyses of computer, software, networking, mobility and professional services companies and the markets in which they participate.

15 "Apple's Tiger, Burning How Bright?", op.cit.

16 The looks of audio chats in Panther consisted of a panel with the list of the names of other chat participants' names and also a sound meter. In Tiger, the soundmeter served additional function i.e. the user not only knew with whom he was talking to, but also provided a visual cue that lets the user to know who's talking.

17 A new standard for upcoming high-definition DVDs, H.264 uses the latest innovations in video compression technology to provide incredible video quality from the smallest amount of video data. This means that it provides the users with crisp, clear video in much smaller files, saving the bandwidth and storage costs over previous generations of video codecs.

18 The interface offers a three-dimensional view, with the two video screens on either end tilted inward toward the third video screen in the middle. The image of each chat participant is reflected beneath their screens, in a look that Apple says is reminiscent of a conference-room table.

19 AppleScript is a system-level scripting language for Macintosh. AppleScript is an English-like language used to write script files that automate the actions of the computer and the applications that run on it. It has always been a fantastic way to create little programs that perform repetitive tasks for instance downloading a gallery of images off the Web and using them to generate a DVD slide show.

20 RSS, or Real Simple Syndication, is an alternative view of a web page that allows its users to subscribe and read the content in RSS newsreader software. Whenever the web page is updated, the newsreader will automatically display the new item.

21 Warrene, Blane "Expo Keynote Highlights Present, Future of Apple", *http://www.macnewsworld.com/*, August 31st 2004

22 "Merrill Lynch: Tiger to boost PC share; New iMacs, eMacs", *http://macminute.com/*, May 2nd 2005

23 "iPod blurs Wall Street's vision of Tiger", *http://www.macworld.co.uk/*, May 3rd 2005

24 "Apple Mac OS X 10.4 Tiger is out", *http://stuff.techwhack.com/*, May 2nd 2005

25 "Special Report: Apple finally poised to take on Windows in 2005", *http://www.macnet2.com*, January 31st 2005

26 Thurrott, Paul "With iPod Success, Apple Takes "Network Effect" from Microsoft", *http://www.windowsitpro.com/*, November 1st 2004

27 "Apple's "Tiger" is aiming to take a bite out of Microsoft", *http://www.industrysearch.com.au*, February 5th 2005

28 "iPod blurs Wall Street's vision of Tiger" *http://www.macworld.co.uk/*, May 3rd 2005

29 "iPod, iMac Fuel Big 2Q Gains For Apple", *http://news.yahoo.com/*, April 13th 2005

30 Schlender, Brent "How Big Can Apple Get?", *http://www.fortune.com/*, May 4th 2005

31 Haslam, Karen "Mac OS X Tiger could polish the Halo Effect", *http://www.macworld.co.uk/*, April 13th 2005

32 "iPod blurs Wall Street's vision of Tiger", op.cit.

33 "Apple's Tiger will rule non-tech innovator jungle for more than a year", *http://www.yeald.com*, March 5th 2005

34 "Halo effect to change balance of desktop sales", *http://www.macnn.com/*, April 27th 2005

35 "Apple earns its stripes", op.cit.

36 "Apple's Tiger, Burning How Bright?", op.cit.

37 JupiterResearch helps companies develop, extend and integrate business strategies across online and emerging channels. Backed by proprietary data, JupiterResearch's industry-specific analysis, competitive insight and strategic advice give businesses the tools they need to exploit new technologies and business processes.

38 "Apple's "Tiger" aims to take a bite out of Microsoft, "Longhorn"", *http://www.channelnewsasia.com/*, April 30th 2005

39 Ibid.

40 Ibid.

41 Ibid.

42 "Special Report: Apple finally poised to take on Windows in 2005", op.cit.

Annexure 1: Spotlight

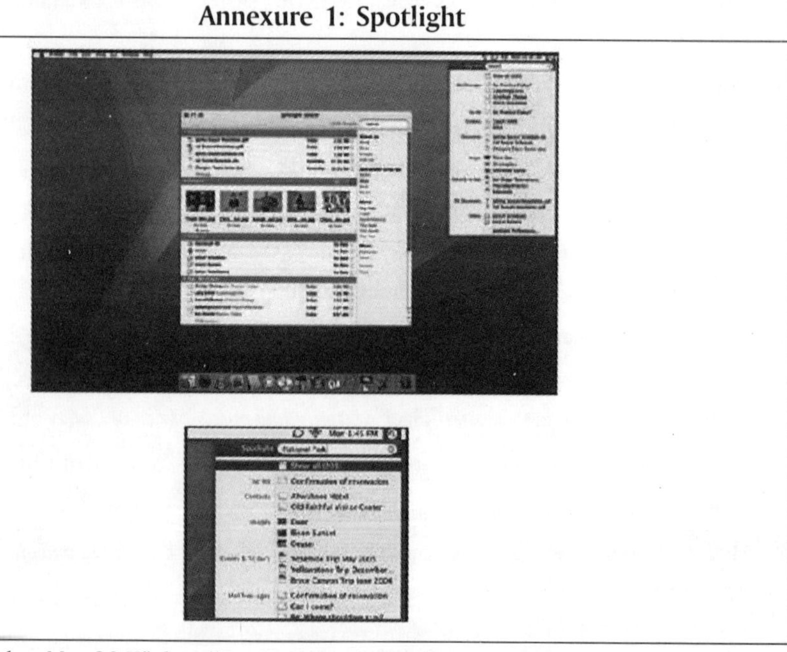

Source: "Apple – Mac OS X", http://www.apple.com/macosx/features/spotlight/

Annexure 2: iChat AV

Featuring a three-dimensional view, iChat AV 3 for Tiger practically puts your colleagues in the room with you, making it easier to follow the conversation. View their faces reflected into space, just as if they were sitting around a conference-room table.

Now Hear This iChat for Tiger allows you to participate in audio conferences with up to 10 participants. High-quality audio compression techniques ensure crystal-clear conversations while full-duplex sound lets everyone speak naturally. Watch as well as listen using particpants' personal sound-level meters. They're a handy visual cue to let you know who's speaking.

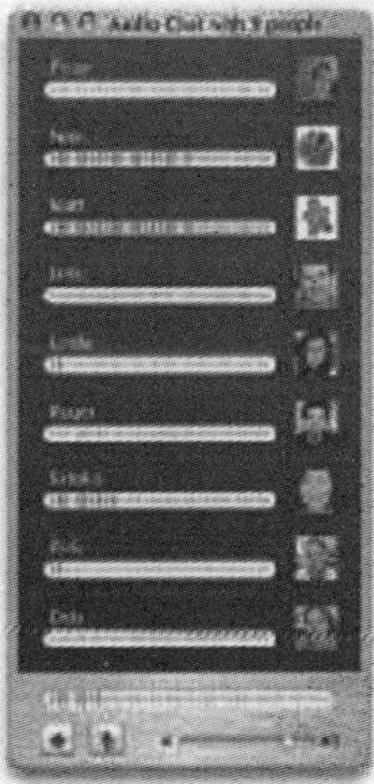

Source: "Apple – Mac OS X", http://www.apple.com/macosx/features/ichat/

<table>
<tr><th colspan="3">Annexure 3: Dashboard</th></tr>
<tr><td colspan="3">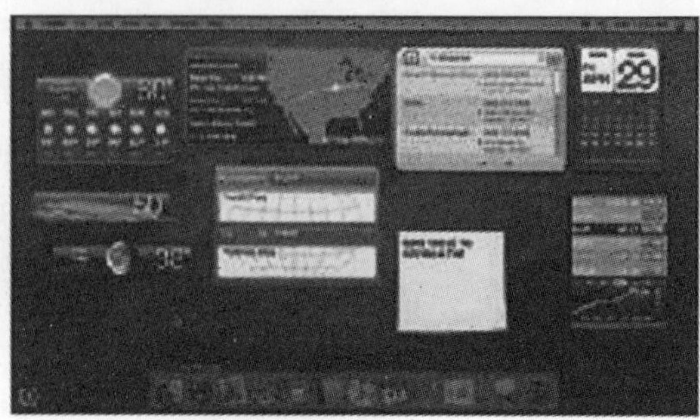</td></tr>
<tr><td></td><td>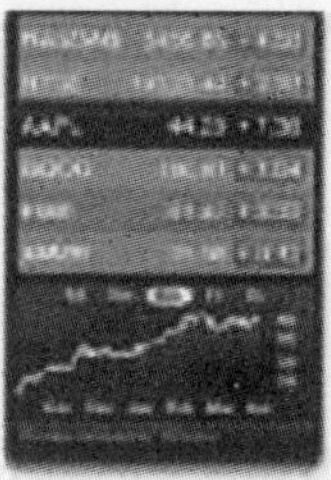</td><td></td></tr>
<tr><td>iTunes
Play, pause, skip forward and backward through songs in your iTunes music library using this simplified</td><td>Stocks
Track changes in your favorite domestic and international stock funds, including recent prices and</td><td>Weather
View weather conditions around the world. Check temperature, expected high and low and a six-day forecast.</td></tr>
<tr><td>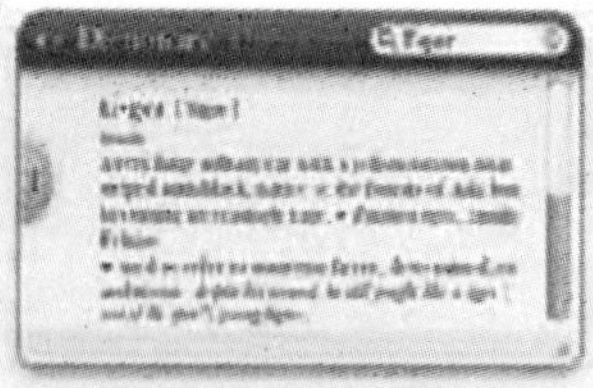</td><td colspan="2"></td></tr>
<tr><td>Dictionary
Quickly find definitions by typing all or part of a word. View the same word in the thesaurus to find synonyms, antonyms and more. Since the dictionary and thesaurus are built into Mac OS X, you don't even need an Internet connection.</td><td colspan="2">Phone Book
Search by name or category to display the phone numbers and addresses for publicly listed US businesses in your area. Click the phone number to display it in extra-large print so you can read it easily while dialing.</td></tr>
<tr><td colspan="3">Contd...</td></tr>
</table>

Contd...

	reminders: don't forget to call dad... flower for mom	
World Clock Check local time anywhere in the world. Open multiple widgets to display the time in different cities.	**Stickies** Jot reminders on as many sticky note widgets as you want. Flip to change the note color and font.	**Tile Game** Scramble a photo and put it back together again. Drag on a new photo to create a different puzzle.

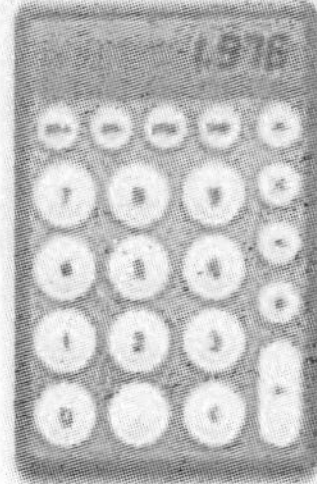	
Calculator Perform basic calculations quickly and easily. The Calculator widget handles addition, subtraction, multiplication and division, and includes a memory function.	**Translator** Translate words and phrases instantly between English, Chinese, Dutch, French, German, Greek, Italian, Japanese, Korean, Portuguese and Russian.

Calendar This colorful widget gives you at-a-glance access to daily and monthly calendars. View the current day and date or click the calendar to reveal the days of the month.	**Flight Tracker** Find and follow flights with the Flight Tracker widget. Enter an airline, flight number and destination or departure city. For flights in progress, a map displays the flight's approximate location.

Contd...

Contd...

Address Book Quickly locate contact information in your Address Book, browse contacts sequentially or search for specific entries.	**Unit Converter** Convert numerous weights and measures, including area, currency, length, speed, temperature, weight and more.

Source: "Apple – Mac OS X", http://www.apple.com/macosx/features/dashboard/

Annexure 4: Mail 2

Apple's Mail application has been significantly updated in Tiger. Apart from User interface issues, in Mail 2, the sliding draw found in previous versions has been replaced by a more traditional column of mailbox folders, like the one seen in Microsoft Outlook, making the application look more professional.

From a functional standpoint, Mail 2 features Spotlight searching. Smart Mailboxes (which are a copy of the Search Folders feature, helps in saving mail searches) and Mac synchronization helps in synchronizing all e-mail accounts, rules, signatures, and Smart Mailboxes to all Tiger-based Macs using the Mac service (subscription rate – $99 a year). Additionally, many of Mail 2's new features are related to iPhoto integration and digital photos. For example, the new photo enables resizing photos before being sent. On receiving the photos in an e-mail message, Mail can display a slideshow. If photos are dragged into a Mail message window, they are stored in the message body with their original size by default. However, a new Image Size drop-down list, available in the lower right corner of the window, enables the user to choose among three different sizes for all of the images in the message.

Mail also offers some new features. There are two buttons next to the attachments line, Save and Slideshow. Save, launches a Finder Save dialog that enables users to copy the attached photos to their hard drive while Slideshow launches a nice Slideshow applet.

On wiggling the mouse during the slideshow, the toolbar is seen. The buttons, from left to right, are Back, Play/Stop, Next, Index Sheet, Fit to Screen, Add to iPhoto, and Close. The Index Sheet option displays all of the photos in the slideshow together on the screen at one time.

Finally, Mail 2 allows the user to easily customize the fields that should appear in a New Message window. To do so, one needs to open a New Message window and then choose *Customize from the Action menu* in the left side of the window (it's the small box next to the Account drop-down list).

Address Book 4.0

In Tiger, Address Book has been updated to version 4.0 (from 3.1 in Panther). Among the new features is a new contacts importer that can import contacts from text files (in addition to vCards and LDIF files). These text files can be in tab-delimited or CSV (Comma-Separated Values) format.

iCal

Mac OS X 10.4 "Tiger" includes a new version of iCal that includes a number of useful new features. For example, one can automatically create a meeting event by dragging an Address Book contact or group of contacts onto an iCal calendar. After doing it, a new meeting appears in iCal on the date and time selected, with those contacts listed as attendees. iCal integrates with Address Book in other ways, too. For example, the user can turn on an optional Birthdays calendar (from iCal Preferences) that finds any of the contacts' birthdays and lists them in the calendar. The Birthdays calendar is read-only. Additionally, iCal now integrates with Mail. The user can configure iCal to automatically grab invitations that arrive via Mail. When such an invitation arrives, the user can reply using the Notifications button in the lower-left corner of the iCal window. This button toggles

Contd...

Contd...

the Notifications pane, which displays any unanswered invitations. The Notifications pane also displays any incoming answers to event requests you've made.

Finally, iCal 2.0 also integrates with Spotlight. This means one can search for calendar events and To Do items directly from the search box in the bottom of the iCal window. Search results appear in a pop-up search results pane.

VoiceOver

VoiceOver is part of OS X's Universal Access features, and it's integrated into the OS's interface, providing another way to access the Mac. With VoiceOver, the user can have Web pages, Mail messages, and word processing documents read aloud; get audible description of the workspace as well as any activities taking place on the Mac. One voice can provide every description, or the user can opt to assign unique and personalized voices to the six different types of information—commands, content, item descriptions, item types, spoken menus, or echoed text—that VoiceOver provides.

VoiceOver also offers keyboard commands for navigating through OS X's interface or controlling application and system commands. A new tool called viewfinder lets the user to control what the Mac says and enables interaction with items on screen via just your keyboard. Using VoiceOver, one can press buttons, drag sliders, select and deselect options, scroll, and operate other on-screen controls that would otherwise require a mouse.

Parental Control

With built-in, system-wide parental controls, one can create a separate user account for a child that restricts his or her computing actions in a wide variety of ways. Parents can limit what programs a child can launch and ban the child from burning CDs and DVDs, changing system preferences, or even printing.

One can restrict a child's Web surfing to the sites he specifies, and limit his or her exchanges of e-mails and instant messages to the people specified. If anyone else sends the child an e-mail, it is forwarded to the parent. If the child wants to send e-mail to a non-approved person, the parent can be asked for permission electronically. The e-mail controls require both the child and the parent to be using Tiger.

Compiled by Icfai Business School Case Development Centre from Thurrott, Paul "Apple Mac OS X 10.4 "Tiger" Review", http://www.winsupersite.com/, April 14th 2005.

Annexure 5: Tiger vs Longhorn

Search: Tiger will feature a built-in local search technology called "Spotlight" (technology built upon the search engines that Apple currently uses to search iTunes and e-mail). Microsoft has said it plans to offer a similar local-machine search engine for Longhorn that will be based on the company's Windows File System (WinFS) technology.

Scripting: Tiger will include a front-end scripting environment known as "Automator." Longhorn will include a new scripting shell (currently in beta test) known as "Monad." Built-in RSS support: Tiger will embed an RSS aggregator into the Safari browser. Longhorn will include an embedded RSS feature in the user interface.

Info-Display Panel: Tiger will have an information-display capability called "Dashboard." Longhorn will have an information-display panel called "Sideshow," to which users can "pin" collections of items of interest.

Integrated Instant Messaging/Video Chat: Tiger will feature a souped-up version of iChat. Microsoft will embed Windows Messenger (a sister to MSN Messenger), which also will likely feature video-chat.

64-Bit Support: Tiger will include extended 64-bit capabilities. Longhorn allegedly will be optimized for 64-bit systems.

Source: Foley, Mary Jo "Longhorn and Tiger: Who's Copying Whom?", http://www.microsoft-watch.com/, June 30th 2004.

INDEX